CRIME AND PUNISHMENT IN REVOLUTIONARY PARIS

Contributions in Legal Studies
Series Editor: *Paul L. Murphy*

Philosophical Law: Authority, Equality, Adjudication, Privacy
Richard Bronaugh, editor

Law, Soldiers, and Combat
Peter Karsten

Appellate Courts and Lawyers: Information Gathering in the Adversary System
Thomas B. Marvell

Charting the Future: The Supreme Court Responds to a Changing Society,
1890–1920
John E. Semonche

The Promise of Power: The Emergence of the Legal Profession in
Massachusetts, 1760–1840
Gerard W. Gawalt

Inferior Courts, Superior Justice: A History of the Justices of the Peace on the
Northwest Frontier, 1853–1889
John R. Wunder

Antitrust and the Oil Monopoly: The Standard Oil Cases, 1890–1911
Bruce Bringhurst

They Have No Rights: Dred Scott's Struggle for Freedom
Walter Ehrlich

Popular Influence Upon Public Policy: Petitioning in Eighteenth-Century Virginia
Raymond C. Bailey

Fathers to Daughters: The Legal Foundations of Female Emancipation
Peggy A. Rabkin

In Honor of Justice Douglas: A Symposium on Individual Freedom
and Government
Edited by *Robert H. Keller, Jr.*

A Constitutional History of Habeas Corpus
William F. Duker

Antoinette Wills

CRIME AND PUNISHMENT IN REVOLUTIONARY PARIS

Contributions in Legal Studies,
Number 15

GREENWOOD PRESS
Westport, Connecticut • London, England

Library of Congress Cataloging in Publication Data

Wills, Antoinette, 1946–
    Crime and punishment in revolutionary Paris.

    (Contributions in legal studies ; no. 15
ISSN 0147-1074)
    Bibliography: p.
    Includes index.
    1.   Crime and criminals—France—Paris—History—
18th century.   2.   Criminal justice, Administration of—
France—Paris—History—18th century.   3.   Criminal
courts—France—Paris—History—18th century.   4.   Paris—
History—Revolution, 1789-1799.   5.   Paris—Social
conditions.   I.   Title.   II.   Series.
HV6970.P3W54   364'.944'361   80-654
ISBN 0-313-21494-8 (lib. bdg.)

Library of Congress Catalog Card Number: 80-654
ISBN: 0-313-21494-8
ISSN: 0147-1074

First published in 1981

Greenwood Press
A division of Congressional Information Service, Inc.
88 Post Road West, Westport, Connecticut 06881

Printed in the United States of America

10 9 8 7 6 5 4 3 2 1

CONTENTS

MAPS AND TABLES

MAPS

TABLES

PREFACE

As an undergraduate studying the history of the French Revolution for
the first time, I remember being baffled by the enigma of eighteenth-
century France: How could the Enlightenment, an age of reason, humanity,
and moderation, culminate in the bloody excesses of the French Revolution? Did reason go wrong? How did moderation become terror?

The current study, written more than a decade after that original encounter, is in many ways a product of what may seem a naive question.
Despite years of formal study of the literature of French history, I have
never found a satisfactory answer to the puzzle.

What I have tried to do in this work is to trace, specifically and in
detail, the connection between changes in abstract ideas in the Enlightenment and changes both in the daily functioning of the institutions of
government and in the daily lives of ordinary individuals.

The reform of the criminal law was a natural choice of subject. It is
one of the clearest cases in which the ideas of eighteenth-century thinkers
took concrete form in the legislation and institutions of the Revolution.
It provided the immediate impact on the daily lives of individuals that I
was looking for. While the subject of this study is specific—it focuses on
six provisional criminal courts of Paris for two years in the early Revolution—my intent has been to see larger questions, larger issues, through
specific details.

Legal history, broadly conceived, is a focal point for intellectual, social,
and political history. I hope that this work will be useful to historians with
a variety of special interests. Furthermore, I hope it will be useful not only
to scholars of the Revolution, but also to undergraduates studying the
French eighteenth century for the first time—and asking naive or basic
questions.

I would like to acknowledge the help of those individuals without whose help this work would have been impossible. My special thanks are due to Marie Benabou for pointing out the significance of the series of documents used here (Archives Nationales, Series Z^3) and for her patience in introducing me to them. Jacqueline Lafon has been most generous with the results of her own research in series Z^3; I wish to express my appreciation for the time she spent with me and the interest she took in my work. To Scott Lytle, David Pinkney, Gordon Griffiths, and Hankins and Joan Ullman, I extend thanks for support, encouragement, and advice throughout my years of graduate training. Others whose advice and whose shared research have been particularly helpful include Robert Darnton, Jeffry Kaplow, Cissie Fairchilds, Alan Williams, Joanne Kaufmann, Patricia O'Brien, and John Wunder. To Suresh Malhotra I extend thanks for assistance with the computer analysis of my data, and to Jerry Dyer for preparing the charts and illustrations. Finally, I could not have completed this work without the support and encouragement of my husband, Mike: every historian should have such a partner.

INTRODUCTION_____

Proceedings of criminal courts are records of compelling human interest. The confrontation between the individual offender and the authority of the state, the dialogue between prosecution and defense, the details of the life-situation of the accused, the infinite variety of offenses (no two of which are ever identical), all tend to provoke reflections on the human condition.

While individual cases are highly anecdotal, collected records of criminal courts provide important information about the life of society as a whole: about the ideas and values groups of people live by, about the structure and functioning of the institutions of government, and about the daily lives of individuals. Some of this information, especially that on the daily life of the poor, the illiterate, the outcasts of society—those most likely to appear in court—can not be gained from any other source.

Recently, historians have taken great interest in court records, and have begun to analyze them systematically as rich sources of information on the legal and institutional life of past societies, the structure of social life, and the nature of daily life and individual experience.[1]

This study focuses on a set of court records that are particularly significant within this growing literature, the records of the criminal courts of Paris in the early years of the French Revolution. The Revolution was a period of self-conscious change, of attempts to restructure French institutions on a rational basis, and to reshape the life of society in accordance with new ideas of justice and equity. One of the most important aspects of this change was the reform of the French criminal law.

The system of criminal justice in France had come under severe attack in the eighteenth century from several quarters. *Philosophes* condemned the existing system as arbitrary, irrational, and inhumane. The power of magistrates was arbitrary, they argued, not bound by any written law defining crimes and punishments. Existing definitions of crime included sacrilege and blasphemy, offenses that could not exist in a rational society. The system of justice allowed inhumane torture of the accused under certain circumstances as part of trial procedure and as a form of execution. Allied with the *philosophes* were many prominent (and some not-so-prominent) government officials and members of the legal profession: presidents of parlements, lieutenants-general of police, successful lawyers, unsuccessful lawyers.[2]

This critique found practical expression in the Revolution. By 1791 France had a new code of criminal justice that provided for a reformed procedure for trials, clearly defined crimes and their corresponding punishments, and a different form for judicial institutions, including jury trials in criminal cases.

In the first half of this book, I examine these changes in law and institutions in some detail, first exploring the nature of the critique of criminal justice as it functioned in the Old Regime, then analyzing the extent to which this critique resulted in real change early in the Revolution.

While the subject is specific, the questions it poses are large. First, and perhaps most controversial, is the relationship of the Enlightenment and the Revolution. I have been intrigued by this problematic relationship since I first studied the French eighteenth century and chose the subject of reform of the criminal law in part because it seemed one of the clearest "success stories" of the *philosophes*. Enlightened ideas were, it appeared, written into law and subsequently applied to daily life. Recently, this relationship has come under question, notably in John Langbein's essay on *Torture and the Law of Proof.*[3]

A related question, equally problematic, concerns transforming ideas into law, turning critiques of existing institutions into new institutions. It is the classic problem of the reformer: What happens to good ideas when they become law? How are they affected by political process? Why did the laws of the Revolution take the form they did? One of the outstanding differences between the Revolution and the Old Regime was the nature of punishment. Recently Michel Foucault has drawn attention to "the birth of the prison" in the Revolution. Why did the prison, not commonly used for punishment before the Revolution, gain instant acceptance?

The final question posed in the first section is the most straightforward: What were the effects of changes in ideas and changes in law on the daily functioning of institutions? How did they affect individuals served by those institutions? The courts of the Old Regime were abolished. Were the new courts substantially different? Crime and punishment were redefined. Were patterns of prosecution and of penalties assigned for various offenses substantially different? The discretion of judges was eliminated. Who were the new magistrates? How well did they observe the new laws? The new system of criminal justice was an experiment. What were the results of that experiment?

Historians have not limited their investigations in court records to the life of the law and of legal institutions. In recent years, social historians have become increasingly interested in persons who live "en marge," at the fringes of society: vagabonds, prostitutes, smugglers, and pickpockets. They have become interested in the history of "mentalités," not just the ideas of elites recorded in abundance, but the ideas of ordinary people who were not in the habit of leaving records for historians but whose participation in events—especially in the Revolution—was significant, even crucial.[4]

The second half of this work focuses on the daily lives of Parisians during the Revolution, at least those who have left records of their activities in court dossiers.

Underlying the reformers' critique of the system of criminal justice were a set of assumptions about crime, and especially about criminals. The identification of the "laboring classes" with the "dangerous classes" so characteristic of the nineteenth century[5] was not present in the eighteenth. Criminals were considered to be evil, extraordinary individuals, defined by their act as having rejected society's constraints. The new system of justice was called for at least in part from a new understanding of the criminal, with more appreciation of the social forces that might have created aggravating circumstances.

I have tried to reconstruct eighteenth-century perceptions of criminality from the arguments of reformers and from popular literature—sources are necessarily sketchy—and to compare it with patterns of criminality revealed in court records. Reformers wished to establish a new system of criminal justice. Was this based on any real understanding of the nature of crime and of criminality?

What was the nature of crime in eighteenth-century France? What changes occurred with the Revolution? Since Durkheim's classic analysis of crime as a "normal" social phenomenon—one present in all societies at all times, subject to change in periods of stress in the same way that birth and death rates change—social analysts have sought to see in patterns of crime reflections of larger aspects of the life of society. What types of crimes are committed? Who commits them? Who are the victims? What happens to "normal" patterns in periods of stress: famine, economic depression, war, revolution?

Answers to such questions drawn from analysis of court records are necessarily tentative because of the small number of crimes prosecuted in comparison to the number committed. Nevertheless, the comparison of court records from one period with those of another can give a good indication of change over time. Examination of individual dossiers allows an opportunity to observe change in the life of society and of individuals in a very real and very vivid way. What effect did the Revolution have on everyday life? What factors in the social environment seem to affect crime rates? Most of those accused of crimes in the eighteenth century were poor. What do court records reveal about the impact of the events of the Revolution on the lives of the Parisian poor?

The reform of the criminal justice system has been counted one of the chief benefits the poor gained from the Revolution. In his *Social History of the French Revolution,* Norman Hampson observed that "Compromises . . . restricted what could be done for the poor by limiting the spoils available for redistribution. Nevertheless, the humbler citizens gained a good deal; they, more than the privileged, benefited from relatively impartial and humane justice. . . ."[6] The records of criminal courts of the Revolution reveal that the poor were not necessarily of the same opinion. As I shall attempt throughout this work to let the accused voice their own opinions on crime, on why individuals commit crimes, on what social factors influence them, I shall also let them express their own opinions of the reform. What was the effect of the new system of criminal justice from the point of view of the accused?

A brief discussion on the sources used in this study, and on my methods of analyzing them, is in order. The records available for historical study of criminal life and criminal justice, at least in the Old Regime, are so vast—proceedings of criminal courts, of police courts, of the numerous petty jurisdictions whose existence was the subject of so much criticism by eighteenth-century reformers—that the historian who ventures into this area must be selective. For the Revolution, the problem is the opposite: most of the records of Parisian criminal courts which functioned during the Revolution were destroyed by fire in 1871.

There is one remarkable exception. Misfiled under courts of the Old Regime in the Archives Nationales is series Z^3, "Tribunal Criminel des

Dix, et Tribunaux Criminels Provisoires." Here, in 116 cartons, are the
complete records of the six provisional criminal courts of Paris, established
in March 1791 to take over the backlog of criminal cases left from the
abolition of the Châtelet and the Parlement of Paris. Although intended
to be temporary, the courts were ordered in September of 1791 to process
current criminal cases until the jury system of criminal tribunals could
begin to function. They continued to do so through August of 1792.
These documents are the heart of this work. With few exceptions, the
cases contained in this series date from the period of the Revolution, beginning in 1789 and ending in 1792. While the records of crimes committed
in 1789, 1790, and 1792 are partial and incomplete—many of the cases
from those years having been tried in other courts—records for 1791 are
substantial. Because these courts replaced the Châtelet, the cases tried
are comparable to records of the Old Regime. Furthermore, since the
records of the only other Parisian court ordered to process criminal
cases in those years, the Departmental Tribunal, were destroyed by fire
in 1871, they form the only remaining record of the application of
changes in laws regulating criminal justice, as well as the only record of
Parisian crime in the early Revolution.[7]

Although this series has been in the Archives Nationales since they
were established, they have been generally unused and unusable before
this time. The documents themselves are not well organized: judgments
are filed separately from the dossiers to which they refer, and cases are
not numbered consecutively as they are in records of the Châtelet and
the Parlement of Paris. There was no known index to the series until
recently when an index drawn up by Emile Compardon in 1859 was
discovered.[8] This index is extremely limited, containing a listing of the
contents of each carton by subject: judgments by date, names of individuals whose dossiers are in the carton, miscellaneous documents, or pieces
of evidence. Another index has been compiled since that time, listing
the names of the accused in alphabetical order and the cartons in which
documents that refer to them are to be found. This index has no date
and the compiler is not identified. By using both of these indexes, I have
reconstructed the records of individual cases, compiling information on
the 1,620 persons accused of crime whose dossiers, judgments, and judgments on appeal are contained in the series.

Poor organization and lack of an index are perhaps the main reasons
these documents have been overlooked. But there is another reason: of

what significance is the information they contain? While it would undoubtedly be interesting, what would it mean? Recent studies of crime in the Old Regime have now made it possible to view the court records of the Revolution in their proper context rather than in isolation and have provided the comparative framework for analysis of social and institutional change from the Old Regime to the Revolution.

The work of François Billaçois and others on the Châtelet records (published under the pseudonym Porphyre Petrovitch[9]) has been most helpful as it provides a full background on criminal life and justice in the Old Regime. For the sake of comparability, I have adopted their methodological model for the quantitative analyses contained in this work. Most of the analysis has involved straightforward frequency distributions or cross tabulations. Unfortunately, a great deal of information is missing. The courts were supposed to demand of the accused his name, age, occupation, birthplace, and residence. Observations are missing in each of these categories. The accused was supposed to sign the judgment of the court or to declare that he was unable to do so. This information is missing in many cases. Where the number of missing observations is very large, in the Petrovitch data or in my own, I have noted this in the text. Conclusions from such data must be considered tentative.

Interpreting the results of this analysis has posed problems. Large numbers of the accused were acquitted. Should analysis of "criminality" be confined to those convicted? Historians have generally chosen to analyze the records of persons accused of crime rather than those convicted, when collecting data from criminal court records. The assumption behind this practice is that since only a small percentage of crimes are ever prosecuted, the larger sample of those accused is better than the smaller sample of the convicted. The best sample is drawn from a point as close as possible to the crime: thefts reported are a better guide to the number being committed than those prosecuted; the group of the accused is more representative of all criminals than those convicted.[10]

Modern criminologists have a variety of techniques to measure crimes committed (but not reported) and types of persons committing them (but never tried). Since this is impossible with historical records, I have adopted the historian's practice—also used by the Petrovitch group—of analyzing all of the accused as at least potential criminals.

A second problem of analysis centers on changes in patterns of crime. To what extent can these be accepted as a change in fact and to what extent to a different manner of reporting? The six provisional tribunals replaced the single criminal chamber of the Châtelet. With increased personnel were they able to judge more cases? The manner of arresting suspects changed in the early Revolution with the disappearance of the royal police: citizen patrols and citizen arrests became more common than police investigations of crimes. How did this affect the number of people arrested?

In considering these problems, I have tried to judge from the conditions under which the new courts were created whether a change in fact, rather than in reporting, is reflected in the data. The Châtelet and the Parlement had a huge backlog of unfinished cases when they were abolished. Since they had become relatively efficient in the period before the Revolution (as measured by delay between crime and judgment: up to one year in 1755; four to six months in 1785), this would seem to indicate that their caseload had increased beyond their capacity. The new courts were created for the sole purpose of clearing up the backlog. An expanded court system seems to have been a direct response to an increase in the number of crimes being committed.

Introductions are not meant to list comprehensively all of the problems involved in writing a work of history, but only to introduce some of them. If I had to describe my method succinctly, I would say that I had tried to achieve a compromise in this analysis between the vividly impressionistic style of Richard Cobb and the statistical and quantitative style of the *Annales E.S.C.* of French history.[11] I have tried to supplement quantitative analysis with sufficient examples from the court records to allow historical actors to speak for themselves in discussing the meaning and causes of crime, the nature of justice, the place of the criminal in society, the causes of crime, and the nature of everyday life in the Revolution.

I owe specific debts to the published works of many persons who have influenced my thought on this subject: Among contemporaries, Restif de la Bretonne and Louis Sebastien Mercier have provided information, observations, and interpretations of Parisian life that have been invaluable.[12] Among historians, the works of Richard Cobb, Jeffry Kaplow, Olwen Hufton, and Louis Chevalier have been extremely suggestive, especially since their interpretations do not all agree.[13] I have found Jeffry Kaplow's concept of the "laboring poor" a useful one to describe the level of Parisian society of most of the accused. Olwen Hufton's studies of the French poor and their struggle for survival have provided a picture of the rural background of many of the urban poor. I have found Louis Chevalier's discussion of the environmental causes of crime provocative. His discussion of the interaction between social perception and the behavior of the working classes and/or dangerous classes has stimulated me to think a great deal about the relationship of crime, real or perceived, to social structure. Richard Cobb's discussion of the value of police documents as historical records has been a useful guide in examining court documents. His depiction of the mentality of the poor has been challenging: the mixture of fascination and disbelief which it originally inspired in me has been at least partially responsible for my choosing this topic for my own research.[14]

My own conclusions have drawn something from each of these, but also a great deal from the opinions of the accused who appeared before the six provisional tribunals. They had their own ideas about crime, about punishment, and about justice. It has seemed to me as fitting to include their thoughts as those of historians and *philosophes.*

Notes

1. The seminal work in this field is Louis Chevalier, *Classes Laborieuses et Classes Dangereuses* (Paris: Plon, 1958), which combines demographic, criminal, and literary records in a discussion of crime and social perception in nineteenth-century Paris. Much research has been done in French judicial archives since Chevalier's work. Andre Abbiateci et al., *Crimes et Criminalité en France 17ᵉ-18ᵉ Siècles* Cahiers des Annales No. 33 (Paris: Colin, 1971) is an excellent collection of studies based on court records and has been particularly important for my own work. Robert Forster and Orest Ranum, eds., *Deviants and the Abandoned in French Society*, trans. Elborg Forster and Patricia Ranum (Baltimore: Johns Hopkins University Press, 1978) contains selections of similar studies taken from the *Annales, Économies, Sociétés, Civilisations* on subjects ranging from prostitution to arson. Both contain bibliographic guides to the literature of criminality in France. The eighteenth century has seemed particularly fascinating to historians as a transitional period when a distinctly modern form of crime appeared. *See* for example, the works of Pierre Chaunu and his students on Normandy, comparing criminal court records of the seventeenth and eighteenth centuries: Bernadette Boutelet, "Étude par Sondage de la Criminalité dans le Bailliage du Pont-de-l'Arche (XVIIᵉ Siècle); de la Violence au vol; en Marche vers l'Escroquerie," *Annales de Normandie* (1962): 235-62; and Jean-Claude Gegot, "Étude par Sondage de la Criminalité dans la Bailliage de Falaise

(XVIIe-XVIIIe Siècles) Criminalité Diffuse ou Société Criminelle?" *Annales de Normandie* (1966): 108-64.
   2. Several good basic works outline the ideas and activities of the re-formers. A classic work, Shelby T. McCloy, *The Humanitarian Movement in Eighteenth Century France* (Frankfort: University of Kentucky Press, 1957) devotes two chapters to the reform movement. More recently, Michel Foucault has focused attention on changing ideas of punishment in his work *Surveiller et Punir*, cited throughout this work as *Discipline and Punish: The Birth of the Prison*, trans. Alan Sheridan (New York: Pantheon Books, 1977). Foucault hardly agrees with the traditional view that the eighteenth century produced a more rational or more humane system of justice and punishment. For an excellent detailed examination of the ideas of the reformers, *see* Joanne S. Kaufmann, "The Critique of Criminal Justice in Eighteenth-Century France: A Study in the Changing Social Ethics of Crime and Punishment" (unpublished Ph.D. dissertation, Harvard University, 1976), cited as Kaufmann "Critique."
   3. John Langbein, *Torture and the Law of Proof: Europe and England in the Ancien Regime* (Chicago: University of Chicago Press, 1976).
   4. The works of Richard Cobb and Olwen Hufton stand out in this field of French history. Their works provide a powerfully evocative re-creation of daily life "en marge" in French society: Richard Cobb, *The Police and the People: French Popular Protest 1789-1820* (London: Oxford University Press, 1970); *Reactions to the French Revolution* (London: Oxford University Press, 1972); Olwen Hufton, *The Poor of Eighteenth-Century France* (Oxford: The Clarendon Press, 1974). On crime as political protest in England, *see* Douglas Hay et al., *Albion's Fatal Tree: Crime and Society in Eighteenth-Century England* (New York: Pantheon Books, 1975).
   5. Chevalier traces the subtle but profound change in the perception of the relationship of these classes in French society, particularly as it was expressed in nineteenth-century literature.
   6. Norman Hampson, *A Social History of the French Revolution* (Toronto: University of Toronto Press, 1963), p. 112.
   7. This series has been largely unknown, although it is listed in standard guides to the Archives Nationales. Richard Cobb has never used the series, despite his interest in the subject of Parisian crime. Jacques Godechot, *Les Institutions de la France sous la Révolution et l'Empire*, 2d ed. (Paris: Presses Universitaires de France, 1968) does not mention the series or the courts. Edmond Seligman, *La Justice en France pendant la Révolution 1789-1792*, 2 vols. (Paris: Librairie Plon, 1901, 1913) has used them and has discussed the history of the six provisional courts briefly. *See* especially vol. 1, p. 572.

8. A preface to this index explains the history of the documents. The preface is in the form of a letter from A. Grun, chief archivist of the legislative and judicial section of the Archives Nationales to the Director of the Archives, dated October 11, 1859. The series was originally misfiled under Z, records of jurisdictions of the Old Regime other than the Châtelet and the Parlement. The present series Z^3 was designated "etcetera: tribunaux criminels extraordinaires," along with records of the Revolutionary Tribunals, the *Haute Cour de Justice de Vendôme,* and extraordinary military courts. The latter were reclassified under W. The provisional tribunals were left under Z but given the separate designation Z^3.

9. Porphyre Petrovitch, "Recherches sur la Criminalité à Paris dans la Seconde Moitié du XVIIIe Siècle." in Abbiateci et al., pp. 187-261. "Porphyre Petrovitch" is a pseudonym for a group of students who carried out a coordinated research project, under the direction of Yvonne Bongert, Pierre Joubert, and François Billaçois. Billaçois is careful to distinguish himself as coordinator and assembler of the work but not sole author. Under his own name he published the model all follow. *See* François Billaçois "Pour une Enquête sur la Criminalité dans la France d'Ancien Régime" *Annales E.S.C.* 22 (March-April 1967): 340-49.

10. For a discussion of the problems of interpreting criminal court records, of dealing with the number of accused rather than convicted, and of the relationship between crime and criminal court records, *see* J.M. Beattie, "Towards a Study of Crime in 18th Century England: A Note on Indictments," in *The Triumph of Culture: 18th Century Perspectives,* ed. Paul Fritz and David Williams (Toronto: A. M. Hakkert, 1972), pp. 299-314.

11. In contrast to and in protest against what he views as quantitative history being carried to extremes, Cobb says of his own writing: "Nothing could be further from my intentions than to drill the *Petit Peuple* into tight formation, march them up the hill, and march them down again." (*The Police and the People,* p. xvii).

12. Nicolas Edme Restif de la Bretonne, *Les Nuits de Paris,* 7 vols. (London, 1788) and Louis Sebastien Mercier, *Tableau de Paris,* 8 vols. (Amsterdam, 1782-1783).

13. Jeffry Kaplow, *The Names of Kings: The Parisian Laboring Poor in the Eighteenth Century* (New York: Basic Books, 1972) differentiates between the laboring poor and the criminal population of Paris in the eighteenth century. He sets off beggars and criminals as a group apart from the laboring poor in chapter 6. Chevalier asserts that they were not so clearly differentiated in the social attitudes of the nineteenth century. Richard Cobb does not pose the question: the life of the poor was violent,

and crime was often a part of it. Olwen Hufton discusses crime as part of the normal economy of the poor, although she also discusses the lengths to which the eighteenth-century Frenchman could go in distinguishing shades of poverty from the "true and honest poor" (le vrai pauvre) to the dishonest beggar and thief.

14. Robert Darnton, "French History: The Case of the Wandering Eye" *New York Review of Books* 20 (April 5, 1973) summarizes this common response to Cobb's writings, and sets his work in the context of others writing on French crime. In light of my own research, I can only say that Cobb's understanding of his subject is profound. However, his fascination with individual human dramas leads him to relate the most interesting stories he finds in the documents, which are often the most extreme rather than the most typical.

CRIME AND PUNISHMENT IN REVOLUTIONARY PARIS

THE CRITIQUE OF CRIMINAL JUSTICE:
The Conflict of Written Law
and Natural Law_____1

> The administration of justice was partial,
> venal, infamous. I have, in conversation with
> many sensible men in different parts of the
> kingdom, met with something of content
> with their government in all other respects
> than this; but upon the question of expect-
> ing justice to be really and fairly administered,
> everyone confessed that there was no such
> thing to be looked for.
>
> Arthur Young
> *Travels in France*[1]

At the time of the French Revolution, the system of criminal justice in
France was regulated by a law more than a century old, the Criminal
Ordinance of 1670. This ordinance did not define what constituted
crime, nor did it set down a table of penalties. It dealt almost entirely
with matters of procedure. While it defined standards of proof in detail,
it left penalties to be assigned for offenses to the discretion of judges,
with the restriction that no new or "unusual" penalties be invented.

Designed to bring more uniform standards of justice to all parts of
France, the ordinance was the most comprehensive legislation that had
ever been decreed on the subject in France. French criminal law, more
than most European legal systems, was heavily dependent on tradition
and learned commentaries. This was possible because the French magistracy
enjoyed the reputation of being well trained and thus capable of using
their discretionary powers wisely.[2]

In 1670 the Great Ordinance had represented substantial progress.
By the late eighteenth century, it was considered hopelessly archaic.

All aspects of the criminal justice system came under attack from various sectors of society, including magistrates, government officials, philosophers and men of letters, lawyers, and others.[3]

The reformist critique showed remarkable unanimity on what was wrong and how it should be corrected. At the time of the Revolution, the reformation of the criminal justice system was one of the most pressing issues demanding attention, as reflected by its frequent mention in the *Cahiers*, and the speed with which the National Assembly acted to reform the criminal law.[4]

In this chapter and the next, I shall only sketch the outlines of the movement for reform and the attempt to restructure French judicial institutions in the first years of the Revolution. Many issues raised in the reform movement are worthy of treatment at length. Fortunately, several substantial studies have recently appeared which deal with one or more aspects of the reform in the detail they merit.[5] Readers who wish to pursue the subject may do so by consulting works listed in footnotes to this text.

Critics of the system of criminal justice in eighteenth-century France focused their attention on three broad areas of law: The proper structure of judicial institutions and the procedure they should follow; the definition of crime and the most appropriate forms of punishment; the causes of crime and the nature of criminality. These three did not receive equal attention: criminal procedure, a familiar topic for lawyers and legal commentators, was discussed frequently and in specific detail; the nature of criminality, a question newly posed by moralists and social thinkers, was not explored in depth.

The basic ideas of the reform movement were defined in two books widely read in enlightened circles: Montesquieu's *Spirit of the Laws* (1748) and Beccaria's *Essay on Crimes and Punishments* (1764).[6] From its beginnings, the reform movement was a joint venture of men of letters and men of affairs. Montesquieu, a member of the French nobility, president of the Parlement of Bordeaux before he resigned to devote his time to writing, symbolized the interaction of lawyers and philosophers who made the reform movement powerful, eloquent, and effective.[7]

Montesquieu had declared the centrality of the criminal justice system to well-regulated society in Book 12 of his treatise: "Political liberty consists in security, or at least in the opinion that we enjoy security. . . . It is therefore on the excellence of criminal laws that the liberty of the subject principally depends." Furthermore, he declared there was no subject more deserving of study: "The knowledge already acquired in some countries, or that may be hereafter attained in others, concerning the surest rules to be observed in criminal judgments, is more interesting to mankind than any other thing in the world."[8]

Chief among the problems of the structure of judicial institutions, as the reformers saw them, were the diversity of jurisdictions, the discretion of magistrates in dispensing justice, and the quality of magistrates considering the venality of judicial office. In his essay on the reform of the criminal law submitted to the Academy of Chalons-Sur-Marne in 1780, Brissot de Warville declared:

> All present tribunals, ordinary and extraordinary, should be suppressed. The cognizance of criminal cases should all go through one tribunal. The multiplicity of tribunals that exist today is a crime. Each locality should have a tribunal, crimes should be judged locally. Each tribunal should have twenty-four judges . . . they should serve seven years and be elected to office . . . by the local citizenry.
>
> They should come from all conditions of life: it should be useless, to be admitted to the status of judge, to have paid 400 *livres* to the University for not knowing anything. . . . The natural law is the common law of men and animals.[9]

Brissot was more radical than many others who called for reforms. Few suggested that all present tribunals be suppressed. Many, however, held up the English system, with its emphasis on local justice, justices of the peace, and jury trials, as preferable to the French system, where the court of jurisdiction might be distant from the crime.

The English system of indictment and trial by jury in criminal affairs was recommended by Brissot as an alternative to the power of magistrates in French courts. Juries had functioned regularly in France before the Ordinance of 1670. Their decline was, in part, due to the regularization of standards of proof by that ordinance.[10] Judges took over inquiry into the facts of the case, declared when proof was sufficient, and rendered judgment.[11] In proposing a panel of "twenty-four judges," Brissot sought to combine the English system and the French. The accused, he proposed, should choose twelve judges to determine the facts in his case. There should be a presiding judge for each tribunal, "with knowledge of the laws of men and of nature," and familiar with local mores. This judge would need only to oversee the application of the law once the facts of the case were determined.

Besides reducing the discretion of magistrates inquiring into the evidence in a case, the adoption of jury trials—or of a system such as Brissot proposed—would resolve two issues which were the subject of much discussion by reformers: secrecy in criminal trials and the use of torture as a regular part of criminal procedure.

Secrecy was basic to French criminal courts in the eighteenth century. The accused was presumed guilty. The object of judicial inquiry was to obtain a confession of guilt, although the accused might not be informed of the charges against him until his trial, or even judgment.[12] Neither the accused nor the public was allowed to know what had been said by whom until the trial was over, and then only if the accused appealed or the judges wished to publicize the case for some exemplary purpose.

Apologists for the existing system argued that secrecy was the necessary basis of the law because it prevented criminal elements of society from conspiring to defraud the system of justice.[13]

Those who wanted to abolish secrecy advanced two arguments: First, that secrecy was unfair to the accused who had a right to know the charges, the witnesses, and the evidence against him, so that he could prepare a defense. Second, that secrecy of criminal procedure was less useful in reducing crime than public trials would be. Prost de Royer, lieutenant-general of police of Lyon, argued that public trials would actually furnish "a school of morality where each will be able to learn his duties" to society.[14]

Torture was the single most criticized aspect of criminal procedure in eighteenth-century France, although the debate was not new.[15] Considered a necessary part of the system of legal proof, torture was an easy target for reformers to attack. It was often treated jointly with the issue of secret proceedings, as in the famous defense of the *trois roues,* by Dupaty, one-time president of the Parlement of Bordeaux.

The affair of the *trois roues* was one of the *causes célèbres* of the late eighteenth century, a highly publicized affair by which the French public became aware of what reformers considered the worst abuses of the criminal justice system.[16] The case involved three men, agricultural workers, accused of assaulting and robbing a man and his wife in their home. The Bailliage of Chaumont had sentenced them to the galleys for life. On appeal to the Parlement of Paris, the sentence was increased to breaking on the wheel.[17] Freteau, one of the judges of the Paris Parlement, wrote to his brother-in-law Dupaty, retired from the Parlement of Bordeaux and very active in the reform movement, asking that he look into the case.

In his *Mémoire Justificatif pour Trois Hommes Condamnés à la Roue* (1785), Dupaty attacked the sentence and the use of torture in the trial to force confessions, demanded reforms to prevent future miscarriages of justice, and made a highly emotional appeal for a more humane justice. He was to repeat this combination of legal, procedural, and emotional arguments in a subsequent defense of seven men condemned in Metz, which he published in 1787, one of the best examples of the rhetorical style of the reformers:

> From the depths of their dungeons, the seven accused prisoners were led in turn into the chambers of the jail, still unaware of their fate. Serenity was on their countenances as innocence was in their souls. . . . The interpreter told them the judgement was to be pronounced; they expect to be absolved. The interpreter speaks out. To three of them he pronounces the *question préparatoire* with reserve of proofs, and to the four others, the *question préalable* and death. What perturbation in the souls of these unfortunates! Their faces dropped; they looked at each other . . . but we are innocent; . . . the die is cast, unfortunates, you must suffer and die. Meanwhile everything is already set in the torture chamber. The court clerk has prepared the instrument of the interrogatory, the executioners that of the torture; the interpreter who must translate the sighs and cries and errors of pain has come; the doctor is there . . . and the magistrate has just entered. "They will perhaps confess," they say, "we shall see." You are going to see. They lead the unfortunates single file via various secret detours from the jail cell to the torture chamber. . . .
>
> The magistrate who has questioned Braun [the youngest of the seven] without success, hopes that torture will be able to draw from his lips the confession he needs, and he gives the signal to the executioners. A terrible cry provoked by the pain suddenly awakened in the poor man's nerves by torture reverberates in the gloomy vaults. The people scattered inside have heard and at this signal the crowd becomes quiet; it is listening . . . ; But what response has pain torn out of Braun? "I was not there; I have no accomplices; I am innocent; May Heaven be my witness . . . Ah! . . ." The judge redoubles his questions; the torturer his torments; the victim his cries and his denials. Magistrate, desist! May you have pity upon a fellow man whose body is shattered with pain. . . . Can words torn out by torture confess or deny, or express anything but suffering? . . . "This *arrêt* must be justified." The torture continues, always with as little success; always—when the sounds that escape the lips of the victim can

be put together to form a word—always they are made to mean: "No, I am innocent, I have no accomplices." Finally the doctor warns that the torturer has left Braun only a last gasp of air; they are quick to unfasten Braun, and spare him for the hangman's rope."[18]

Public defense of accused criminals was a highly acceptable activity for eighteenth-century reformers, both lawyers and *philosophes.* The language of the publicist was reason, moderation, humanity, and justice. The system of criminal law provided opportunities for satire, drama, and attacks on other aspects of French society that touched on the criminal justice system. Voltaire, for example, became involved in the cause of reform through his writings on the Calas case, an affair which interested him originally because of his opposition to the Catholic church.[19]

While reformers may have labeled their tracts *Cri de l'humanité . . . ,* there were limits to the philosophic "love of humanity." While it often appeared that the reform movement brought together men from very different classes of society, their common interests were more apparent at a distance than face-to-face. In 1764 Voltaire wrote to Necker about meeting a shoemaker he had helped to gain release from a galleys-sentence: "I saw your shoemaker. Truly he is an imbecile. If his friends are just as dimwitted, as I presume, they are as certain of paradise in the other world as they are of the galleys in this."[20]

The right of the accused to an effective defense, the reformers argued, included not only the right to know the charges against him and not to be tortured into confession, but also the right to have an advocate in the courtroom, to have a lawyer present for the defense, paid by the state if necessary. The accused should also, they asserted, receive a copy of all the documents in the case, especially the interrogation, to see that the evidence was being recorded accurately. In 1783, thirty-two lawyers in Toulouse organized the *Conférence de Charité* to provide legal defense for the poor. Bertrand Barère, who would become famous in the Revolution, was part of the group and left extensive, but unpublished, notes critical of existing practices denying defense to the accused.[21]

Defense counsel, like juries, had been forbidden by the Ordinance of 1670 as unnecessary, given the new standards of proof. Minimum proof needed to convict the accused, according to the ordinance, was the testimony of two eyewitnesses testifying in agreement. Recognizing that eyewitnesses are not always available, the statute defined various categories

of "clear proof" and "partial proof" that could be complemented by confession of the accused. In contrast to the English system, there was no
plea of "guilty" in France: a man's confession was not sufficient to convict him.[22] The court still required "clear proof," such as eyewitness
testimony and physical evidence of the crime. When this was lacking,
a complete proof could be achieved if there were sufficient "partial proofs,"
such as witnesses who had seen the accused flee the scene of the crime
even though they had not seen him commit it. The use of partial proofs
was a subject of criticism, even satire. Voltaire claimed that, since credibility
was given to witnesses who had heard of, but not witnessed, the guilt of
the accused, it was possible that if eight people heard the same wild rumor,
this constituted proof under the Ordinance of 1670.[23]

If this was true in theory, it was rarely true in practice. If judges did not
have sufficient proof to convict or acquit the accused, they could sentence
him to remain in detention, or to be released, pending more evidence being
obtained.[24] Torture could be used to complete proof by obtaining a confession only in cases which potentially required capital penalties. For the
most serious crimes, like murder and armed robbery, it could even be
ordered after judgment to force the convicted individual to name his accomplices. The amount of criticism directed against these practices was
not a function of their frequency—torture was infrequent—but of their
unacceptability in a humane judicial system. All forms of torture were
abolished by royal decree before the Revolution, in the *lit de justice* of
May 1788.[25]

Other criticisms of the procedure followed in criminal cases concerned
the *serment* and the *sellette*. The first required the accused to swear in
court that he would tell the truth. This meant that either he perjured himself and broke an oath, or that he testified against himself. While there
was no recommendation that the law should protect a man from self-
incrimination—even the reformers believed that the guilty should confess—the specific requirement of the oath was criticized. The *sellette*,
a low stool on which the accused had to kneel before the judges during
final interrogation, was used only in serious crimes to make the accused
physically uncomfortable in the hope that he would confess. Reformers
criticized this practice not only as an abuse of the rights of the defense,
but also as an affront to the human dignity of the accused.[26]

Beyond such specific procedural changes, reformers called for general
principles to be incorporated in the law: A man's wealth, they argued,

should not influence his treatment in prison or the final outcome of his trial. The accused should be considered innocent until proven guilty. Justice should be speedy, and should be carried out in the locality of the crime, to set a public example. The trial should be a matter of community concern, with the general public participating in some way.[27]

The sum of these changes would constitute a new era in French criminal justice—although some argued that it would only restore the rights Frenchmen had enjoyed before the Ordinance of 1670 took effect.[28] While Louis XVI and influential members of the legal profession were in sympathy with many of the reformers' criticisms, only piecemeal changes were made before 1789. The total change in judicial institutions reformers called for could only be carried out in the Revolution.

The problems of what constituted crime and what penalties were appropriate to each offense were more subtle and complex than the problems of procedure and judicial institutions. The definition of crime and the determination of punishment were dictated by tradition, not by statute. While the reformers agreed on general principles, few were able to draw up model codes of law that showed in detail how principle would be transformed into practice.

In Diderot's *Encyclopédie,* crime was defined as a matter of natural law and of jurisprudence. In natural law, "Crime is a harmful action, committed with conscious intent, which does harm directly or indirectly to the public interest or the rights of the individual citizen." In jurisprudence, crime is defined as "an action which is forbidden by law and brings punishment by the state."[29] In defining the nature of crime and punishment, the problem for *philosophes* and for lawyers was to reconcile these two definitions.

What "harmful actions" should be forbidden by law? The two types of offenses that were universally agreed upon as "crimes," were assaults against persons in which the victim suffered physical injury, and offenses against property resulting in loss to the victim through removal or destruction of his goods.[30] These were in fact the most frequently prosecuted offenses in French criminal courts. In Paris, for example, property offenses made up from 80 to 95 percent of cases and assaults on persons from 5 to 20 percent of cases tried in the decades before the Revolution.[31]

By and large the reformers agreed with existing practice that the age, sex, and servile status of the accused should be considered in defining the seriousness of his offense. Courts regularly ruled that the youth of the defendant diminished his responsibility for his act; that the fact of being female diminished responsibility for crime, especially if there were male accomplices who were assumed to have instigated the act; that a domestic was not to be held responsible for crimes committed under the orders of master or employer.[32]

Penalties assigned for crimes varied not only with the person of the accused but also with the person of the victim and circumstances of the act. In practice, if not in law, rape, seduction, and debauch were crimes only when committed on females under the age of sixteen. A thief who stole in broad daylight was not as severely punished as one who stole at night. A lone individual was not punished as severely as one who acted with accomplices. A servant who stole his master's silver was more severely punished than a stranger who broke in during the night and made off with it.[33] In these cases reformers also generally agreed with existing practice.

One area in which reformers disagreed violently, however, was in the special treatment accorded those with money or social status. A bourgeois woman arrested for shoplifting was likely to be acquitted; a poor woman, sent to the Hôpital.[34] Outrage at this practice was not confined to men who lacked wealth and privilege. In 1784, the Société Royale at Metz, a traditionally conservative academy with a large aristocratic membership, awarded a prize to Lacretelle for his essay discussing the legal as well as unwritten social privileges enjoyed by the rich in which he demanded the repudiation of inequitable class justice.[35]

In regard to the definition of crime, reformers voiced their greatest opposition to law and practice in matters of religion. There had been several sensational cases in the eighteenth century in which offenses against religious beliefs were punished by the state, as in the case of the Chevalier de la Barre, or in which religion was an issue, as in the Calas Affair.[36] Even in "ordinary" cases, such as a theft of sacred objects used to celebrate mass (often made of gold or silver), the act was punished not only as theft but also as sacrilege. Reformers attacked the crimes of blasphemy and sacrilege as having no place in a rational judicial system. Furthermore, they objected to the special privilege granted to clergy who committed ordinary crimes, but were tried in ecclesiastical, rather than royal, courts.

Like blasphemy and sacrilege, sorcery and witchcraft were condemned as nonoffenses, superstitious beliefs that the state had no business prosecuting. There had been few trials for witchcraft or magic in the eighteenth century, but if these "crimes" had ceased to exist in fact, they had not yet been abolished in law.[37]

Vagabondage posed a difficult problem in the definition of crime. The chronic poverty of the masses of Frenchmen in the Old Regime made vagabondage an economic necessity for the rural poor and begging a common activity in cities. The problem of distinguishing the "honest poor" from the dangerous brigand became particularly acute in the economic crises of the decades before the Revolution. As far as the state and the criminal courts were concerned, "by the end of the 18th century, begging was not considered a moral concern but a question of law and order."[38] Beggars, vagabonds, and those with no visible means of support were regularly detained, not for any offense they had already committed but for what it was feared they would inevitably do.

This "preventive detention" was criticized by reformers on two grounds. First, it violated the principle that an individual was to be presumed innocent until proven guilty of an offense. Second, reformers allied with the physiocratic school of thought saw crime as "a disease of the social order," and begging and vagabondage as symptoms of the same disease. Neither charity nor prison would solve the problem: the poor must be given work. As intendant at Limoges, Turgot had tried to reduce the begging population by establishing public workshops, although he intended them for the "deserving poor" rather than for "idlers." Diderot, Guillaume LeTrosne, and others recommended work as the cure for the instability in the lives of the poor that led to crime: public workhouses would employ the deserving poor, add to the general wealth, and instill a love of honest labor in the beggar.[39] Brissot called for a redistribution of national wealth as a way to eliminate the armies of beggars in France, arguing that this was one of the most basic ways to prevent crime.[40] In an ideal society, which the *philosophes* hoped might someday exist in France, poverty and vagabondage would be eliminated, and society would be free of the crime associated with them.

The extent to which expressing opinion was a crime against the state or society was similarly complex. Many *philosophes* had been restricted in the free circulation of their ideas by government censorship. Nevertheless, there was no general demand for freedom of opinion in speech or press. There was some fear that a completely free press would have the capacity to undermine the government or public morals. Public opinion was recognized as a powerful force, one that could be turned to evil as well as to good.[41]

The discussion of what constituted crime tended to emphasize a statement of general principles rather than specific actions, although some reformers, especially Brissot and Valazé, drew up extensive tables and classifications of crimes and their appropriate punishments.[42] One distinction that was made almost universally, and had been set forth by Montesquieu, was that not all offenses were crimes to be prosecuted by the state. Montesquieu had distinguished four classes of offenses: those that offend religion, morals, the public tranquility, and security of the subject. He had also set forth the principle that there should be a "just proportion between crimes and punishments," and that "criminal laws should derive each punishment from the particular nature of the crime." Offenses against religion, therefore, should be punished by God; those against the public order, by the state.[43]

While Montesquieu did not go as far as others in calling for a code of crimes and punishments, he has been credited with establishing the principle of determinate sentencing, still fundamental to the French criminal justice system. Those who called for a penal code sought not only to reduce the discretion of judges in assigning penalties but also a way to educate society in the knowledge of right and wrong, a law that would enable men to weigh the consequences of their actions before committing a crime.[44]

Insofar as the judicial system in eighteenth-century France can be said to have had a theory of punishments, it rested on two principles: First, punishment was to be exemplary: harsh, corporeal punishments, carried out in public, were intended to discourage others from committing the same offense. Thieves were branded with a hot iron in the Place de Grève in Paris. Murderers were placed on "the wheel" to have each of their bones broken in sequence. A servant convicted of stealing from his master might be publicly burned.[45] Second, punishment was not directed in any way to reform or rehabilitate the accused, but rather to gain a public apology, or to illustrate the power of the sovereign over those who offended society. Before being branded with a *V* (for *voleur*) a thief might be assigned to make the *amende honorable*, kneeling before a church and apologizing to God, and then ordered "banished from Paris and the presence of the King" for a set term or indefinitely.[46]

The reformers proposed a new theory of punishment, based on a different view of society:

> The harshness of penalties does nothing but multiply crimes. It is around the scaffold that murderers come to study murder, to see how one makes men suffer.... It is above all in seeing the sad condition of the people in all corners of the universe, in seeing the balance of evil turn always in their direction, that I demand the suppression or amelioration of harsh penalties. The rigor of the law weighs them down in their misery, and it is misery which drives them to commit crimes.[47]

The reformist critique attacked harsh penalties, especially those that sought only to inflict pain on the body of the criminal, on two grounds. First, they argued that severe penalties did nothing to prevent crime and that harsh punishments might actually increase crime. If the death penalty were prescribed for theft, robbers would always murder their victims, since they incurred no worse a punishment for doing so and stood less chance of being caught. Second, they argued that punishment could indeed be exemplary, but proposed a different approach to public education than simple intimidation.

One of the causes of crime, according to the reformers, was lack of individual restraint: where men were ruled by their passions, whether lust or greed, they committed crimes. The state, if it sought to reduce crime, should establish institutions to help men control their passions, not set an example of punishments based on vengeance. Ideally, they argued, penalties should be based on restoring the damage done to an individual or to society.[48]

For this reason and others, many reformers argued that the death penalty should be abolished. Beccaria had argued against capital punishment, as had Rousseau, Montesquieu and Robespierre. There were two kinds of reasoning behind these arguments. For some reformers, death was too easy a way out for the criminal. "You will punish him better, you will avenge society better, by forcing him to do good" wrote Philipon de Madelaine, a Jesuit-turned-lawyer from Besançon.[49] For the most part, however, the arguments against the death penalty were couched in terms of concern for humanity and for human dignity: all forms of death which involved torture were barbarous, injurious to society, and unfitted to a civilized nation. Reformers spoke from practical experience when they declared that the spectacle of public torture and execution, rather than inspiring fear of the law, actually hardened the sensibility of the average Frenchman to the sight of human suffering, and even might arouse a blood-lust in those already so inclined.[50]

What should be substituted for the brandings, banishments, and beatings of traditional punishments? The reformers had no single answer, but those who went beyond general principles shared a conviction that once the accused was found guilty of an offense through a fair trial, punishment should not be gentle. Brissot proposed that those convicted of serious crimes be put in the deepest dungeons of prisons:

> ... [T]hose who are to be deprived of their liberty or who are waiting to be transferred to public works, to the galleys, or to the mines ... should have a bed of straw, bread and water, and kept in chains. Twice a year, the public should be admitted to visit the prisons to see the fruits of crime.[51]

For lesser offenses, Brissot proposed lesser degrees of severity within the same prison—each locality would have its own. Prisoners would be provided with work and with religious instruction, the lack of which, Brissot believed, were the most general causes of crime.

Few reformers went as far as Brissot in proposing prison as the most effective punishment for a variety of different crimes. In the eighteenth century, prisons were for those awaiting trial, not for the convicted. They were also for noncriminal offenders: debtors, persons confined by *lettre de cachet.*[52] Women and young offenders were commonly ordered to a term in the *Hôpital,* not officially, but in effect, a prison. Most reformers directed their attention to the means of entering prison—criminal procedure, *lettres de cachet*—rather than to what should happen to the person sent there.

Since the nature of prison was to remove punishment from the public eye, other reformers preferred more public forms of exemplary punishment. Philipon de la Madelaine suggested public spectacles based on shame, rather than pain, but spectacles nonetheless. He proposed to "make for the victims of public vengeance days yet more marked with affliction and ignominy," when they would be "brought to the temples of the God of all Justice." There, they would be exposed "to the broiling heat of summer or the ice and snows of winter, stirring at the same time the indignation of men and the rage of animals, displayed with horror like ferocious beasts, heaped with curses from those who pass . . . [D]raining drop by drop before the eyes of all the cup of shame and suffering, they would lead men to the love of order" far more than the spectacle of executions and wheels.[53]

Whether the public would respond as Madelaine's moral sense assumed is open to considerable question. But his proposal shows the extent to which the Old Regime was to be abandoned. In the future, the system of criminal justice, from public trial to public punishment, was to be a school for society. With a clear and simple code of laws defining crimes and punishments, men could learn virtue from the system of justice, or at least rationally calculate the benefits to be derived from criminal acts against the penalties that followed from them.[54]

Punishment was not simply, or even primarily, a school for virtue, however. Reformers never lost sight of the need to protect the public from those who had broken the law. This was perhaps the most compelling reason behind the widespread rejection of banishment as an appropriate form of punishment. Sentencing a convicted criminal to three years' ban was compared to "letting a mad dog loose upon society."[55] Furthermore, removing a man from his familiar surroundings, his employment, and his family was likely to change him for the worse: every day the criminal courts were creating the vagabonds the police were so concerned to arrest.

If banishing men was seen to be counterproductive, sending them to the galleys was seen as a useless anachronism. Prisoners condemned to the galleys no longer rowed the king's warships in the eighteenth century: they did heavy labor in ports and coastal towns. While the reformers did not object to the principle of forced work as a punishment, they argued that the galleys no longer were effective or useful since they removed the convicted man from the scene of his offense and therefore diminished the public example of punishment.[56]

In support of these new modes of punishment, the reformers wished to see several general principles written into the law. The most important was punishment based on individual responsibility. There should be no distinctions in the penal system because of the social rank of the accused.

Only the criminal should suffer, his family should not be affected. There should be no confiscation of goods unless the money would benefit the victim of the crime or charitable institutions. There should be a Penal Code, so that the same crime would always receive the same penalties.

In the nineteenth century, those who identified themselves with the principles laid down by the eighteenth-century reformers constituted the "Classical School of Criminology." They stressed defects of the institutional system, rather than defects of the individual, as the cause of crime. They concentrated on problems of procedure and designed codes of criminal law, rather than trying to identify types of individuals or social environments that tended to crime.[57] In this they reflected the major emphasis of the reform movement, the critique of institutional abuses. But underlying this critique, and justifying proposed changes, the eighteenth-century reformers had sought to define the social causes of crime and even argued that it could be eliminated in a more perfect society. This emphasis in their writings is important as an idea whose formal expression was lacking in European social thought before the eighteenth century.[58]

"Crime is the result of poverty, misery, and unhappiness" wrote Marat.[59] In asserting this doctrine, and in the discussion of the natural rights of men, the eighteenth-century reformers defined a new attitude to criminals, to crime, and to the place of crime in society. Old Regime justice served a society which presumed guilt in the accused, took misery and human suffering for granted, punished the body harshly, and viewed crime as the product of morally defective or evil individuals. Brissot proposed a new approach: "the criminal is a sick and ignorant person; it is necessary to heal him, to instruct him, not to repress him."[60] The accused was still a human being, with at least the potential for human dignity.

Reformers realized that a total solution to the problem of crime would require attention to more than institutions, to more than individual offenders. Criminal disorders had been shown to arise from faults of social organization: if government would deal with the problems of poverty, unemployment, and underemployment, society would be better served than if it simply punished criminals after the fact. Where a man could support his family by his own labor in a simple society, close to nature, Montesquieu had argued, crime was at a minimum. Where there was virtue in public life, as in the early Roman Republic, there was no serious problem of crime because the moral sense and public spirit of citizens would not allow it. The corrupting factors of French society were seen to be the uneven distribution of wealth, the lack of good morals among the rich, who set an example for society, and the excessive taxation of the fruits of honest labor.

Cities, especially Paris, were believed to be places of corruption. Men were removed from nature. They were frequently desperate and in need. Opportunities for crime were abundant, and organized fraternities of criminals and beggars were assumed eager to tutor the inexperienced. Women fell easily into prostitution, and then to crime.[61] Brissot proposed a seven-point program for reducing crime:

1. The government should attempt to arrange itself to deprive the ordinary citizen of as little as possible of the products of his work. Presently the court, the military, the church, and the nobility do the opposite.
2. Government should strive to improve the morals of society. . . . The countryside is the reserve of moral strength but it is being corrupted by the cities. The worst examples are set by the wealthy who are idle and corrupt.
3. There should be a reform in national education. . . . Wives and children should be taught to respect their husbands and fathers; men taught to respect the king. . . .
4. Arts and letters should be encouraged by the state because of the power they have to shape opinion.
5. Poverty should be eliminated by a more equal distribution of the national wealth.
6. There should be enough police to discourage crime, but they should be respected, as the English police are, for their fairness. The fewer crimes are committed, the fewer injustices of the authorities will be perpetrated on society.
7. Some crimes could be eliminated by better charitable institutions. Infanticide would not be so frequent if there were more orphanages.[62]

Those critics who had been in a position of public authority had often tried to implement one or another of their ideas on a local scale: as lieutenant-general of police in Lyons, Prost de Royer had been instrumental in setting up a Bureau des Nourrices for abandoned children, a growing problem in many cities in France.[63]

The reformers spoke in large social terms, they proposed long-range projects, but they never faced directly the ambiguity of their position that poverty was the root of the problem of crime. Attitudes toward the poor in eighteenth-century France were dual. There were the honest poor, especially widows and children, who deserved charity from all who had food or clothing to spare. But those who turned to begging or crime because they did not wish to work were to be treated more harshly. Montesquieu had declared "A man is not poor because he has nothing, but because he does not wish to work. If he has a trade, he will always be able to find employment."[64] Those who did not wish to work were idle, idleness was the root of crime, therefore the government should counter an evil character (laziness) with good habits (the love of work) in public workshops and projects.

Failure to resolve this ambiguity did not diminish the influence of the eighteenth-century reformers on French law and society in the nineteenth century. While they had proposed a new idea, that the criminal might be a product of his milieu, they had not been able to take this idea very far.

> One cannot say that they were the founders of modern criminal sociology but only its precursors. Yet their ideas were not without effect, since they challenged traditional ideas, and in the first 75 years of the nineteenth century, their ideas dominated French thought.[65]

Nor did this failure diminish the immediate impact of the reform movement. In 1788, Louis XVI sounded the call for reform of the criminal law in the *lit de justice* of May. The goal of this reform, he declared,

> is to reassure innocence in protecting it by those forms most fitting to establish it; to render punishments inevitable by eliminating excessive severity, which tends to the toleration of crime . . . ; and to punish malefactors with the restraint that humanity demands, and the interests of society permits the law.[66]

The king's speech was not a concession of all that the reformers had called for. The *Cahiers* drawn up for the meeting of the Estates General were more comprehensive, and nearly unanimous in their call for reform, including: emptying the prisons, and improving conditions in those not immediately destroyed; public attendance at criminal trials; defense counsel for the accused; access to the documents of the case for the accused; abolition of torture and the *sellette;* and limitation of the death penalty to the crimes of premeditated murder and arson. These reforms were called for immediately. For the longer term the *Cahiers* called for jury trials, a written code of crimes and punishments, differentiation of crime from sin or vice, and abolition of crimes based on privilege—especially the decriminalization of smuggling. The idea of the fundamental rights of man, including his rights when charged with criminal offenses, appeared in the *Cahiers.*[67]

The movement for reform of the criminal justice system had achieved a great deal in a relatively short time. Although the publicists of the reform movement had dealt with exceptional crimes, like the Chevalier de la Barre, and exceptional abuses, like torture, they had convinced many Frenchmen, including influential persons in the judicial system who were not publicly committed to reform, that drastic changes were needed. French criminal law had depended on tradition, learned commentary, and royal ordinances. It was now to be restructured by the light of reason, in accordance with the natural law. Early in the Revolution, the effect of the reformers' arguments was seen in the establishment of legislative committees to deal with judicial power, criminal legislation, mendicity, and the problems of the poor. These reflected the conviction that if the legal and social system could be changed, crime would disappear of itself, without attention to the individual criminal. Failure to achieve this goal in the Revolution and beyond did not diminish the important influence the ideas of the eighteenth-century reformers continued to exert into the nineteenth century.

Notes

1. Arthur Young, *Travels in France During the Years 1787, 1788, 1789,* ed. Bentham-Edwards (London: George Bell & Sons, 1900), p. 320 (Originally published, 1792).

2. Adhemar Esmein, *Histoire de la Procédure Criminelle en France* (Paris, 1882) is still the basic reference work on criminal law and trial procedure, with special emphasis on the Ordinance of 1670. Gerard Aubry, *La Jurisprudence Criminelle du Châtelet de Paris sous le Regne de Louis XVI* (Paris: Librairie Général de Droit et de Jurisprudence, 1971) supplements Esmein, but deals only briefly with procedure. On the respect given to French magistrates, *see* John Langbein, *Torture and the Law of Proof: Europe and England in the Ancien Regime,* p. 59.

3. The most comprehensive study of the movement is Joanne Kaufmann. "The Critique of Criminal Justice in Eighteenth-Century France: A Study in the Changing Social Ethics of Crime and Punishment." Good

brief summaries are included in Michel Foucault, *Discipline and Punish: The Birth of the Prison*, and in Shelby T. McCloy, *The Humanitarian Movement in Eighteenth Century France*.

4. Albert Desjardins, *Les Cahiers des Etats Généraux en 1789 et la Legislation Criminelle* (Paris, 1883).

5. Notably the works of Kaufmann, Langbein and Foucault already cited. These works and others raise the question "How humane was the party of humanity?", i.e., beyond the rhetoric of the Enlightenment, what were the realities of the daily contact of *philosophes* and people, what were the effects of their ideas? A very interesting approach to this question is Harry C. Payne, *The Philosophes and the People* (New Haven: Yale University Press, 1976). Payne traces the evolution of the relationship between two groups who confronted each other "across a wide social gulf." His basic theme is the ambiguity the *philosophes* faced and never resolved. They wished to remain aloof but felt their involvement was necessary. They struggled to remain distant from the "stupid," "miserable" people, while reshaping them into something better for the future.

6. Charles Louis de Secondat, Baron de la Brede et de Montesquieu, *De l'Esprit des Lois*, 2 vols. (Paris: Éditions Garnier Frères, 1973), especially books 6 and 12. Cesare Bonesana, Marquis de Beccaria, *An Essay on Crimes and Punishments*, n.t. (London: Hodson, 1801). *See* especially Marcello T. Maestro, *Voltaire and Beccaria as Reformers of the Criminal Law* (New York: Octagon Books, 1972) on the seminal influence of Beccaria on Voltaire, whose reputation as a publicist was already established when he "discovered" the cause of reform of the criminal law through his involvement in the Calas affair.

7. Kaufmann's work is particularly valuable for the biographical background and the analysis of ideas of lawyers involved in this movement. She is interested in analyzing lawyers who wanted to break out of the traditional modes of their profession, especially when they spoke and wrote "en philosophe."

8. Montesquieu, *Esprit des Lois*, vol. 1, p. 202. Book 12, pt. 2 discusses the relationship between political liberty and criminal law.

9. J. P. Brissot de Warville, *Théorie des Loix Criminelles* 2 vols. (Paris: J. P. Ailland, 1836) 2, pp. 263-70. This is a republication in two volumes, with notes, of Brissot's essay of 1780. The quotation given is a summary of his discussion.

10. Montesquieu, *Esprit des Lois*, vol. 1, pp. 80-150. Book 6 includes discussion of the jury system of France. Esmein states that the regulation of standards of proof in the Ordinance of 1670 was one of the major causes for the decline of the jury: it was no longer considered necessary.

11. Lloyd Weinreb, *Denial of Justice: Criminal Process in the United States* (New York: The Free Press, 1977) is an excellent introduction to the differences between the French "magisterial" procedure and the Anglo-American jury trial, and puts some of the eighteenth-century debate into context by showing the different legal systems that resulted.

12. Esmein, *Procédure Criminelle,* pp. 3-42 summarizes criminal procedure. In Appendix 1, I have compared trial procedure before and during the Revolution.

13. Esmein, *Procédure Criminelle,* p. 377.

14. *See* Joanne Kaufmann, "In Search of Obedience: The Critique of Criminal Justice in Late Eighteenth Century France," *Proceedings of the Western Society for French History* (1978). Cited as Kaufmann, "Search."

15. Langbein, *Torture,* gives the impression, in his presentation of the "fairy tale" version of the abolition of torture, that historians have consistently presented the change as sudden, and as somehow due to a change of heart among European rulers struck by the ideas of the Enlightenment. I do not find this "fairy tale" in any of the standard works on the reform movement in France. Esmein, Kaufmann, McCloy and others have appreciated the relationship of the abolition of torture and the changes in standards of proof as Langbein has. The reformers recognized that an attack on torture was not new: Montesquieu said that he would not discuss the subject because the case against judicial torture had been so well made already. It attracted the attention of critics perhaps because that case was so established, and out of all proportion to its frequency in daily judicial practice.

16. These cases were undoubtedly good tools of public education, but they gave a distorted picture of how common were the abuses they attacked.

17. This was one of the more gruesome forms of public execution: a prisoner was tied to a frame, frequently in the shape of a wheel, to have his bones broken in sequence until he died. For a vivid description of the inventiveness of executioners, see the description of the execution of Damiens in Foucault, *Discipline and Punish,* pp. 1-7.

18. Dupaty, *Justification de Sept Hommes Condamnés par le Parlement de Metz en 1769* (Paris, 1787) as cited in Kaufmann, "Critique," p. 134. Dupaty's career is summarized pp. 83-89. He became involved in the reform movement after being denied the presidency of the Parlement of Bordeaux, from which he was then forced to resign. "His own experiences may have intensified his concern for victims of injustice," according to Kaufmann, p. 88.

19. Maestro, *Voltaire,* ch. 1.

20. Payne, *Philosophes,* p. 1.

21. Kaufmann, "Critique," p. 201. Muyart de Vouglans, a conservative legal commentator of the eighteenth century, defended the prohibition of lawyers from court, arguing that lawyers had never done anything to establish the truth in a trial but had always served only to complicate the proceedings (cited in Esmein, *Procédure Criminelle,* p. 390).

22. Esmein, *Procédure Criminelle,* p. 275. For a discussion of the Theory of Legal Proof *see* pp. 260-75.

23. Esmein, *Procédure Criminelle,* p. 369. Among the reformers, Brissot was almost alone in dealing with the tangled issue of legal proof. *Théorie,* vol. 2, pp. 86-171. Even Beccaria found himself unable to deal with this question. In chapter 14 of his *Essay* he says "It is much easier to feel the moral certainty of proofs than to define them exactly. . . . To judge of [the facts of the case] nothing is wanted but plain and ordinary good sense, a less fallacious guide than the knowledge of a judge, accustomed to find guilty, and to reduce all things to an artificial system borrowed from his studies.", p. 53.

24. This was an order of *plus ample information,* commonly abbreviated *PAI* (an abbreviation I will use frequently in chapter 3). Technically it is not a sentence at all but simply a part of trial procedure. In fact, persons held for months or a year on this order were effectively punished.

25. Aubry, *Châtelet,* p. 34, and Esmein, *Procédure Criminelle,* p. 387.

26. Desjardins, *Cahiers,* p. 84.

27. This was most generally expressed as a call for public trials, which already existed in civil cases. *See* Kaufmann, "Critique," p. 190.

28. This was especially true in the early works of the reform movement, which favored arguments from historical precedent and classical morality. By the time of the Revolution, arguments tended to be made more frequently in the name of natural law and absolute human rights. This evolution of argument is outlined in Kaufmann, "Critique," chapters 4-6.

29. M. le Chevalier de Jaucourt, "Crime," *Encyclopédie, ou Dictionnaire Raisonné des sciences, des arts et des métiers,* ed. Denis Diderot, (1751-1765), vol. 4, p. 466. In the eighteenth century, crime was defined by tradition rather than by law. *See* appendix 3 for a comparison between crimes prosecuted by the Châtelet in the eighteenth century and those defined by the Penal Code of September, 1791.

30. Marat is an exception to the universal acceptance of an absolute right to property. In his *Plan de Legislation Criminelle* (Paris, 1790), he questioned whether a starving man should be prosecuted for stealing from a rich one, whose wealth might have been gained illegally. Ultimately he concluded that since property gained by honest labor must be protected, theft must always be considered a crime in law, if not in morals.

31. Porphyre Petrovitch, "Recherches sur la Criminalité à Paris dans la Seconde Moitié du XVIIIe Siècle," p. 208.

32. Petrovitch, "Recherches," pp. 226-38. *See also* Aubry's discussion of penalties assigned by the Châtelet.

33. Alan Williams, *The Police of Paris 1718-1789* (Baton Rouge: Louisiana State University Press, 1979), p. 192 states that the police especially were of the opinion that domestics were to be carefully surveyed and severely punished. Lenoir believed that domestic servants were an idle class who, because they were living within the homes of the rich, were a greater danger even than the city's vagabonds and beggars.

34. Olwen Hufton, *The Poor of Eighteenth-Century France,* discusses the problem of crime, punishment, and social status in chapter 8. She cites the specific case of a bourgeois woman arrested for being a pickpocket who was released on the basis of her social status, p. 245.

35. Kaufmann, "Critique," pp. 119-21. Lacretelle was a lawyer, as his father had been, and a successful one. In the revolution he would become premier *élu* of the Commune. The academy awarded a prize to Robespierre in the same year for an essay on a similar theme.

36. For brief descriptions of these and other famous cases of the eighteenth century *see* Jean Imbert, ed., *Quelques Procès Criminels des XVIIe et XVIIIe Siècles*, Travaux et Recherches de la Faculté de Droit et des Sciences Economiques de Paris, Serie "Sciences Historiques" No. 2 (Paris: Presses Universitaires de France, 1964).

37. Aubry, *Châtelet,* pp. 53-54, describes a prosecution for magic before the Châtelet in 1779. The penalty imposed by the court was simply a warning not to repeat the offense. This was raised by the Parlement of Paris, on appeal of the government, to *amende honorable* in a church (i.e. ritual apology to God, performed standing before a designated church). The case involved three men claiming to be exorcists. The Châtelet judges stated that they and the family who had hired them to exorcise their daughter were more to be pitied than to be blamed.

38. Hufton, *The Poor,* p. 244. This problem is also discussed at length in Williams, *Police,* chapter 5. For changing ideas about, and resources for charity, poor relief, and beggars *see* Cissie Fairchilds, *Poverty and Charity in Aix-en-Provence 1640-1789* (Baltimore: Johns Hopkins Press, 1976).

39. Payne, *Philosophes,* discusses the efforts of men like Turgot and Diderot to establish such workshops in chapter 7. Kaufmann, "Critique," focuses on Guillaume le Trosne's physiocratic critique of crime as a disease of the social order, and his nostalgia for a simple life as a cure for crime, pp. 69-70. *See also* Hufton, *The Poor,* chapter 1, for the conflict of the Catholic idea of charity with the Enlightenment social program.

40. Brissot, *Théorie,* pp. 84-90.

41. The expression of opinions that stirred men to armed rebellion against the authority of the state, for example, was not to be allowed. Desjardins, *Cahiers,* pp. 125-35.

42. Kaufmann, "Critique," p. 100.

43. Montesquieu, *Esprit des Lois,* Book 6, pt. 16, and Book 12, pt. 4. Brissot proposed a similar division: "There are three sorts of crimes. Sin is an infraction of the divine order, for which punishment is reserved to God. Vice is a disorder inflicted on oneself, and should be punished by shame. Crime is injury to one's neighbor, and is punished by society." *Théorie,* vol. 1, p. 103.

44. Kaufmann, "Search," draws this theme out of the writings of many of the reformers. It is also basic to Foucault's work, although he is more interested in changes in the style of punishment, the attempt to make mind and body conform to social norms after a crime has been committed rather than before.

45. Aubry, *Châtelet,* pp. 178-79.

46. Foucault, *Discipline and Punish,* pp. 48-59 discusses punishment as a ritual "to restore an injured sovereignty" as well as a punishment of individual offense.

47. Brissot, *Théorie,* vol. 1, p. xix.

48. Restif de la Bretonne, although hardly in the same class intellectually as most of the men discussed here, had one of the more interesting plans for making punishment suit the crime. On his nightly wanderings about Paris he saw many crimes being committed. A stern moralist, he proposed that those convicted of serious crimes be considered as having excluded themselves from consideration as members of society—and almost as human beings. In a code for punishment of unmarried men (married men would have their own), he proposed that murderers be sold into slavery, with the purchase price going to benefit the family of the victim; that poisoners be subjected to different kinds of poisons and their antidotes until they die; that arsonists be forced to rescue people from burning buildings; and that rapists be sold into slavery, or castrated, or made subjects for experiments with venereal diseases—unless the victim chose to marry her attacker. *Les Nuits de Paris,* vol. 4, pp. 1548-54. Restif was called a "philosophe sauvage," even by his friends, but his opinions may reflect more of the opinion of "the common man" than more socially prominent *philosophes.*

49. Kaufmann, "Critique," p. 255.

50. Restif wrote of this frequently, as he often went to public executions. *See Nuits,* vol. 1, pp. 91-92.

51. Brissot, *Théorie,* vol. 1, p. 192.

52. Although there is not yet a study of the subject, it may be that more people were confined on *lettres de cachet* at the request of their

families than at the will of the king. Williams, *Police,* pp. 103, 226-27 describes the numerous requests the police received from husbands wishing their wives incarcerated, and offering to pay all expenses, or of parents wanting their errant sons and daughters confined.

53. Quoted in Kaufmann, "Critique," p. 259.

54. Kaufmann, "Search," refers to this as an attempt to instill "The Wisdom of Obedience." Foucault calls the attempt at social conditioning "the gentle way of punishment." In both, there is the idea of the "search for the rational criminal," a term I prefer as describing the still mythical individual to whom the reformers and legislators directed their efforts in reshaping the law.

55. Brissot, *Théorie,* vol. 1, pp. 192-96. Desjardins, *Cahiers,* p. 35.

56. Desjardins, *Cahiers,* p. 63.

57. Leon Radzinowicz, *Ideology and Crime* (New York: Columbia University Press, 1966), chapter 1 summarizes twelve basic points of eighteenth-century thought, drawn primarily from Beccaria, and discusses their continuing influence in the nineteenth century.

58. Henry Levy-Bruhl, "Evolution du Crime et du Peine," *Déviance et Criminalité: Textes,* ed. Denis Szabo (Paris: Colin, 1970), pp. 50-75.

59. Marat, *Plan,* p. 5.

60. Brissot, *Théorie,* vol. 1, p. xx.

61. Hufton, *The Poor,* chapter 8 discusses the transition a migrant entering Paris penniless might make from patterns of rural crime to urban, and asserts that "close-knit criminal fraternities" of persons from the same provinces operated in Paris to initiate newcomers to crime, p. 256. Restif plays on the theme of the innocent peasant being corrupted in the city constantly in his works, although his interests are frequently prurient and many of these tales simply pornographic.

62. Brissot, *Théorie,* vol. 1, pp. 40-100. Beccaria outlined a similar plan in chapters 41-47 of his *Essay.*

63. Kaufmann, "Critique," p. 80.

64. Montesquieu, *Esprit des Lois,* Book 12, pt. 29 argues that if a man does not work it is more a failure of will or training than of the economic system. The causes of unemployment were not understood in his argument, which he expanded as follows: "The man who without any degree of wealth has an employment is as much at his ease as he who without labor has an income of a hundred crowns a year. He who has not subsistence, and yet has a trade, is not poorer than he who, possessing ten acres of land, is obliged to cultivate it for his subsistence. The mechanic who gives his art to his children has left them a fortune. . . ." One could work very hard in Paris and still not be able to feed one's family. Restif

de la Bretonne defended low wages as necessary for the control of the working classes. If they earned enough to live by working only three days, he argued, they would spend their life in idleness and corruption, as they did in the few opportunities they had currently. For a discussion of Restif's ideas on work, *see* Mark Poster, *The Utopian Thought of Restif de la Bretonne* (New York: New York University Press, 1971), ch. 4.

65. Levy-Bruhl, "Evolution," p. 56.

66. Desjardins, *Cahiers,* p. 20.

67. Desjardins, *Cahiers,* ch. 2.

REVOLUTIONARY LEGISLATION:
The Search for
the Rational Criminal _____ 2

Despite the popularity of the movement for reform of the criminal law, France had a viable, if complicated, set of judicial institutions at the time of the Revolution. They were not abolished solely through the pressure of the reformist critique, but rather as a consequence of political power struggles, beginning with the conflict between the Parlement and the monarchy which preceded the Revolution.[1]

The issues of political power and legal reform were associated as early as May 1788. By the *lit de justice,* Louis XVI suspended the Parlements and established new courts to take their place. At the same time, he decreed specific changes in the law on other subjects, including several changes in criminal procedure to take effect immediately, as a prelude to a complete overhaul of the Ordinance of 1670. The *sellette* and the use of torture in any form and at any stage of the trial of the accused was abolished; judges were ordered to specify the crimes of the accused in their judgments before assigning penalties; a majority of three judges was needed to order a death sentence; a delay of at least a month was to pass between the ordering of a death sentence and its execution (previously the sentence had been carried out as quickly as possible); and all orders of acquittal were to be printed at the expense of the accuser or of the state and made public.[2]

Lesser courts of the Old Regime were disbanded soon after, again for reasons both philosophical and political. As part of the abolition of feudal privileges on the night of August 4, 1789, the National Assembly eliminated seigneurial courts; condemned the sale of judicial office; and called for the free availability of justice. Serious work to overhaul the entire judicial system of France began soon afterwards. Not all parts of the new system of justice so painstakingly worked out in committees

early in the Revolution were realized. In this chapter I shall highlight
only those that were instituted before the end of 1792, when the September massacres in the prisons of Paris gave a very different meaning to
justice than the reformers had ever intended.

On August 17, 1789, Nicolas Bergasse[3] presented a report on the proposed reorganization of the judicial power to the Assembly in the name of
the Committee on the Constitution. He set forth the general principles
of the new system and proposed a plan that was not significantly modified
in the legislation that followed in 1790 and 1791. Justice was to be de-
centralized, with both civil and criminal justice administered by local
courts. This guaranteed that judicial reform would have to wait for the
administrative reorganization of France. Judges were to be named by
the king, but only from lists of candidates elected by the people. Venality
of office was forever outlawed. The basis of the criminal justice system
was to be the *juge de paix* (justice of the peace), a locally elected official
who would hear the initial complaint of an offense and the first defense of
the accused. The justice would have the power to dismiss the charge or to
send the case to higher courts.

The language of Bergasse's report was one indication of the new attitude toward persons accused of crime the state was to adopt: "le juge
de paix avertira la cour suprême de justice *qu'il a mis un citoyen sous
la puissance de la loi.* "[4] The form of the higher court was another: Each
local tribunal would have two judges, one of whom would prepare the
documents of the case. Judgment of guilt or innocence, however, was
to be determined by a "jury of peers" of the accused. The administration
of justice was to be free, with costs borne by the state. Legal counsel
would be provided without charge to the poor. Court proceedings, after
certain preliminary hearings, were to be public.

Bergasse's report was accepted without debate and with applause.
The consensus of public opinion shown in the *Cahiers* was apparent also
in the first stages of reform in the Assembly. Although Bergasse was
counted a conservative in the Assembly, his report assumed that the
existing court system would have to be completely dismantled. Good
government, he argued, was founded on the separation of powers. Existing courts, notably the Parlements, confused the legislative and the judicial powers and, therefore, would have to be replaced.[5]

The Declaration of the Rights of Man and Citizen, adopted by the
Assembly on August 26, further defined several aspects of the new

meaning of justice: Article seven abolished arbitrary arrests; article eight, arbitrary punishments; and article nine declared that all men were to be considered innocent until proven guilty.[6] It was relatively simple to declare the new principles. The task of writing laws which would guarantee their execution was assigned to a Committee on Criminal Legislation, formed September 14, 1789.[7]

On September 29, the committee presented its first report, dealing primarily with questions of procedure to be followed in criminal trials. Briois de Beaumetz, speaking in the name of the committee, prefaced his remarks by observing the fundamental ways in which the problems of criminal law were joined with the rights of man. Echoing the Declaration, he urged the Assembly to take special care to protect by law the rights of defendants "because the people are so agitated and willing to join the accusers."[8] The report proposed to do no more than remedy the worst abuses of the present system: criminal trials were to be open to the public, the accused was to be guaranteed the right to counsel, and any evidence the accused wished to submit for defense or justification was to be admitted as part of the court record.

In support of these principles, new rules of judicial procedure were to be established. If the complaint were the result of denunciation, the person supplying information had to be named, and the accused had to be informed of his identity. To protect the privacy of the accused until the validity of the complaint was established, the first part of the trial was to be conducted in private, but not in secret. Two *notables*, citizens of at least twenty-five years of age and able to sign their names, were to be present at all private hearings of the evidence in the case. (The institution of the *notables* as witnesses to court proceedings was the first step toward a jury.) Judges and *notables* were required to sign each page of the court record. When the decree of *prise de corps* (*see* Appendix 1) was issued, the rest of the trial was to proceed in public with the doors of the courtroom open. The decree of *prise de corps* had to be signed by at least three judges (a measure intended to prevent arbitrary arrest). Failure to observe any of these points of procedure would result in the case being declared null, after which the judges would determine whether the trial should begin again or the accused should be acquitted.

Although they had not been instructed to examine the issue, the committee decided to add an article on residence: persons having a fixed domicile were not to be subject to a decree of *prise de corps* unless the

accusation against them was serious. Free and responsible citizens, the
committee delcared, should not be put into prison for minor causes.
At the time the order for arrest was issued, the accused was to be given
a copy of all documents relating to his case. In all there were twenty-
seven articles, including one forbidding judicial torture.

Debate on the proposed law began on October 5, 1789, but had
to be postponed because of disturbances in the Assembly chamber.[9]
It is a measure of the importance of this issue that the Assembly continued trying to resolve it in the midst of the upheaval of the October
Days. On October 8, the first fifteen articles were adopted. But on October
9, debate on the rest of the articles had to be postponed because the king
ordered the Assembly to move to Paris. After the move, the remaining
articles were adopted with little debate.

Additional articles proposed by other members of the Assembly,
notably Dr. Guillotin, had to be postponed. Guillotin proposed that
the principle of equal penalties for equal crimes, regardless of the social
rank of the accused, be written into the law, that the death sentence
always be carried out by decapitation, that the family of the accused
not suffer any penalties, that there be no confiscation of property in
criminal trials, and that the body of the executed person be returned
at the request of his family.[10]

On December 22, two reports were presented to the Assembly in the
name of the Committee on the Constitution. In the first, Adrien Duport[11]
presented a summary proposal of the fundamental principles of police
and of justice. His report reflected the reformist critique in its call for
proportionate penalties and a fixed schedule of crimes and punishments,
but it also reflected the legislator's point of view:

> It is above all to the prevention of crime that social institutions
> should apply themselves. The things one should wish to do on this
> subject for humanity's sake, are also good politics. It is easier,
> simpler, and safer to maintain order than to try to restore it once
> disturbed.[12]

Exactly how this was to be achieved was not explained.

The report of Jacques-Guillaume Thouret on the project for the new
judicial organization was more specific. The system would be based on
juries and justices of the peace, as outlined by Bergasse. The existing in-

stitutional structure was to be dismantled, with a target date for the new system set for 1792.[13] Thouret proposed that the Assembly begin work immediately on a Penal Code, because the juries would not be able to function without one. Duport's report, and Thouret's, were statements of principle; they were not debated or acted upon.

By the end of 1789, the Assembly had produced a precise law on changes in judicial proceedings in criminal cases, effective immediately. Changes to be made in the judicial system as a whole had been outlined, and the principles on which the new system was to operate clearly stated. During the next two years, the Assembly debated proposals on specific points of criminal law, judicial organization, and organization of the police. Issues were dealt with piecemeal, evolving from questions of procedure to the structure of new institutions. Decisions, votes, and debates were neither so quick nor so unanimous as they had been in 1789. And change began to produce unanticipated problems.

In the matter of restructuring the institutions of justice, for example, it was six months between the time the Assembly adopted a decree ordering a new structure (March 24, 1790),[14] and the time it ordered the suppression of all tribunals of the Old Regime (September 6, 1790).[15] It decreed that criminal trials were to be by jury (April 30, 1790),[16] but kept civil cases in the hands of the judges of the new departmental tribunals (August 1790).[17] The details of the new jury system were not worked out at the time the old criminal courts were suppressed. Therefore, as one of the last articles of the law creating the new departmental (civil) tribunals, almost in the nature of an afterthought, they were ordered to try criminal cases as well as civil until the juries should begin to function.[18]

Establishing the jury system for criminal cases was complicated by the need for a fully defined Penal Code before they could begin to function. Final legislation on juries and on the penal code was not adopted until September, 1791, a year after the old courts had been suppressed. The juries did not begin to function until April of 1792. Meanwhile, criminal justice in France was in a shambles, and Paris was in a crisis.

On March 13, 1791, Duport spoke to the Assembly about the problems of the capital:

> Sirs, you know that there are now 1800 persons in the prisons of Paris, . . . awaiting trial in more than a thousand cases. The new tribunals are, with good reason, adhering religiously to the new forms

[of judicial procedure] which you have decreed. . . . [T]hey cannot keep up with new cases. . . . It may be four or five years before all of these [current and backlogged] affairs can be judged. It is in the public interest that these cases by processed more quickly, because from the moment that one loses sight of the individual arrested for crime, and that the punishment becomes too long separated from the offense, the whole effectiveness of judicial proceedings is lost.[19]

The Departmental Tribunal of Paris had been divided into six courts, to try to provide capacity to deal with the volume of cases arising in the city. From the beginning, this had not been enough: the judges of the district tribunal petitioned the Assembly during the first month of their existence for relief in some form.[20] In February 1791, the Assembly had decreed that a new criminal tribunal be established for each department of France.[21] The problems of Paris were so pressing, however, that it was clear more was needed.

Duport proposed that Paris have an additional court—one tribunal in two chambers, or two tribunals—to deal with cases arising before January 25, 1791 (date of the installation of the departmental tribunal). Another member of the Assembly, Martineau, observed that with two chambers only, the new court would need at least eighteen months to process the backlog. Martineau proposed that the number be raised to six so the problem would be cleared up quickly. This proposal was adopted: the six provisional tribunals were expected to be functioning by the end of March and to continue for perhaps six months. They were to be staffed by seven judges each, drawn from the forty-two departmental tribunals closest to Paris. The salaries of the judges would be paid by the tribunal from which they were appointed.

The six provisional criminal courts of Paris, created by the law of March 13, 1791, were intended to be no more than a footnote to the history of judicial reform. Events dictated a different role for them. The courts did their work well; by September they reported that they had finished, or nearly finished, the backlog of cases assigned to them. Since the juries were still not operating, they were ordered by a decree of September 29, 1791, to take charge of current criminal cases pending before the regular departmental tribunals as well as all new criminal cases until the installation of the juries in Paris.[22] They continued to do so until August of 1792, disbanding shortly before the prison massacres of September—and the events that followed from them—gave a very different meaning to crime and to justice than the one the Assembly was defining with such care in 1791.

The activities of the six provisional courts will be examined in detail in chapter three. Although they were intended only as a short-term solution to a pressing problem, they became an important part of the new system of justice. They responded to changes in law; they sought to follow the letter and spirit of the reform. For the moment, however, they were to be forgotten. The emergency in Paris taken care of, the Assembly returned its attention to the larger problems of the new law.

Two major aspects of the new judicial system were established by legislation in 1791: organization of the police, including judicial procedures for trying petty crimes and misdemeanors; and establishment of juries for criminal trials, including formulation of a Penal Code for their use.

Bergasse had outlined the structure of the new police in his report in August 1789: There should be a separate department within the police for the prevention and prosecution of crimes, and others for matters of health, safety, and so forth; and the police should be under the control of the local government, that is, the municipal administration. The duties and limitations placed on the police were also defined: the justices of the peace should be the judges in police matters; and a code and a law for the police, setting forth the limits of their powers, the duties of the justices of the peace, the type of actions which they are competent to punish, and the forms of appeal from their judgments should be drawn up.[23] The Law on the Organization of the Municipal Police of July 22, 1791, adhered closely to these principles. It provided for two types of police to be established under the control of the municipal government. The *police municipale* would serve to maintain order and tranquility in all places. The *police correctionnelle* would be responsible for controlling acts which, while not meriting the severe penalties of the Penal Code, "trouble society and tend to crime." The *police correctionnelle* had the specific duty to punish offenses against good morals; problems stemming from the practice of religion; insult and violence to persons; disturbing the public tranquility by mendicity, tumult, and unlawful assembly; and threats to private property by theft and larceny, simple theft, swindling, and problems in gambling houses.[24] Those committing these offenses would be brought before a justice of the peace, who would hear the evidence and order them detained or released. If they were ordered detained, they were to be brought before the tribunal of the *police correctionnelle* within three days. This tribunal would be composed of several justices of the peace (nine in Paris, to meet every day, in three chambers if necessary). The accused would have the right to a public defender. The only sentences which the tribunal could order would be a fine, confiscation of the object of the crime, or a prison sentence not to exceed two years in a *maison de correction.* The tribunal might also decide that the crime did come under the Penal Code and send it to the regular criminal tribunal. The accused could appeal a sentence from the tribunal of *police correctionnelle* to the regular criminal courts.

The debate on the new Penal Code was more extended than that on the police. The Penal Code adopted by the Assembly in September-October 1791, consummated the break with traditional French criminal law which had been legislated piecemeal since 1788. It was the keystone of the new "rational" system of French justice. It was supplemented by a law establishing juries, voted on September 16,[25] and by a law defining procedure in criminal trials, adopted October 21.[26] While much of the Code could have been predicted from demands made by eighteenth-century reformers and by the writers of the *Cahiers* (such as the elimination of banishment as a penalty), there were some surprises. The most notable surprise was the extent to which the new Code established prison sentences as the punishment for most crimes. This major change in penal philosophy and practice was accomplished with little debate on prison as punishment, *per se.* The most important areas of debate in the new Penal Code were the abolition of the death penalty, and the acceptability of forced labor as a punishment.

The first report on the project for a Penal Code was delivered by Louis-Michel Le Pelletier Saint-Fargeau,[27] in the name of the Committees on the Constitution and on Criminal Legislation, on May 23, 1791. The proposed Code had two parts: part one defined legal penalties; part two defined what constituted crime and which penalties were to be assigned to each crime.[28] In place of the discretion of the Old Regime, judges and juries were to be given rules that were precise, fixed, and inflexible. The right of the King to pardon, or to interfere in any way with the rules established by the Assembly, was abolished. The new Code had two objectives: to prevent arbitrary decisions by magistrates and to simplify the judicial process. The juries would need only to determine the facts in a case; the crime and its appropriate penalty would then be located in the Penal Code and assigned.

In the four months that the Assembly debated the provisions of the new Code, the intentions and aspirations of the legislators were articulated clearly. As the *philosophes* had argued that the old system of penalties was actually a cause of crime, framers of the new Code consciously tried to design a legal instrument that would prevent crime while punishing it. This was clear from the first, as Le Pelletier Saint-Fargeau began his report by declaring the fundamental principles of the new law:

1. "All penal law should be humane." Since this has usually been forgotten, it is important to state it clearly. Law is less effective as it is less humane, because one hesitates to apply it.
2. To be an effective deterrent to crime, penalties should be graduated in accordance with the severity of the crime.
3. The precise relationships between aspects of crime and consequent punishment must be clearly expressed in the laws. Physical pain should attach to violent crime; work should be the penalty for idleness.
4. "Equal penalties for equal crimes" is a necessary corollary of this.
5. To be an effective deterrent to crime, penalties must be durable, they must be public, and they must be applied in proximity to the scene of the crime.
6. The aim of the penal system must be "to *punish the guilty and to improve him.*" The most ordinary source of crimes is need, the child of idleness. The system of penalties then should be based on work. Work should not be punitive, it should not be hateful to the convicted man but should prepare him to reenter society.
7. Penalties should be temporary. Despair is the most barbaric of punishments and one that society has no right to inflict.[29]

He proceeded to criticize specific practices of the present and to show the directions in which the new Penal Code would change them.

1. The death penalty is, in and of itself, in violation of the basic principles of the new penal law, since it is permanent. It must be debated. If it is retained, it should never be allowed to be the public spectacle it is now.
2. The galleys as a sentence now produce useful work. But it is done in small maritime towns and loses the power of example. It should be changed to hard labor in the vicinity of the crime.

3. Most punishments are now accompanied by beating and branding. Beating or whipping is not a very effective punishment. Branding raises a number of questions. It serves a useful purpose in identifying a known criminal, and the new law recognizes that habitual criminals should be severely punished. But the branded criminal is unable to return to society and make an honest living. The *mark* violates the principle that penalties should be temporary. In the future, better records will be kept of each individual, his birthplace, family, etc. Thus vagabonds will stand out more readily in the future and the *mark* will be unnecessary.

4. Mutilations, other than the *mark*, are rarely practiced now but the law should declare that they never be repeated.

5. Banishment is universally condemned as a penalty more injurious to society than to the criminal.[30]

The report continued, giving more detail on the new penalties to be established. But the question of primary importance, and one which would determine other elements of the Code, was the question of abolishing the death penalty.

In his report, Le Pelletier Saint-Fargeau presented arguments for and against the death penalty, but concluded that it was not an effective deterrent to crime and should be abolished:

Criminals also have their philosophy. Among the chances of their fate they calculate coldly on what they call the "terrible quarter hour." More than once on the scaffold this secret has escaped: no, they say, the fear of death has never deterred us from a single crime; only the wheel makes the most ferocious of us fearful.[31]

Examining the death penalty in English law and classical Roman law, he concluded that the general moral state of society and the guarantee of certain and speedy justice were more effective deterrents to crime than the existence of the death penalty. He proposed that the convicted man should be deprived of all of life's pleasures, but allowed to live. He proposed prison as an alternative to death: The criminal would be "locked in a dungeon [*cachot*], given bread and water and a bed of straw, bound hand and foot with chains, and kept in solitary confinement." He would not be allowed to work at first. Once a month, the public would be allowed to come see him, weighed down in his chains. This punishment would continue for twelve to twenty-four years, with each year bringing some consolation, some lessening of the penalty. The prisoner would be allowed to work a little at first, then for several days a week, but always alone.

The single exception that the law could allow would be for the leader of a rebellion: since he posed a greater threat to society than a murderer and since the person of the leader was important to the rebellion, such a man should be executed if his death were necessary to suppress the uprising.

If there is a moment in French history that marked "the birth of the prison," it was this. In the first report of the Revolutionary Penal Code all the elements of later prisons are defined, including the isolation of serious offenders and their public example, even though they are hidden in a deep dungeon. The *cachot* was only the most severe form of the prison: others outlined by Le Pelletier involved less rigorous conditions of confinement, allowing more light and air, better food, more labor, and association with other prisoners.

The significance of the moment, however, is more apparent in retrospect than it was on the May afternoon when the new Code was first presented to the National Assembly. A single voice of protest was raised against the extent to which prison was being proposed as the just punishment for a variety of crimes. M. Chabroud, deputy from the Third Estate of Dauphine, argued:

> If I betray my country, I am imprisoned; if I kill my father, I am imprisoned; all crimes imaginable receive the same punishment. . . . It seems to me that punishments should be more nearly matched to the nature of the offense.[32]

Duport replied that Chabroud's suggestion was inadmissable. The old system of punishments needed to be replaced as soon as possible, the juries needed a clear table of crimes and punishments to function, and there was not time to revise the proposed Penal Code to the extent suggested. It would be an infinite task and a futile one, leading to a legal system with a maze of rules and exceptions instead of a simple system of graduated penalties. The discussion was cut short, and the Assembly moved on to what was seen as the more important and more fundamental question—the abolition of capital punishment.

On this issue, and on others, the Assembly as a whole was more conservative than its committees. The debate on the abolition of the death penalty set the tone for the rest of the debate on the Penal Code. The same two opposing positions appeared on each issue: the philosophical, humanitarian arguments of the eighteenth-century reformers on one side and the pragmatic, "realistic" arguments of the century's legal apologists on the other.

On the issue of death, the speeches of Prugnon and of Robespierre defined the views of the two sides. Prugnon spoke first, in favor of retaining the penalty. He showed his familiarity with the arguments of the reformers, citing Montesquieu and Beccaria, but concluded in favor of death on nonphilosophical grounds: if the death penalty was not a deterrent to crime, neither was any other penalty. Criminal justice was already too generous to the accused, he declared, and predicted that in twenty years France would be a jungle. Comparisons with other societies, he argued, were not valid or had been misused by the philosophers. When the death penalty had been abolished in large states, it had always been reinstituted after a few years.[33]

Robespierre spoke in favor of abolishing the penalty. It was unjust, he argued, as if a nation victorious in war should murder its defeated enemies, or as if a grown man should beat an infant. It multiplied crimes rather than diminishing them, for it was a crime committed by the state.[34] The speech of Prugnon was applauded, while that of Robespierre was greeted with murmurs and suggestions that he should go make his speech in the forest of Bondy (just outside of Paris, reputed to be a den of thieves and highwaymen) to see if he came back alive. The vote was taken on June 1, 1791. The death penalty was retained.

The same day, the practice of branding convicted criminals with a hot iron, the *mark,* was abolished. The "pragmatists" had been influenced by the critics of the Old Regime at least to this extent. There was little debate on abolishing the *mark*; opinion seemed to be unanimous. Although the Penal Code did not take effect until January of 1792, the abolition of the *mark* was effective the day of the formal vote on that article in the Penal Code, September 29, 1791.

While the report of Le Pelletier had originally tied the issue of prison to the abolition of the death penalty, the retention of capital punishment did not mean the rejection of prison. Prison terms were a necessary alternative to the two most frequently assigned sentences of the old courts, the galleys and banishment.

Prison was, in many ways, the ideal solution to the problem of punishment for the new France. "How could the prison not be the penalty *par excellence* in a society in which liberty is a good that belongs to all in the same way. . . . Its loss has therefore the same value for all; unlike the fine, it is an 'egalitarian' punishment . . . the clearest, simplest, most equitable of penalties."[35] It was easily subject to precise gradation according to the seriousness of the offense: prison terms could be graduated by time, as well as by greater or lesser severity of the conditions of confinement.

While confining men to prison was not debated in the Assembly, what should happen to them once they were there was argued at length. The heart of the debate was the problem of forced labor: whether prisoners could be or should be forced to work, and what effects this would have on them. Duport argued against the principle, because it did not serve the purpose that work was supposed to achieve:

> The essence of the question is whether a sentence of forced work can be useful or not, if it is a means of improving the criminal. Because instead of inspiring in him a love of work, you inspire a hatred of work. . . . You cannot make men work except by beatings and this makes the punishment arbitrary because it is in the hands of the jailer.[36]

His view was overruled. On June 2, the Assembly decided that the principle of forced labor should continue, against the recommendation of its committees.

While forced labor was to continue, the galleys were to be abolished. Because galley convicts were sent to coastal towns to work, the sentence violated the principle that punishment should be carried out near the scene of the crime. Furthermore, the isolation of the galley convicts from society and the concentration of the worst felons in one small place was judged a school for crime, not for individual improvement.

Le Pelletier had proposed that prisoners be able to choose the work they would do. This proposal was rejected on the grounds that they would surely choose to work with tools that would allow them to escape. Work would have to be authorized by prison authorities. Furthermore, the Assembly decided, prisoners would not be allowed to work together without the permission of prison authorities, for fear they would conspire to overcome their guards and escape.[37]

The Penal Code not only ordered terms and conditions of incarceration for particular offenses, it also went far to define the nature of prisons to be built in implementing its provisions: each locality was to have its prison, and each was to be locally controlled by the municipal authorities with departmental supervision; separate prisons were to be maintained for those awaiting trial and for those convicted; appropriate provisions were to be made for those confined in maximum security and solitary confinement; men and women were to be separated; no one was to be detained without due process of law; prisoners were to be treated humanely and given sufficient food and clothing; prisons were to be kept clean.[38] Jeremy Bentham's plan for a prison system, the *Panopticon,* was ordered printed at government expense, and a French architect, Giraud, was commissioned to draw up plans for more sanitary institutions. Nothing came of these actions: no new prisons were built following the plans.[39]

While much of the debate on the Penal Code showed a desire to ameliorate the harsh nature of the Old Regime, the logic of the reformers led them to abolish at least one practice that had served as a corrective in that system: the power of the king to pardon the convicted person, and to free him during trial by a letter of grace. On June 4, the Assembly debated whether the king should retain these powers that might provide individual "justice" but upset the normal judicial procedure. Those on the right in the Assembly argued, following Montesquieu, that the king should reserve this right because mercy was an important quality of kings. The representatives of the committees drafting the new law argued that there would be no need of mercy in the new system, because the system would be just; the innocent would not be convicted and the guilty did not deserve special treatment.[40] The committees' proposal was ultimately accepted; the royal power to pardon was denied.

In these debates of early June, the guiding principles of the Penal Code were determined. For the next three months, debate continued on specific articles of the Code, but the basic arguments had been made and the underlying principles established in the first week of debate. The result was a law similar in form to that proposed by the joint committees but different in spirit. The emphasis on the need to protect society, on the public example of prison, far outweighed any concern for the rehabilitation of individual offenders. Further actions to implement the new law, such as appropriations for the new prisons that would need to be built, would be vitiated from the start, in terms of achieving Le Pelletier's original purpose. In fact, few such acts followed once the Penal Code was adopted.

The second part of the Penal Code, which dealt with the definition of crimes, did not arouse as much debate as the first part. The crimes of the Penal Code were, for the most part, the crimes of the Old Regime—personal injury, theft, or damage to private property—with some predictable exceptions. No type of religious crime was retained in the new Code; a theft of the sacred vessels from a church was a theft like any other and no longer involved sacrilege. Crimes of opinion were specified in the Code but were confined to political opinion expressed in such a fashion as to be dangerous to the state. The Code carefully defined crimes of rebellion and treason and ordered death as their penalty. Crimes by public officials in the exercise of their office formed a new category of offense.

In the cases of the two most frequent types of crime, crime against persons and against property, the Code retained traditional judicial practice of modifying the penalty according to circumstances of the time and place of the crime, the person of the victim, the number and character of the accused.[41] The principle of equal penalties for equal crimes was modified by the age and especially the sex of the criminal: women were sentenced to years of confinement and labor, but did not wear chains or do heavy forced labor as men did. The length of sentences was the same for men and women, but the conditions of their imprisonment were different.

Despite the efforts of the committees to make the new Code scientific and complete, the Code allowed a certain amount of discretion to the judges. There were a few unresolved problems that the judges petitioned the Assembly to clarify, such as what was to be done in a case where a crime had been attempted but not completed. The Code contained a provision that was supposed to deal with these problems and allow the judges some discretion in applying it. When an act did not fit the specific descriptions of crimes of the Penal Code, the law of correctional police was to be applied. The records of the six provisional tribunals show that they used their own discretion in defining crimes, if not penalties, to make them fit this provision of the otherwise inflexible Penal Code.

The changes made in the criminal justice system of France in the first two years of the Revolution show that many of the assumptions of the reform movement were shared by legislators in the Assembly. Crime was believed to be caused at least in part by factors external to the individual, especially by the large problems of poverty. In his report on the Penal Code, Le Pelletier Saint-Fargeau had included a vision of a future in which the punishments just set forth might be unnecessary. In the France of the future, under the new law and the new structure of society and government, the state would provide for all laborers, and would thus remove the primary cause of crime—idleness. The grandchildren of the present generation would be better educated, and would have a civic spirit lacking in the present generation. Existing inequalities of income and the distribution of wealth would gradually lessen, and all classes of citizens would enjoy a greater well-being.[42]

But that moment had not yet arrived. And if crime was sometimes the product of poverty, it was also a matter of free will. Not all poor men turned to crime. The Penal Code of 1791 was designed for a rational criminal, capable of calculating the rewards of his act against the punishments he would receive. When justice was fair but certain, and ignorance of the criminal law was replaced by clear knowledge of a simple code of crimes and punishments, the law itself would act as a deterrent to crime. This, at least, was the vision that inspired the Assembly in 1791.

Notes

1. Edmond Seligman, *La Justice en France pendant la Révolution,* vol. 1, ch. 2. The issues of political power and reform of the criminal law were essentially separate issues. They became joined in this period because the judicial institutions exercised considerable political power.

2. Adhemar Esmein, *Histoire de la Procédure Criminelle en France,* pp. 401-02.

3. Most of the men who worked on restructuring the judiciary were lawyers, often connected with the Parlement of Paris or of their region. They were men of comfortable means, sometimes even great wealth. I will give brief notes identifying them as they appear. The most comprehensive work on the reform of the criminal law, culminating in the Penal Code of 1791, is Frédéric Masson, *La Révolution Pénale de 1791 et ses Précurseurs* (Nancy, 1899). Unfortunately, I have never seen a copy of this work; it was out of place at the Bibliothèque Nationale and does not appear to be available in the United States.

Nicolas Bergasse, a lawyer from Lyon, had lived in Paris for several years before the Revolution, becoming a lawyer to the Parlement. Among his friends were other men who worked on the reform of criminal law in the Revolution, notably Target. He also knew Brissot, who did not become involved in this issue during the Revolution, despite his earlier interest. Bergasse published a *Discours sur l'Humanité des Juges* in 1773, in which he spoke of the disadvantages suffered by the poor under the present system of justice. Politically a member of the moderate right, he believed that the program he proposed for judicial reform simply summarized what had been said in the *Cahiers.* He left the Assembly in

September of 1789. For an account of his life and thought see Louis Bergasse, *Un Défenseur des Principes Traditionnels sous la Révolution: Nicolas Bergasse* (Paris: Perrin, 1910).

4. France, *Archives parlementaires de 1787 à 1860,* J. Mavidal and E. Laurent, eds. First Series, 1787-1799, 90 vols. (Paris, 1867). Italics added.

5. Bergasse, *Un Défenseur,* chs. 4-5.

6. *Collection Général des Lois 1788-An II* 23 vols. (Paris: De l'Imprimerie Royal, 1792), 5, pp. 1213-16. The Declaration was included in the Constitution of September, 1791.

7. There were seven original members of this committee:

Bon-Albert Briois de Beaumetz, president of the Conseil Supérior of Arras, deputy for the nobility of Artois. Politically associated with the moderate left, he was anticlerical.

Emmanuel Marie Michel Philippe Fréteau de St-Just, counselor of the Grand-Chambre of the Parlement of Paris, deputy of the nobility of the Bailliage of Melun, has already been mentioned in connection with the affair of the *trois roues* whose case he brought to the attention of his brother-in-law, Dupaty. Politically an Orleanist, he had been arrested in 1788 as a supporter of the old Parlements. He joined the Third Estate before other members of his Estate. In 1791 he became a judge of the Tribunal of the Second Arrondissement.

Trophine-Girard, Comte de Lally-Tollendal, a captain in the regiment of *cuirassiers* before the Revolution, was elected a deputy of the Nobility of Paris. He joined the Third Estate after the oath of the Tennis Court but said that he would not speak in the Assembly because he did not have a mandate to do so from the *Cahiers* of his constituency. He was also named a member of the Committee of the Constitution in July 1789.

Andre-Benoit-François Hyacinthe Le Berthon, deputy of the Nobility of Bordeaux.

Guy-Jean-Baptiste Target, lawyer to the Parlement of Paris, and member of the Conseil Supérieur of Bouillon, had been a member of the French Academy before the Revolution and was considered one of the most brilliant lawyers in France. Elected deputy from the Third Estate of Paris, he was also a member of the Committee on the Constitution. He was not a good speaker in the Assembly, and is considered to have had little political influence.

Jacques Guillaume Thouret, a lawyer from Rouen, deputy of the Third Estate of Rouen, was active in the cause of the popular party and was politically on the left in the Assembly. He was named a member of the Committee on the Constitution in September 1791.

François-Denis Tronchet, lawyer to the Parlement of Paris, elected deputy by the Third Estate of Paris, was a respected member of the bar, politically moderate and unremarkable. He was a member of the Committee on the Constitution after September 1789. The Committee on Criminal Legislation was made up of lawyers or men with legal training and experience (except for Lally-Tollendal). They were predominantly deputies elected by the Third Estate whose political sympathies were moderate to left. Several members of this committee also served on the Committee on the Constitution. The two committees worked together on the issue of judicial reform. (*Biographie Moderne, ou Dictionnaire Biographique de Tous les Hommes Morts et Vivants* 4 vols., second ed. [Breslau: Korn, 1806]; Armand Brette, *Les Constituants* [Paris: Société de l'Histoire de la Révolution Francaise, 1897]).

8. *Archives Parlementaires,* 9, 213. See Appendix 1 for a comparison of procedure under the Old Regime and under the Revolution. Most procedural reforms were embodied in the laws of October 8-9, 1789, which were a product of this report. Beaumetz summarized the spirit of the legislative reform: "Public security ought to be established. The passions which give birth to crime should be repressed by fear; but humanity, sacred humanity, ought to be respected. Above all, innocence ought to breathe easily under the shelter of the laws. How happy if these principles shall be imprinted on our work as they are engraved in our hearts!" (*Archives Parlementaires,* 9, 214).

9. *Archives Parlementaires,* 9, 348. A crowd of women were demanding that the Assembly do something about the grain crisis. When the *president* closed the debate on the subject and opened debate on the criminal law, the women screamed out "What is this! What difference does it make to us what the criminal laws are if Paris is without bread!" They were removed from the Chamber with great difficulty.

10. *Archives Parlementaires,* 10, 346; 11, 278. These were debated and adopted between November 30, 1789 and January 21, 1790.

11. Adrien Duport, counselor to the Parlement of Paris and deputy of the Nobility of Paris to the Estates General, was not an original member of the Committee on Criminal Legislation. He became a member soon after its formation. He was antimonarchist, in sympathy with the left, and very active in the reform of the criminal law. On March 30, 1790, he presented the project for the organization of the judiciary in the name of his two committees. (*Biographie Moderne,* vol. 2, pp. 160-61.)

12. *Archives Parlementaires,* 10, 745.

13. Ernest Lebegue, *La Vie et l'Oeuvre d'un Constituant: Thouret 1746-1794* (Paris: Felix Alcan, 1910), ch. 12, on the reform of the judiciary, provides a good idea of how heated this debate was. Duport wanted juries for both civil and criminal affairs. The vehemence of feelings on this subject, and the criticism of the date set by Thouret as too far away, does not come through as strongly in the *Archives Parlementaires.*

14. *Archives Parlementaires,* 12, 344-49.

15. The Parlement of Paris had been ordered to remain permanently *en vacance* on November 3, 1789. The Châtelet continued to function until January 1791, when the new departmental tribunals began.

16. *Archives Parlementaires,* 12, 343.

17. *Archives Parlementaires,* 18, 115.

18. As an emergency measure, the Assembly had set up a tribunal of ten judges to handle cases left over from the Parlement which required immediate attention: these were primarily sentences of *plus ample information* that had reached their designated time limit, and cases under appeal. Jacquelin Lafon, "Recherches sur la Fin des Juridictions d'Ancien Régime pendant la Révolution: le Châtelet et le Parlement de Paris" (Ph.D. thesis, Faculty of Law, University of Paris, 1972), pp. 115-21 summarizes the functioning of the *Tribunal des Dix.* Much more work of this type needs to be done before the institutional realities of the French Revolution are fully understood. By doing a great deal of searching in judicial archives, including series Z^3, Lafon has attempted to trace the effects of changes in law on daily institutional life. She has traced the resolution of the cases left pending before both the Châtelet and the Parlement in part I of her study. In part 2 she has traced the activities of the officials of the Châtelet and Parlement after their positions were abolished.

19. *Archives Parlementaires,* 24, 67.

20. Much of the history of the departmental tribunals depends on A. M. Casenave. While researching his comprehensive but uncompleted *État des Tribunaux à Paris 1789-1800* (Paris, 1873), he did extensive work in the department archives, which burned in 1871. Casenave's work is limited to the first volume, on the Old Regime. Working from his notes, one of his students completed a work on the civil tribunals of the Revolution: A. Douarche, *Les Tribunaux Civils de Paris pendant la Révolution 1791-1800,* 2 vols. in 3 parts (Paris: Cerf, 1905-1907).

21. *Collection Général des Lois,* 3, 755-56.

22. *Collection Général des Lois,* 5, 1385-86.

23. *Archives Parlementaires,* 28, 425 ff. There is a summary of the new organization of the police in Seligman, *La Justice en France,* vol. 1, p. 451. Very little has been written on the police during the Revolution. A good introduction is Henry Buisson, *La Police: Son*

Histoire, 3rd ed., (Paris, 1950), pp. 130-49, and Philip John Stead, *The Police of Paris* (London: Staples, 1957), ch. 4. *See also* Alan Williams, *The Police of Paris 1718-1789.* Although Williams does not include the Revolution in his study, he gives a good idea of what needed to be replaced when the lieutenant-general of police handed over his power to the municipal authority in 1789. After the fall of the Bastille, the National Guard became the effective police force of the city, and police became a municipal, rather than royal, responsibility. There was a two-year hiatus of formal police structure, from July 1789 until the Law of Municipal Police in July 1791.

24. *Collection Général des Lois,* 5, 424-52.

25. Jury trial for criminal affairs was made part of the Constitution in September, 1791. *Collection Général des Lois,* 5, 1252-65.

26. *Collection Général des Lois,* 6, 536-622. Included in this law are the forms the juries were to use for *informations, plaintes,* judgments, etc. While the language of court proceedings had been standardized by tradition, it had never been dictated by law.

27. Louis Michel Le Pelletier Saint-Fargeau, formerly *président à mortier* of the Parlement of Paris, elected a Deputy of the Nobility of Paris to the Estates General, was known for his philosophical liberalism before the Revolution. He was a wealthy man with a reputation for philanthropy. It was said that he had taken an oath never to vote a death sentence while a member of the Parlement of Paris. He joined the Committee on Criminal Legislation in January 1790 and was one of its most active members. When he was assassinated in the Palais Royal in January 1793, Robespierre eulogized him in the Assembly. (*Biographie Moderne,* vol. 3, pp. 169-70). An account of his life and of some of his works, including this project for a Penal Code, was published by his brother, Felix Lepeletier, ed., *Oeuvres de Michel Lepeletier Saint-Fargeau* (Brussels: Arnold la Crosse, 1826).

28. The Penal Code was to become effective when the juries began to function on January 1, 1792. When they were not in place by that date, the six provisional tribunals were ordered to apply the Code to cases they judged.

29. *Archives Parlementaires,* 26, 321-23. The full report is pp. 319-45. This is a summary of his remarks, not a direct quote.

30. Ibid., 323.

31. Ibid., 326.

32. Ibid., 618. In a strictly literal sense, Chabroud was wrong. Treason was the only crime for which the death penalty was proposed. His protest might have been taken more seriously and discussed in greater detail if legislators had any idea of the future development of the prison system,

such as Michel Foucault describes in *Discipline and Punish*. But prison as a total institution was not understood; it was barely outlined. The term "rehabilitation" was used in the Code, but only to describe civic rehabilitation that a prisoner might request after serving a prison term. The intention to "resocialize" the prisoner was clear though, especially in debate on the problem of forced labor in prisons.

33. Ibid., 620.

34. Ibid., 622.

35. Foucault, *Discipline and Punish,* p. 232.

36. *Archives Parlementaires,* 26, 712.

37. Ibid.

38. *Collection Général des Lois,* 6, 110-58.

39. McCloy, *The Humanitarian Movement,* chapter 7 deals with prison reform during the Revolution. Most histories of prisons in this period actually deal only with the Terror. It seems that this could be a fruitful area for further research.

40. *Archives Parlementaires,* 26, 734-39.

41. *Collection Général des Lois,* 6, 536-622. Title II of the Penal Code specifies these distinctions. For thefts committed at night, for example, two years were to be added to the basic sentence for the fact of the offense being committed at night. Another two years were to be added if there were accomplices. Theft by a person employed in a house from the master of that house was more serious than the same theft by a stranger to the house.

42. *Archives Parlementaires,* 26, 331.

MAGISTRATES AND PEOPLE:
The Judicial Response
to Change_____3

Changes made in the criminal law evoked varied responses. Those who
had previously been excluded from the courtroom welcomed the new
procedure enthusiastically. Courtrooms were packed with spectators, not
only for *causes célèbres* but also for ordinary trials. A new type of period-
ical appeared: judicial chronicles reporting on the daily proceedings of
various courts. A criminal bar was formed, with men from the best families
vying to speak for the prosecution or for the defense.[1]

Those who had been part of the old system and had to adjust to the
new rules recognized the practical problems of implementation that each
change in the law created and responded more moderately. In October
1789 the judges of the Parlement of Paris complained that public trials
and the participation of lawyers in criminal cases resulted in longer trials
and in delayed justice. By June 1790 the chief prosecutor of the Châtelet
complained that the new standards of proof were making conviction un-
duly difficult: "Justice now has few means of acquiring certain proof
against the accused. . . . The prisons are no longer sufficient [to confine
the criminal elements] . . . . Those who are released for lack of proof
necessarily increase the number who must be admitted, to be released in
their turn. . . . This contributes to the corruption of that all-too-numerous
class of men who cannot be restrained except by example."[2]

These complaints, however, were a product of compliance with the
new law, not resistance to it. The judges constantly petitioned the Assembly to clarify points of the new law. Did the new rules apply to petty
crimes and misdemeanors as well as more serious offenses? (The Châtelet
was divided into two jurisdictions: the *Grand Criminel* and the *Petit
Criminel*.) By a decree of April 22-25, 1790, clarifying certain points of
criminal procedure, the Assembly responded that only the *Grand Criminel*

was affected. Were the judges of the Châtelet and Parlement, educated men from good families, to submit to supervision by the *notables*, men of no legal training? They did, and with few problems, except those of finding enough observers to fulfill the letter of the law. The Assembly decreed that where the *notables* were unable or unwilling to serve, the judges might proceed without them. Where was there room in the old courts for a public audience? What was to happen when the public became unruly, or when publicity in the early stages of the trial violated the right of the accused to protect his good name? Questions from the judges to the Assembly were numerous. Few were answered.[3]

In January of 1791, the Châtelet of Paris ceased to function. Pending cases were sent to the new departmental tribunals of Paris, and to a special court of ten judges (the *Tribunal des Dix*) established to deal with cases needing immediate attention—primarily those in which the accused was being held on an order of *plus ample information* (PAI) whose time limit had expired.[4] The backlog was substantial: 1,238 cases from the *Grand Criminel* and an unknown number from the *Petit Criminel.* In addition, the new courts had to deal with 286 cases being judged on appeal left from the Parlement of Paris, which had been abolished in October of 1790. The new courts were overwhelmed. In March 1791, the six provisional criminal courts were established in Paris to help reduce the backlog of cases and quickly inherited most of them.

Called together to judge individual offenders, and to clear the prisons of Paris, the new courts found themselves confronted immediately with a much larger problem—to judge the extent to which the courts of the Old Regime had managed to accommodate themselves to the new laws of the Revolution. Had the judges of the Châtelet followed the new rules of procedure? Had their judgments been fair? Had they assigned appropriate penalties to those convicted? The overwhelming answer from the new judges was no, they had not.

The new laws on judicial procedure passed in October of 1789 ordered that in cases where the new judicial forms were not followed in criminal trials, the entire proceeding was to be nullified and the accused either released or ordered retried. In the first six months of 1791, the new courts nullified 70 percent of the cases sent to them from the Châtelet on the grounds of procedural error. Their decision aroused a storm of protest. The editor of the *Gazette des Nouveaux Tribunaux,* founded to keep the public informed of the activities of the new courts, described the dilemma: while the judges were right to respect the laws, the nullification of such large numbers of cases already partially tried would overburden the courts terribly and lead to greater suffering rather than better justice for those being held in prison awaiting trial.[5] The public prosecutors expressed themselves in even stronger language in a letter they addressed to the Assembly in May. They complained that the Châtelet cases were being nullified on trivial grounds and that the tribunals were not being consistent with each other. This defeated the intention of the law which had established the tribunals, prolonging the imprisonment of the accused, overburdening the prosecutors, and making the accused stand trial twice.[6] The judges themselves were well aware of the problems they were creating and petitioned the Assembly for clarification of the rules of procedure requiring nullification. Their statement shows that they were genuinely torn between the desire to adhere to the letter of the law and the desire to carry out its spirit:

> The horrifying state of the prisons of Paris has determined you to call on the judges of the Departments neighboring Paris. Called together by the law of March 14, we have come to give justice the necessary attention, to stop crime by the prompt and rigorous application of the laws.
> However, sirs, the laws will not be able to realize their strength, justice will not recover its empire, if you do not lift the obstacles which surround us, which hold us back at every step.[7]

The total backlog, they estimated, was now 1,200 to 1,500 cases. Were irregularities in signatures serious? Was the failure to advise the *notables* of the names of the accused and of the witnesses (so that they could declare whether they had a conflict of interest) truly grounds for nullification? If they adhered strictly to the law, they would have to declare almost all 1,500 cases null with the result that "in six months there will be many judges but no justice." This would be foolish, it would be expensive, it would be inhumane, and it would be extremely dangerous.

> Even though we were called to empty the prisons we have effectively closed their doors. Soon there will not be room for those whom error, misery, and crime will order to enter there.
> Do you not fear, Sirs, that this violent state of affairs will lead to some great misfortune? It must be said that the prisoners are in a state of agitation that will lead to insubordination and revolt. We have seen this in the courtroom.[8]

On this issue, the limits of legislative power and of judicial discretion were being defined for the new courts, although not in a conscious process. The judges sought clarification of standards of proof as well as procedure, because at the moment, they said, each tribunal determined its own standards, one overturned what the other had ordered, and none were certain which cases should be ordered retried. The Assembly could not respond to such specific requests. The judges were forced to rely on their own discretion. In this instance, they conformed to the letter of the law. The months of May and June 1791 were given over almost entirely to declaring the Châtelet proceedings null, acquitting some of the accused but ordering most to remain in prison for retrial.

Procedural delays were the most visible problem of the new courts, and one the Assembly did little to resolve. Less complex, but equally bothersome, were institutional problems. The old courts had been abolished before the new were ready. Problems of volume and procedure were compounded by general confusion and understaffing in the new courts. Problems as simple as office space took months to resolve. In February, the secretary of the tribunal of the Second Arrondissement (one of the regular departmental tribunals) complained that he could not perform his functions because he had no room of his own.

> I have had the disagreeable task for the last two weeks of working twelve hours a day trying to bring order out of the chaos occasioned by the meeting of this court. The judges are mixed every day with workers of every sort, and with the present state of public discontent I am subject to reproach daily, although [I am] innocent [in causing delays].... Great numbers of prisoners are suffering because of this overburdening. In the public interest, which is always my first concern, have the architects build a room for the secretary.[9]

In July the *commissaires du roi* of the six provisional tribunals petitioned the minister of justice to grant that each secretary have two assistants, stating that this understaffing was the major cause of the slowness of the new tribunals. Their request was granted.[10]

The confusion and delay accompanying the installation of the new tribunals took its toll on the good will of the citizens toward them. The *notables,* whose presence in court was so important, served without pay. Since they were chiefly businessmen and merchants, good will was important They complained as early as April 1791 of their frustration, of the delays

of the new courts, and of their irregular activity. They had better uses for
their time, they said, than sitting around the Palais de Justice waiting to
be called into court.[11] Nevertheless, they took their duties seriously. The
six provisional tribunals were always able to find the *notables* they needed
and suffered no delays on their account.

A final cause of delay at the first meetings of the new courts, and one
that never resolved itself in time (as did the problems of nullifications,
understaffing, and general confusion) was the problem of the absence of
the lawyers for the defense. This was a minor legal problem, because the
new laws did not require nullification if the defense counsel were not
present at either the judgment or the appeal, but it was a major moral
problem. The new laws of judicial procedure guaranteed the accused the
right to counsel but made no provision for paying lawyers to serve indigent
clients. There was a small group of lawyers who served all the accused tried
by six provisional tribunals. Although the law allowed it, they did not
normally accompany the accused at each stage of the trial. They were rarely
in court until the final interrogation of the accused, just before judgment
was passed, and they tended to appear only for the judgment in first instance or on appeal. The lawyers were "chosen" by the accused with little
or no knowledge of their abilities and seem to have had little influence on
the outcome of the trial.[12]

At first the judges of the six provisional tribunals attempted to take
the presence of the lawyer for the accused seriously, holding up the judgment if he was not present. In their address to the Assembly, the judges
cited the problems this could cause:

> Recently, a woman . . . was brought before one of our tribunals. At
> the time that her case was about to be concluded, her counsel aban-
> doned her. She was appointed another counsel and told she would be
> judged the next day; but apparently a day is a century in prison. The
> unfortunate woman broke into tears, cried out, beat her head against
> the bar in cursing the judges; and the public who was witness to the
> scene saw her led out of the court by two soldiers.[13]

The delay was short, but the effect on the woman and on the spectators
in the courtroom was profound. Furthermore, the time spent searching
for the lawyer who could not be found could not be used for hearing
other pending cases. The frequent failures of the lawyers to appear soon

led the judges to ignore the fact of their absence. Occasionally, lawyers sent word that they could not appear in one of the courts because they were appearing at the same time in another.

The problem, apparently, was not always with the lawyers. There were frequent complaints, especially from private attorneys, that they were not notified of the day their client was to be judged, with the result that they could not help missing their court appearance, no matter how zealous they were for their client's interest. A sample of the notations of presence of lawyers, from the Fourth and Fifth Tribunals, tends to confirm this complaint. In the Fifth Tribunal, judges declared the lawyer present in 56 percent of cases judged in first instance, and 45 percent of cases judged on appeal. In the Fourth Tribunal, figures were only 40 percent in first instance and 32 percent on appeal. This disparity could be explained by the difference in the efficiency of the court secretary in notifying attorneys of the court calendar.[14] It might also be affected by the ratio of public defenders to private attorneys serving the court, but court records give no indication whether the attorney was serving with or without a fee. It seems clear, however, that one of the most important guarantees of the new laws on criminal procedure was vitiated by the failure of the Assembly to provide funds for the lawyers of the poor and its failure to provide assistants for the secretaries who had the responsibility of informing the lawyers of their clients' court dates.

Between the disappearance of the old courts and the effective functioning of the new, there was a hiatus in court proceedings of nearly six months: from January to June 1791, there were, as the new magistrates had pointed out, "more judges than justice." By the end of June 1791, however, many of the problems of confusion and delay had been resolved and the six provisional courts began to resolve cases at a respectable rate.[15]

It is at this point that change between the old courts and the new becomes measurable. I shall examine three areas of change from the old courts to the new in order to see the effects of the reformist critique at the point when it was finally implemented in the daily activities of the courts. First, I have considered the change in personnel. Who were the new magistrates? Judges of the departmental tribunals were elected. Were these men members of the former judiciary, lawyers, or "new men" with no legal training? Second, how did the sentences they handed down differ from those of the old courts? Were they more lenient or more severe? How did the new courts judge cases on appeal from the old? What was the effect of the Penal Code? Finally, did the relationship between magistrates and people change with changes in the law? How did the new legal attitude to the accused manifest itself in court? Did the accused see themselves benefiting or suffering from the changes? Public opinion received the changes in law enthusiastically in 1789. How was the judicial experiment viewed after it had been in operation a few years?

Elections of judges to the newly decreed departmental tribunals were held across France in November 1790.

> The choices made seem to have been excellent; throughout the country voters elected reputable men of the law, not only for their abilities but also for their devotion to the new ideas. In Paris, the first elected was Freteau, one of the chief promoters of the reform of the criminal law... also Thouret, Target, Treilhard, Lefevre d'Ormesson, Tronchet. . . . Versailles elected Robespierre. . . . In Montpellier, the judges of the *Cour des Aides,* suppressed by the Assembly, found a new place in the district Tribunal. . . . At Nerac, on the other hand, all the judges elected were new men.[16]

The judges of the Civil Tribunal of Paris were prominent men, lawyers, deputies of the Assembly. For the provisional tribunals, however, for all the records that remain, there is no indication of the identity of the judges beyond their names and the tribunals to which they were originally elected: Pulleu, of Chaumont-en-Vexin; Guesnier, of Gisors; Saladin, of Amiens; Dubourg, from Beauvais; and so on.[17] Did the departmental tribunals send their best members to Paris, or their most expendable? Lacking any firm evidence, I can only assume that the judges of the six provisional courts, like their colleagues in the departmental tribunals, were a mix of members of the old courts, of lawyers, and of "new men." Their dedication to the reformed law, however, is overwhelmingly clear.

Despite the demands and confusion of the first months of operation, the judges of the new courts showed themselves to be filled with the spirit of the reforms, enthusiastic about the Revolution, and zealous for the interest of the persons who would come before them for trial. At the installation of the six provisional tribunals on April 1, 1791, the judges spoke of their dedication to the letter and spirit of the new law. The president of the First Provisional Tribunal, le Maître, began his address to the municipal officers in attendance with praise of the Revolution:

If it is glorious for us to come and occupy places whose function is to maintain the law and the public tranquility, it is even more glorious that we should exercise those functions in the heart of that capital which has captured the precious liberty men have sighed for so long.

Dear citizens, we owe you a great debt for this happy Revolution, which you have begun and which guarantees your well-being and our own.

... You should not doubt our patriotism and our civic spirit. We have left our homes, our families, and our affairs to show proof of our submission to the law, and our sincere desire to render ourselves useful. . . .[18]

One of the members of the Second Provisional Tribunal, Saladin, expressed the new attitude toward the criminal held by the judges:

We have been raised, by the choice of our fellow-citizens, to the rank of their judges, charged with the honorable task of reconciling the differences that arise between them by the just and wise application of the law. . . . It is, above all, when we are required to judge on the life and the honor of the citizens who come before us that our task is the most difficult and thorny, and we must exercise the utmost care. Torn between the interests of society, which demand the punishment of crime, and the interests of the men who come before us, who are always touching in their suffering, the judge must find a just path between the interests of the two. . . . If, listening to the voice of sentiment, . . . [the judge] tries to distinguish the guilty man from the man whom misery has forced towards the precipice, he takes the risk of assuring the impunity which makes men bold to commit further crimes and he returns to society those dangerous men who have troubled its tranquility and security. If, adhering too closely to the principles of a justice too exacting, he merges crime with misery, if he believes that he must impose exemplary punishments for the benefit of society's health, and he punishes indiscriminately and with equal severity the man who makes a habit of crime and him for whom crime was only a momentary error, has he not increased the deplorable list of the victims of a monstrous set of laws?[19]

The judges promised to work hard to accomplish the task assigned them. The president of the Sixth Provisional Tribunal expressed this sentiment:

We have nothing to offer but an ardent zeal, an unbounded devotion to our duty, an untiring effort from which nothing can distract us. . . .

A powerful motive draws us to the service which we are about to
render to you: it is suffering humanity which calls out to us. . . .
We shall descend to those places where humanity is injured; we
shall make every effort to restore to society those who have been
victims of calumny, and to punish those who have broken the law.[20]

With such expressions of hope and intent, the judges were extremely
frustrated when, for the first two months, they could do little to resolve
cases pending and instead had to spend much of their time on procedure.

By July, however, they were able to turn their full attention to judging
evidence, not procedure. By September they had cleared up the backlog
of cases completely. For their industry they were rewarded with an additional year's absence from their homes, when the Assembly ordered
them to take on current cases.

In the eighteen months that the six provisional tribunals functioned
in Paris, they judged 1,620 persons accused of 1,064 crimes.[21] They were
empowered to judge in first instance and on appeal—from a decision of
the old courts, or from one of the departmental or provisional tribunals.
Change was apparent from the first: the pattern of penalties assigned by
the new courts was distinct from the old, even before the Penal Code
took effect in January 1792.

The six provisional tribunals received 439 cases that had been begun
in the Châtelet and other courts of the Old Regime.[22] Of these, ninety-
three were to be judged on appeal, involving a total of 178 individuals.
Examining the disposition of these cases on appeal provides one clear
measure of change from the old courts to the new: the new judges had
only to review the records and declare whether the punishment was just.
Their decisions would be based on three criteria: whether the court
procedure had been correct; whether the evidence was sufficient to prove
the charge against the accused; and whether the punishment had been appropriate to the crime. Only three cases were nullified, and ordered retried, on procedural grounds. For the rest, the new judges declared that
the courts had been fair in the trial, but showed a strong tendency to
change the penalties assigned to crimes.

Table 1 indicates the types of crimes the 178 individuals appealing
their sentences had committed. Table 2 shows the penalties assigned to
them by the Châtelet and the Parlement, and the changes made on appeal to the six provisional tribunals. For all the debate over the death
penalty in the Assembly, it was not a penalty frequently assigned in the

TABLE 1

Crimes committed by individuals, judged in first instance by courts of the Old Regime, judged on appeal by the six provisional criminal tribunals.

Type of Crime	No. of Accused
Crimes against property	
Theft in a private place	95
Theft in a public place	37
Suspected theft	11
Swindling	2
Domestic theft	1
Crimes against persons	
Homicide	13
Violence	6
Morals	1
Miscellaneous	10
Observations missing	2
TOTAL	178

Source: Archives Nationales, $Z^3$2, 3, 24, 43, 60, 72, 100.

TABLE 2

Comparison of sentences rendered in first instance by Old Regime courts with those rendered on appeal by the six provisional tribunals.

Sentence in First Instance	Sentence on Appeal
9 Death	6 Death
	1 Galleys
	1 Prison
	1 Observation missing

TABLE 2 (cont.)

Sentence in First Instance	Sentence on Appeal
53 Galleys	6 Death
	27 Galleys
	1 Prison
	1 Banishment
	4 *Blâme*
	2 Acquitted
	2 *Plus ample information*
	3 Other
	7 Observations missing
8 Prison	4 Prison
	3 *Blâme*
	1 Other
26 Banishment	2 Galleys
	1 Prison
	4 Banishment
	6 *Blâme*
	6 Acquitted
	5 *Plus ample information*
	2 Observations missing
12 *Blâme*	1 Death
	1 Galleys
	1 Prison
	5 *Blâme*
	3 Acquitted
	1 Observation missing
24 Acquitted	1 *Blâme*
	10 Acquitted
	2 *Plus ample information*
	11 Observations missing
44 *Plus Ample Information*	3 Galleys
	1 *Blâme*
	29 Acquitted
	8 *Plus ample information*
	3 Observations missing
1 Other	1 Galleys
1 Observation missing	

Source: Archives Nationales, Series Z^3 2, 3, 24, 25, 43, 60, 72, 100.

Old Regime. Nine persons in this group were ordered to die: five for murder and four for theft. Six of the nine death sentences were confirmed on appeal. In addition, the new courts ordered seven penalties of death for persons sentenced to lesser punishments. A thief whom the Châtelet had ordered branded—but with no banishment or prison term defined—was sentenced to death on appeal. He had been an accomplice in an armed robbery. This increase in severity shows that the new tribunals were keeping their promise to punish crime firmly in cases where guilt had been clearly proven.

Most of the individuals in this group of 178 had been sentenced to the galleys.[23] Their crimes were generally thefts, with one case of armed robbery and one homicide. Half of these men had their sentences confirmed on appeal; three were ordered simply to witness the punishments inflicted on their accomplices in crime. The new courts tended to reject sentences of galley terms, a frequent punishment in the Old Regime. They showed approximately equal tendencies in the twenty-six sentences overturned to increase and to decrease sentences on appeal, depending (sometimes months and years after the offense) on the amount of evidence available in the case.

Banishment as a punitive measure was rejected by the new courts. It had been the single, most frequently assigned penalty in the Old Regime. (*See* Table 3.) The twenty-six banishments ordered by the old courts were reduced on appeal to four; the new courts ordered banishment of only one other individual in the group of 178, for a total of five.

The order of *plus ample information,* a procedural order but also a punitive sentence, had been criticized by reformers as an abuse of the power of the court to imprison men whose guilt could not be proven. Persons so held were generally acquitted after a certain length of time. Of the forty-four persons ordered held pending further evidence by the old courts, twenty-nine were acquitted by the new. Eight had their original sentences confirmed on appeal, one was sentenced to *blâme* and three to the galleys. Since the rate of acquittals for persons so sentenced was normally high, this does not show excessive leniency on the part of the new judges.

The provisional tribunals tended to confirm acquittals ordered by the former courts. Acquittals were normally appealed by the prosecutor, in this case the *procureur du roi*, rather than by the defendant. Sometimes, individuals acquitted in cases where others had received heavy

TABLE 3

Sentences rendered in first instance by the Châtelet:
1755, 1765, 1775, 1785.

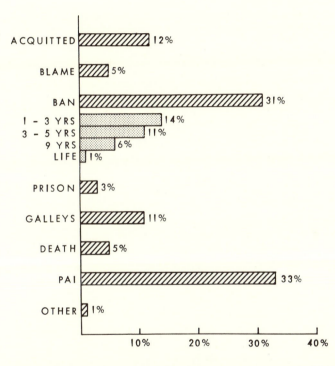

Source: Porphyre Petrovitch, "Recherches sur la Criminalité à Paris dans
la Seconde Moitié du XVIIIe Siècle," *Crimes et Criminalité
en France 17e-18e Siècles*, Cahiers des Annales No. 33 (Paris:
Librairie Armand Colin, 1971), p. 227.

sentences found themselves in court as the whole case was appealed. None of the individuals acquitted had their sentences significantly increased on appeal (two were ordered PAI, but at liberty). Overall, the new courts acquitted one-third of those whose cases came to them on appeal. Most (thirty-nine out of fifty) had been acquitted or ordered PAI the first time.

The new courts confirmed less than half of the sentences of the old, (42.1 percent). They increased penalties for one person out of ten (10.7 percent), and decreased sentences for almost half (45.6 percent). Of this last group, however, a large number were acquittals from original sentences of PAI.[24]

The judgment of these cases on appeal was only the first indication of the extent and direction of change from the old courts to the new. It shows that elected judges did not entirely reject the actions of the past. A large number of the decisions by the now abolished courts were accepted as fair; their procedure in cases brought to completion generally accepted as correct. The new courts increased the severity of penalties on appeal when the evidence in the case justified the action, and acquitted persons being held on little evidence. The new judges rejected some traditional penalties, notably banishment, and rejected certain forms of others: no person sentenced to death was ordered broken on the wheel; all were ordered hanged. These changes are even more evident in a comparison of patterns of sentences assigned in first instance by the new courts with sentences ordered by courts of the Old Regime.

Patterns of sentences assigned by the new courts must be considered in two parts: those assigned before the Penal Code went into effect in January 1792, and those issued in accordance with the new code. In 1791 the judges of the new courts exercised as much discretion in assigning penalties as they had in the Old Regime, relying on traditional penalties. Continuity with the punishments of the Old Regime during this period was to be expected, tempered to the extent that the reform movement had been effective in changing the outlook of those who exercised judicial authority. In 1792 the Penal Code established fixed penalties for precisely defined crimes. Tables 3, 4, and 5 summarize the pattern of sentences ordered in first instance by the Châtelet, by the new courts in 1791, and by the new courts in 1792.

In 1791, the six provisional tribunals and the departmental tribunals of Paris judged 533 individuals in first instance. The most outstanding

TABLE 4

Sentences rendered in first instance by the six provisional tribunals: **1791**

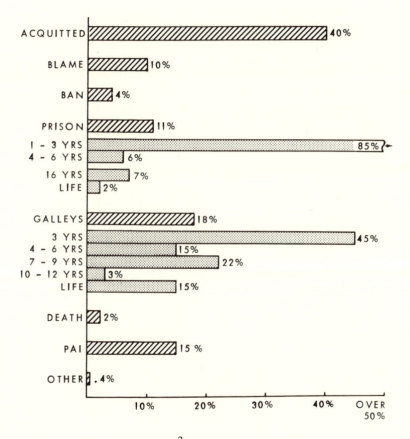

Source: Archives Nationales, $Z^3$2, 24, 43, 62, 72, 100.

TABLE 5

Sentences rendered in first instance by the six provisional tribunals: 1792

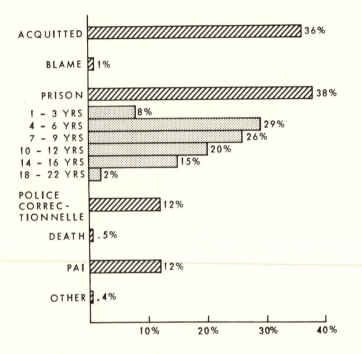

Source: Archives Nationales, $Z^3$3, 25, 43, 60, 72, 100.

difference between the pattern of their sentences and those of the Châtelet is the high number of acquittals: 215, or 40.3 percent. This does not necessarily show greater sympathy for the accused on the part of the new judges; the figure is artificially inflated because of the problems of transition from one court system to another. The large numbers of Châtelet procedures declared null produced a large number of acquittals. (Fifty-seven persons were acquitted without retrial, thirty-six were acquitted after retrial, thirteen more were acquitted on appeal.) The delays involved in shifting the cases from the Châtelet to the departmental tribunals and then again to the six provisional tribunals resulted in acquittals. As dossiers were moved from court to court, documents were lost; as the delay between crime and judgment increased, witnesses disappeared.

Acquittal was small comfort to a person who had already spent a year or more in prison awaiting trial. It did not restore disrupted lives and damaged reputations. The suggestion made in the *Cahiers* that the state should pay an indemnity to persons acquitted of criminal charges was never seriously considered. While the problems of transition were a highly visible cause of acquittals, they were not the only cause, since the number of acquittals remained high in 1792 when many of the problems of transition had been overcome. Of 839 persons judged in first instance by the new courts in 1792, 303 or 36.4 percent were acquitted.

In both 1791 and 1792 the rise in the number of acquittals was in part a product of the decline in the number of orders of *plus ample information*. Judges were not specifically forbidden by the new laws on procedure and penalties to use an order of PAI to hold a person who was highly suspect, but against whom there was little evidence, yet they showed themselves opposed to preventive detention in principle and in practice. In the eighteenth century, 33 percent of the accused were ordered PAI, sometimes at liberty but usually in prison. This figure dropped to 14.6 percent of the accused in 1791, and 12 percent in 1792. In addition, the period of detention ordered tended to be short: 80 percent of persons ordered PAI were held for six months or less. At the discretion of the judges, the accused was ordered to remain in prison or at liberty for the duration of the PAI: 78 percent were ordered to remain in prison, while 22 percent were allowed their liberty.

Thus despite the guarantee of freedom from arbitrary arrest in the Declaration of the Rights of Man and Citizen, preventive detention continued to be part of the reformed judicial system. It continued to be an abuse of the rights of the accused: 67 percent of all persons held pending further information by the new courts were acquitted on appeal or when the PAI expired; only 10 percent were sentenced to prison or the galleys; the remaining 23 percent had their order of PAI confirmed on appeal and the final resolution of their cases is not known.

Banishment for a period of time was the single penalty most frequently assigned by the Châtelet in the eighteenth century: 31 percent of all the accused were banished. Even before the Penal Code eliminated the practice of banishing convicted criminals, the new courts had rejected banishment in favor of prison terms. In 1791 the judges of the six provisional tribunals had reduced the number of sentences of banishment from 31 percent to 4 percent of all judgments in first instance. A short term of banishment, three years, was favored by the Châtelet, although this was more favored in 1755 than in later years when longer terms became more common.[25] The new courts favored short sentences: 60 percent of all bans were ordered for three years. The branding of convicted criminals with a V on the right shoulder was an important part of the old system of banishment. It allowed the police to keep track of convicted felons before national record keeping was possible. This practice was eliminated in the Revolution, forbidden by law after September 29, 1791.

Prison terms were rare in the Old Regime: only 3.1 percent of all the accused were sentenced to prison by the Châtelet. Prisons were for persons who did not fit existing categories of criminal offenses, debtors, persons confined by *lettres de cachet* or for those awaiting trial. As a punishment, prison was reserved for women and for juveniles and was ordered as an alternative to the galleys.[26] Forced labor had been a frequent penalty in the Old Regime with more of the convicted men sent to the galleys for longer terms, as the century progressed.

In 1791 the judges of the new tribunals sentenced 11 percent of all the accused to prison terms and another 18 percent to the galleys. This is a significant increase from the Châtelet. While prison terms tended to be short—85 percent were for three years or less—galley terms tended to be long—25 percent were for life and only 45 percent for three years or less.

In 1792, the Penal Code made prison terms the primary form of punishment for crime, established varying degrees of harshness, and abolished the galleys as a punishment. The Penal Code established seven forms of prison to be assigned according to the seriousness of the crime committed. For rape, a man was to be bound in chains. For armed robbery, he could be ordered to hard labor or solitary confinement. (*See* appendix 3 for forms of prison.) The galleys were replaced by years at hard labor, bound in leg irons, but not restricted to coastal towns. In 1792, 38 percent of all the accused were sentenced to prison terms. Unlike 1791, these terms tended to be long: 29 percent were for four to six years, 25.8 percent were for seven to nine years, and 20.5 percent were for ten to twelve years. Life sentences did not exist.

The six provisional tribunals increased the severity of penalties for crime as compared to the Old Regime both before and after the Penal Code was adopted. More people were sentenced to prison and the galleys for longer terms. The debates on the Penal Code indicated that prison was intended to be, at least potentially, a form of rehabilitation as well as punishment. In fact, persons sentenced to prison in Revolutionary Paris suffered a very severe punishment and experienced little rehabilitation. Whereas French society might or might not have been able to absorb those banished in the eighteenth century, it was clear that the prisons could not absorb those sent there during the Revolution. They were overcrowded, rumors of prison plots and violence were common, escapes were frequent—some prisoners simply walked out with their visitors—and unsuitable buildings were pressed into use as temporary prisons.[27]

The Penal Code contained a provision for a sentence of *police correctionnelle,* a mild prison term, for simple crimes without aggravating circumstances (for example, simple theft, without accomplices or property damage, in broad daylight). In 1792, 12 percent of all the accused were ordered "by the law of Police Correctionnelle" to mild prison terms of no more than two years. In case of repeated offenses, the time was doubled. This raised the total number of individuals sentenced to prison in 1792 to 50 percent of all the accused, and also increased the number assigned to short terms. The distinctions between prison and *police correctionnelle* were important. Not only were the actual conditions of imprisonment better under *police correctionnelle*—no irons, no solitary confinement, more varied work available, work to be done in groups rather than individually—but the provisions on recidivism in the Penal Code, usually requiring a doubling of the sentence for a second offense, did not consider *police correctionnelle* as prison or persons so sentenced as felons.

The provisions on *police correctionnelle* allowed the judges more discretion than any other part of the Penal Code, for the application of the rules of prison or of *police* were entirely dependent on the definition of the crime. If the judges declared that the facts of the case did not constitute a crime as qualified by the Penal Code, they were free to apply the lesser penalty. They did this in 12 percent of all cases. Theoretically, these cases should have been taken care of by the justices of the peace or the police tribunals at the time of the arrest and not been sent to the regular criminal courts. The judges thus exercised a good deal of discretion under a Penal Code designed to leave them very little. The figure of 12 percent is not unreasonable, however, and probably did not constitute an abuse of their discretionary powers.

The most serious penalty, the death penalty, was rarely ordered in the early Revolution. While the pattern of sentencing convicted persons to prison terms shows that the new courts believed in punishing those convicted of crimes, the death penalty had come under sharp criticism as a useful means of punishment. In the Old Regime, 4.6 percent of accused criminals were sentenced to death in first instance. In 1791 this figure was reduced to 1.9 percent, to be carried out by hanging or decapitation rather than the forms of slow torture that had become so infamous. In 1792 this figure was further reduced to .5 percent of all penalties. The Penal Code reserved the death penalty for treason and rebellion against the state, manufacturing counterfeit money, premeditated violence or murder, arson, poisoning, parricide, and castration. Because the powers of judges to assign penalties had been so largely discretionary, no meaningful comparison can be made for the eighteenth century as a whole.[28]

Blâme, or admonition, was a very mild penalty in the Old Regime and the Revolution. The accused was found guilty, but the crime was declared not to be serious or the involvement of the accused was found to be slight (as in the case of an unwitting accomplice). The punishment consisted of calling the convicted person before the judges in open court and warning him to be more careful of his actions in the future. The object of the punishment was to subject the criminal to public shame. In some cases the person was ordered to spend time tied to a post, or in the stocks, in the public square nearest to the scene of the crime, with a notice of his crime clearly posted beneath his head.[29] The Châtelet assigned this penalty to 4.9 percent of accused criminals. In 1791 this number was in-

creased to 10 percent. The Penal Code did not specifically provide for
blâme but the judges occasionally called the prisoner to the bar to be
warned against future offenses. This occurred in 1 percent of the sentences
ordered in 1792, for offenses not qualified as "crimes" under the Penal
Code.

After final judgment had been declared in open court and the sentence
pronounced, (it is not clear if the accused was present in the court at this
time), the secretary visited the accused person in prison, read the sentence
of the court, and asked if he wished to appeal the decision and to which
tribunal. It is difficult to compare the number of appeals from sentences
of the new courts, where the right was carefully guaranteed, with the number from sentences of the Châtelet.[30] Five hundred thirty-six persons appealed the sentences rendered in first instance by the new courts (out of
1,442 judged in first instance). Many of the appeals are missing either
because they came late in 1792 and the court was abolished before they
were decided or because they were appealed to the departmental tribunal and no record remains of the decisions. Almost one-third of the
appeals are missing (167 out of 536, or 31.3 percent). Of the appeals
judged, and of which records remain, 49.6 percent (183 out of 369)
confirmed the sentence originally ordered. The tendency to decrease
sentences on appeal was slightly stronger than the tendency to increase
sentences on appeal. Ninety-three individuals had their sentences decreased (25.7 percent), while seventy-two individuals had their sentences
increased (20.5 percent). In addition, twenty-one individuals were ordered
retried on appeal, because of procedural errors in their first trial. There
does not seem to be a pattern of increasing or decreasing sentences between any two courts. The number and pattern of appeals from one
court to another cannot be explained by a pattern of leniency or strict-
ness on the part of one or another of the tribunals. For the most part,
persons who appealed their original sentence had it confirmed on appeal.
If it was not confirmed, they had almost as much chance of having it
increased as of having it decreased. Few persons were able to appeal
successfully on the grounds of procedural violations.

In trying to gauge the severity of punishments of the new courts
as compared to the old, it would be most useful to be able to relate
penalties assigned to types of crimes committed. Unfortunately, this
is not possible. The discretion of magistrates under the Old Regime
made each case a law unto itself: sentences varied not only with the

TABLE 6

Sentences ordered in first instance by the six provisional tribunals in 1791 and 1792, by type of crime committed.

Type of Crime	Sentence: 1791	Sentence: 1792
Thefts		
Domestic	3 Acquittals	9 Acquittals
	1 *Blâme*	
	2 Prison	23 Prison
	4 Galleys	
	1 PAI	
Private Place	40 Acquittals	56 Acquittals
	5 *Blâme*	1 *Blâme*
	9 Banishment	
	28 Prison	166 Prison
	54 Galleys	25 *Police correctionnelle*
	1 Death	
	33 PAI	26 PAI
	2 Other	1 Other
Public place	57 Acquittals	65 Acquittals
	23 *Blâme*	1 *Blâme*
	6 Banishment	
	22 Prison	78 Prison
	26 Galleys	45 *Police correctionnelle*
	22 PAI	34 PAI
Suspected and attempted	41 Acquittals	63 Acquittals

70

	Column A	Column B
	7 *Blâme*	1 *Blâme*
	3 Banishment	24 Prison
	8 Galleys	14 *Police correctionnelle*
	10 PAI	25 PAI
		1 Other

Swindling, abuse of confidence

Column A	Column B
18 Acquittals	23 Acquittals
7 *Blâme*	1 *Blâme*
1 Banishment	8 Prison
1 Galleys	3 *Police correctionnelle*
4 PAI	2 Death

Counterfeit money

Column A	Column B
9 Acquittals	32 Acquittals
2 *Blâme*	
2 Banishment	
1 Prison	8 Prison
1 Galleys	
2 Death	1 Death
2 PAI	6 PAI

Offenses against public authority

Riot or resisting the guard

Column A	Column B
29 Acquittals	3 Acquittals
1 *Blâme*	2 Prison
	4 *Police correctionelle*
	1 PAI

Seditious opinion

Column A	Column B
	2 Acquittals

Crimes against Persons

Morals

Column A	Column B
2 Acquittals	5 Acquittals

TABLE 6 (cont.)

Type of Crime	Sentence: 1791	Sentence: 1792
	1 Prison	2 Prison
		2 PAI
Violence	11 Acquittals	17 Acquittals
	4 *Blâme*	6 Prison
	2 Prison	6 *Police correctionnelle*
	2 Death	5 PAI
	5 PAI	1 Other
Homicide	1 Acquittal	6 Acquittals
	1 Prison	
	2 Galleys	1 PAI
	5 Death	1 Death
Insult	3 Acquittals	3 Acquittals
	1 *Blâme*	
	2 Prison	
Kidnapping		5 Acquittals
Other		
No crime specified		8 Acquittals
Destruction of property	1 Prison	1 Acquittal
Abuse of public office	1 Galleys	2 Acquittals
Vagabondage or begging	1 Acquittal	1 Acquittal
		1 Prison
Counterfeit documents		2 Acquittals

Source: Archives Nationales, Z^{3}2, 3, 24, 25, 43, 60, 72, 100.

type of crime but also with the age, sex, employment, and residence of the accused, as well as with the amount of proof against him. In chapter 4 the pattern of crimes committed in the Revolution, as revealed in court records, will be compared with the pattern of crimes in the Old Regime. The pattern of crimes changed less than that of punishments. Beyond the changes in punishments outlined in this chapter, it is not possible to compare changes in penalties assigned, by types of crimes committed, for the old and new courts.[31] However, it is possible to do this for the new courts, by considering the penalties assigned before and after the Penal Code went into effect in January 1792.

Theft was the single most frequent crime tried by the criminal courts, in the Old Regime and in the Revolution. In 1791 and 1792, approximately 30 percent of persons accused of theft were acquitted. The rest were sent to prison or to the galleys, banished or sentenced to *blâme*, in conformance with the Penal Code or by the discretion of the judges. In 1791 more thieves were sentences to *blâme* than in 1792, but in 1792 many were sentenced to short prison terms under the law of *police correctionnelle*. The rate of acquittal for suspected and attempted theft was predictably higher than that for theft: in 1791, 66 percent of suspected thieves were acquitted and 44 percent of those charged with attempted theft were acquitted. These figures dropped in 1792 (to 53 percent and 30 percent respectively) but the rate of sentencing to *plus ample information* for these crimes rose. Swindlers and counterfeiters had a better chance of escaping punishment than thieves, with over 50 percent of the persons accused of these crimes acquitted in both years. However, they, too, might suffer a harsh penalty under the Penal Code: in 1792 two swindlers and one counterfeiter were sentenced to death for their crimes. Morals offenses were difficult to prosecute: over 50 percent of all persons so charged were acquitted in both years. Violent crimes, especially homicide, were punished more severely in 1791 than in 1792. Persons accused of "violence" were more likely to be acquitted than those accused of murder. Much "violence" was declared to be no more than a brawl or a quarrel between workers, usually drunk, and thus not done with criminal intent. In 1791, 45 percent of persons charged with violence were acquitted; in 1792 this figure was 48 percent. Another 40 percent were sentenced to *blâme* or PAI in 1791, and 35 percent to PAI and *police correctionnelle* in 1792. Homicides were rarely acquitted in 1791; only one person so accused (out of eight) was acquitted while five others were sentenced to death. In 1792 nine persons were charged with homicide, but six were acquitted and only one was sentenced to death.

The numbers of individuals involved in these comparisons is often too small to allow any explanation of these differences (as in the case of the death penalty) beyond the amount of proof available in the case. By and large, however, the effect of the Penal Code is clear: sentences were simpler, more consistent in form. Fewer options were available to the judges of 1792 than were available in 1791.

The debate over the reform of the criminal law had raised the problem of how to be more humane to the accused while protecting society. The records of the Parisian courts show that the solution achieved by the legislators was far from perfect. The spirit and the letter of the law had changed, as had the structure and the personnel of judicial institutions. The judges of the new courts showed themselves to be dedicated to the reformed law. They rejected certain penalties even before they were abolished in the Penal Code. The small number of persons banished in 1791 reflects the desire of the judges to protect society. The large number of persons acquitted on procedural errors shows their desire to protect the rights of the accused. Accepting the principle that the guilty were to be firmly punished, the judges assigned numerous galley terms in 1791 and long prison sentences in 1792.

Overall, the new courts were probably more harsh than the old. While certain abuses had been abolished, such as breaking on the wheel or a life sentence to the galleys, the new system of punishments was never fully developed. In order for the longer prison terms to achieve any kind of individual rehabilitation, the French prison system would need to be expanded and overhauled. This would be a long-term project and was not even begun in the Revolution.

The accused was probably better off under the new rules of procedure. At least he was able to defend himself, and to know who his accusers were. He stood a good chance of being acquitted. Once convicted, however, he was more harshly punished by the new courts than by the old, in most cases. Whether that harshness served a rehabilitative purpose remained an open question.

Analyzing the pattern of sentences assigned by the new tribunals is one way of measuring the change in judicial institutions in the Revolution, but for an understanding of the daily reality of the new system of justice, it is necessary to examine the individual dossiers of the accused. Some problems that have already been discussed, such as the problem of standards of proof, were left unresolved by the legislators, yet they had to be dealt with in court every day. The new Penal Code was not the scientific compendium of crime and punishment it sought to be—much was still left to the discretion of judges. (Although once the Penal Code took effect they exercised this discretion more in the definition of crimes than in the determination of penalties.) Court proceedings were highly ritualized: standard questions often evoked standard answers (especially denials). Yet there are cases that offer more: insight into the attitudes of the court to the accused, and of the accused to the court.

Individual dossiers reflect the ways in which the early organizational problems of the courts affected the lives of the accused. Even persons not affected by the problems of nullifications of Châtelet procedures suffered long delays in coming to trial. Cases also were delayed when they were shifted from court to court. Some prisoners seemed to get lost for months. The case of Julie Le Roux, accused of stealing a tablecloth in a tavern in February 1791, is one example. The secretary's inventory of her dossier shows the grounds for the prisoners' frustration:

1. February 25, 1791. *Procès-Verbal* of arrest. By the *Commissaire* of police, *Section des Lombards*.
2. March 7-11, 1791. *Interrogatoire d'office.* (Preliminary interrogation of the accused. Tribunal of the Third *Arrondissement*.)
3. March 11, 1791. Declaration of *Plainte* by the public prosecutor of the Tribunal of the Third *Arrondissement*.
4. March 31, 1791, *Information* made by one of the judges.
5. July 4, 1791, Decree of *prise de corps*. (Although this was the formal order for arrest, Julie had been in prison since her arrest.)
6. July 6, 1791. Report of the surgeons. No mark.
7. July 6, 1791. The evidence in the case is read to the defendant. She chooses counsel.
8. July 6, 1791. *Interrogatoire sur décret*. Questioning of the accused in open court.
9. July 13-19, 1791. *Réglement a l'extraordinaire.* The *reglement* was confirmed December 29, 1791, by the third provisional tribunal.
10. March 2, 1792. The Third Provisional Tribunal orders this case pursued.
11. April 10, 1792. Notice of death of one of the witnesses.
12. April 11-26, 1792, and June 1. Order for *récolement des témoins*.
13. June 1, 1792. Confrontation of witnesses and the accused.
14. May 24, 1792. Notice of absence of one of the witnesses.
15. May 26, 1792. Notice of wrong address of one of the witnesses.

16. July 3, 1792. Conclusions of the public prosecutor.
17. July 3, 1792. Conclusions of the *commissaire du roi.*
18. July 3, 1792. Final questioning of the accused in the presence of her lawyer.
19. July 3, 1792. Judgment. Eight years in prison.
20. July 3, 1792. Judgment read to the accused. She appeals to the First Provisional Tribunal.[32]

The judgment of the appeal in Julie's case is missing. It may not have been judged before the courts were disbanded.

How typical was Julie's case? A speedy trial had been praised by the reformers of the eighteenth century as one element of a good criminal justice system, given that proper procedure was observed in court and the rights of the accused were protected. The Châtelet had become "efficient" in the late eighteenth century (compared to mid-century) and resolved most criminal cases within six months. After the period of initial confusion following the abolition of the Châtelet, the new courts compare favorably with the old in the speed of processing criminal cases. The case of Julie Le Roux was not typical. Half of all the cases handled by the new courts were brought to judgment in first instance within seven months of the crime, and only 15 percent took more than a year. Appeals were judged quickly: 60 percent were judged within three months and only 10 percent waited seven months to a year. Within ten months after the crime, 61.4 percent of all the accused whose cases originated in the new courts had their cases judged definitively, including appeal.

In some cases the judges of the new tribunals put too much emphasis on speed of judgment and violated the rules of procedure in doing so. Jean Louis Roussel,[33] a miller, was accused of stealing a handkerchief in the public audience of the Sixth Tribunal in June 1791. Within a month he had been tried and sentenced to three years in the galleys. On appeal to the Fifth Tribunal his sentence was reduced to two hours in the stocks outside the Palais de Justice, branding *V*, and three *livres* fine. The case was appealed to the Tribunal de Cassation. It, in turn, declared that there were many violations of procedure, including failure to appoint a counsel for the defendant and lack of proper signatures on the documents in the case. The case was ordered retried.

While the judges had declared their intention to observe the new rules of procedure to the letter, in at least one case the facts of the case were declared more important than the fine points of procedure. A case of

TABLE 7

**Delay between crime and judgment in first instance:
Crimes committed in 1791-1792, judged in first instance
by the six provisional tribunals.**

Delay in Months	Number of Cases	Percent of Cases
0	9	1.4
1	22	3.5
2	34	5.4
3	41	6.6
4	42	6.7
5	46	7.4
6	53	8.5
7	58	9.3
8	49	7.8
9	40	6.4
10	33	5.3
11	46	7.4
12	43	6.9
13	33	5.3
14	17	2.7
15	18	2.9
16	11	1.8
17	7	1.1
18	3	.5
TOTAL	605	96.8
Missing observations	20	3.2

Source: Archives Nationales, $Z^3$2, 3, 24, 25, 43, 60, 72, 100.

murder tried in the tribunal of the First Arrondissement, involving a
woman who had murdered her lover in the Palais Royal, was appealed
to the Tribunal of the Second Arrondissement on the grounds of procedural errors. On appeal the judges confirmed the sentence of death by
hanging, and said "We have not thought it important to cling to mistakes
of form, in the case of such a flagrant offense, and one in which the crime
was so atrocious."[34] In general, however, the new courts were conscientious
about procedure. Only twenty-one individuals (out of 536 total appeals)

TABLE 8

Delay between judgment in first instance and judgment on appeal: Crimes committed in 1791-1792, judged in first instance by the six provisional tribunals.

Delay in Months	Number of Cases	Percent of Cases
1	47	27.0
2	17	9.8
3	39	22.4
4	22	12.6
5	18	10.3
6	13	7.5
7	6	3.4
8	4	2.3
9	1	.6
10	2	1.1
11	1	.6
12-14	4	2.3
TOTAL	174	100.0

Source: Archives Nationales, $Z^3$2, 3, 24, 25, 43, 60, 72, 100.

had their judgments nullified on appeal on grounds of procedural errors committed by the new courts.

The most difficult procedural problem for the new tribunals was that of standards of proof. While the Ordinance of 1670 had dealt with this problem at length, the laws of the early Revolution did not deal with it at all. Since the Ordinance of 1670, the minimum acceptable proof of a crime was the testimony of two eyewitnesses and some physical evidence that a crime had been committed. When this was lacking there were other forms of proof that could be substituted, with "sufficient proof" left to the discretion of the judge. The new courts were no more successful than the old had been in developing firm standards of proof. Some crimes were more difficult to prove than others. Cases of rape or seduction, especially of very young girls, were difficult to prosecute because proof of the crime rested on the testimony of a child, but children's testimony was not acceptable without other evidence. Generally, evidence needed to prove rape was the development of venereal disease in the child and the evidence of venereal disease in the accused. Even if the accused had substantial proof that the child's story was impossible, the presence of disease generally resulted in conviction. Cases of swindling and counterfeit money were also difficult to prove because the law required that there had to be intent to commit crime, as well as the illegal act itself, on the part of the accused. Many persons charged with passing counterfeit money, especially women, were acquitted when they demonstrated that they could not read or write, or that they had just arrived from the provinces and could not differentiate bad Parisian money from good. (The court attempted to

TABLE 9

Delay between crime and definitive judgment: Crimes committed in 1791-1792, judged in first instance by the six provisional tribunals.

Delay in Months	Number of Cases	Percent of Cases
0	4	.6
1	19	3.0
2	20	3.2
3	28	4.5
4	36	5.8
5	31	5.0
6	47	7.5
7	61	9.8
8	53	8.5
9	49	7.8
10	36	5.8
11	44	7.0
12	47	7.5
13	40	6.4
14	27	4.3
15	22	3.5
16	18	2.9
17	11	1.8
18	9	1.4
19	3	.5
TOTAL	605	96.8
Missing Observations	20	3.2

Source: Archives Nationales, $Z^3$2, 3, 24, 25, 43, 60, 72, 100.

have them identify the source of the money in this case but was not able to bring charges against the person named as the source without other evidence.)

The infinite variety of thefts, attempted thefts and suspected thefts resisted simple criteria of proof. Standards of proof varied with the age, the character, the family, the residence, the employment, and the previous record of the accused. One can guess the outcome of the case of Louis Philibert[35] without even opening his dossier, for on the cover the secretary has written not only his name and the date of judgment, but also "suspected of being already branded" and "pieces of evidence: one sheet." Louis Philibert, a twenty-eight-year-old carpenter, was convicted of stealing a sheet from his hotel room in the rue de la Tannerie and was sentenced to eight years in irons.

Ideal criteria for conviction of theft included the following:

1. Proof that a crime had been committed and
2. Proof that the accused committed the crime, with conscious intent. These kinds of proof required the testimony of two eyewitnesses. Adult witnesses were preferred but the testimony of children was admissible. Witnesses should have seen the crime, not just the aftermath (for example, the accused running down the street, people shouting "thief"). Proof also required connection of the accused to the crime by some piece of tangible evidence, preferably possession of the stolen goods. If the goods had already been sold, the testimony of the second-hand dealer who bought them was admissible.
3. Proof that no one had planted the evidence to bring false charges.

Two cases, however, show that standards of proof could be affected by the age, employment, and family situation of the accused. In his first report on the proposed Penal Code, LePelletier Saint-Fargeau had specifically denied that these should have any effect on the punishment of crime: equal crimes should have equal punishments. But in the daily operation of the courts this ideal was rarely observed.

Marie Anne Adelaid Le Normand, a twenty-one-year-old shop clerk, was accused of stealing linens from her employer in December 1791.[36] Testimony was taken from everyone in the shop, whether she had the opportunity and the intention to steal, and from her former employers, whether they had ever suspected her of theft. The stolen goods were found in her room, but she denied the theft in court. She was acquitted of the charges because her employer had searched her room and found the stolen goods in her absence and thus might be falsely accusing her. There was some evidence to convict her, including her admission—according to some friends—that she had stolen certain goods to get money to run away with her boy friend. The crucial factor in this case appears to have been the active intervention of her stepfather, a "responsible citizen" (not further identified) who first tried to convince her employers not to prosecute her and then was able to have her released on her own recognizance while awaiting trial. Sufficient doubt of her guilt, combined with family interest in her welfare, apparently led to her acquittal.

Bernard Salles was not so fortunate. Twenty-seven years old, an unemployed domestic, he was charged with theft from his former employer.[37] During his employment, he had been in charge of the key to the silverware drawer. One evening, a month after he had ceased to be employed, he had come back to visit the other domestics. A watch and some silverware disappeared. Bernard did not have a key to the drawer in his possession, did not have the silverware, and objected to the testimony of the witnesses, none of whom had seen him take anything. He was ordered detained in prison for six months on an order of PAI by the Second Tribunal, the sentence confirmed on appeal by the Fifth Tribunal.

Problems of standards of proof often arose from problems in the definition of crime. Nanette Savignon,[38] a thirty-six-year-old day laborer, was sentenced to fourteen years in prison for a series of thefts carried out in January 1790. The testimony of the witnesses proved that she, herself, had not stolen the goods; it was likely she had two male accomplices who did the stealing. She was in possession of the stolen goods and could not render a good account of how she got them. The sentence by the Second Tribunal was confirmed on appeal by the Fourth Tribunal.

Attempted crime and crime by means of surrogates and accomplices had always been a problem for the courts. Crime by surrogates was defined in the Penal Code and was to bring the same punishment to the instigator as to the executors of the crime. (In the case of Nanette, the men had been acquitted because they did not have any of the stolen goods in their possession.) If no one had claimed the goods as having been stolen from them, Nanette also would have been acquitted.[39] If she had not had accomplices but had merely been in possession of stolen goods, she would not have received such a long prison term.[40] The courts petitioned the Assembly to clarify the law on attempted crimes, suspected crimes, possession of stolen goods, and possession of false keys. The response was slow in coming and the courts continued to exercise their discretion based on the same factors (age, family, previous record, and so forth) that influenced standards of proof.

The traditional penalty for these crimes was the order of *plus ample information.* In 1792 the courts also applied the law of *police correctionnelle* in cases of dubious crimes. Persons found in suspicious circumstances, with false keys, in possession of stolen goods, or having too many handkerchiefs in their pockets could be sentenced to one or two years of prison by this law. The judges declared first that the crime was not a crime as defined by the Penal Code, but that some offense had been proved, and then applied the penalty of up to two years in "a correctional institution."

Precise definition of the crime was important because the results could be very different for similar acts, as in the cases of François Mathieu[41] and Louis Servail.[42] Both were judged by the Second Tribunal. François Mathieu, forty years old, a writer, was accused of entering the room of a washerwoman in the rue Boucher in July 1791 and stealing a package of handkerchiefs. The only eyewitness was a seven-year-old girl. Nevertheless, he was convicted of simple theft and sentenced to one year of prison by *police correctionnelle* in June 1792. Louis Servail, thirty-four years old, a carpenter, was accused of entering the room of a washerwoman in the rue Montmartre and stealing a package of linens. The victim surprised him in the act. She also swore that she had locked the door and two eyewitnesses said that they had seen him throw away a key as he ran. The key was introduced into evidence but was not proved to be a "false" key.[43] Neither was it proved to be the key to anything Louis Servail owned nor the key to his residence. He was sentenced to ten years in irons for "theft with a false key." If the theft had been declared "simple," not qualified by the Penal Code, the sentence could have been the same as that of François Mathieu.

The case of François La Marre[44] raised a problem that was submitted to the minister of justice for clarification. La Marre, a forty-two-year-old bookseller, was arrested in October 1791 for "making plates for the purpose of printing false Leave papers for soldiers." In his defense, he said that he thought that now that the press was free he could print anything he wanted and hadn't done anything wrong. Despite the attention given to crimes against the security of the state in the Penal Code, this specific crime had not been defined and the accused was acquitted by the Fifth Tribunal in April 1792.

There are some indications that the judges of the six provisional tribunals resisted the fixed schedule of punishments dictated by the Penal Code. They stated their protest against it in their judgments on a few occasions. They besieged the minister of justice with individual cases, (although this might be seen as a desire to adhere strictly to the law rather than to protest it), they exercised considerable discretion in declaring that no crime had been committed, and used the law of *police correctionnelle* in cases where the Penal Code clearly applied. Penalties were a problem for the judges in many ways, but especially after the introduction of the Code. Longer prison terms were mandated by law than had been dictated by tradition. Two cases show that even after the introduction of the Code, judges could use their discretion in assigning penalties.

Louis Rigolet and Nicolas La Forge[45] were arrested in December 1790 for stealing the sheets from a room they were renting in the rue des Deux Ponts. In November 1791, they were sentenced to three years in the galleys by the Fourth Tribunal. Their appeal to the Third Tribunal was judged in February 1792. In accordance with the Penal Code they were sentenced to eight years in irons. La Forge had died in prison, saying that it was misery and the bad advice of Rigolet that had made him steal. In this case, age, sex, family, employment, and domicile seemed to determine whether the Penal Code was applied and in what manner. Rigolet was an unemployed domestic with no fixed residence. He was punished for stealing the sheets from a lodging house with an accomplice. Joseph Michel and his "wife" Marguerite Gauthier[46] were arrested in July 1790, accused of stealing the sheets from a lodging house the previous February. The case was badly tried, with long delays. The testimony of the witnesses was not heard in court until October 1791. Joseph was released from prison in August 1791 on the grounds that there was no evidence against him. He complained that at the time of his release he had been in prison almost a year without even being questioned. Marguerite was not released. She had confessed the crime when arrested and there were two valid witnesses against her. After Joseph gained his release from prison, he petitioned the court to release his wife, on the grounds that she had two children, one of whom was blind and needed her help. Furthermore, her father had died and she needed to settle the family's financial affairs. The landlord had been persuaded to drop his complaint, after testifying against them in court. (Dropping the complaint was not always followed by acquittal of the accused.) Largely because of Joseph's petitions, his wife was released from prison in February 1792. Their case was exceptional because her guilt was so clearly proved, but it shows that the courts took account of factors other than the nature of the crime, although this became more difficult once the Penal Code became law.

While the individual cases would seem to indicate that the attitude of the judges toward the individual accused could influence the outcome of the trial, it is difficult to assess those attitudes on any general basis. Had the relationship of the courts and the accused changed with the new law? The ritualized forms of court procedure make it difficult to tell. The form of the dialogue was dictated in part by law, and in part appears to have been a secretarial convenience, using standard phrases instead of verbatim transcripts. Again and again, when asked about specific charges, the defendants are reported to have said, "Il n'y a rien de plus faux." One might expect their denials to have more color and variety. The judges rarely allowed themselves to express an opinion or a personal comment on a case, but their attitudes may be inferred from the patterns of courtroom dialogue and from the final sentences they rendered.

One of the most important changes the reformers had tried to bring about was the legal assumption of innocence instead of guilt during the trial of the accused. The patterns of interrogations of the accused show that this may have been the law but it was not reality in the courtroom. Most persons accused of crimes denied their guilt, if not in their first interrogation then in the later ones. The judges often warned them to tell the truth because their guilt was proved by the testimony of the witnesses, or pointed out that they had already admitted the crime and warned them to tell the truth. This was more in the hope of getting a confession than of declaring a fixed opinion of guilt. Even when the judges told the accused their guilt was proved, they often acquitted them for lack of proof. The judges of the six provisional tribunals were conscientious about observing the new rules of procedure designed to guarantee the rights of the defense.

The strongest factors influencing the attitude of the courts toward the accused were the age and previous record of the accused and the nature of the crime. The judges tried not to make hardened criminals out of children who had committed crimes at the urging of others, or from some unintentional indiscretion, as was the case with Jean Joseph Bernardin[47] a fourteen-year-old cowherd in Neuilly. Jean had been hired by a vineyard owner in Neuilly to help tread the grapes to make wine. He was charged with stealing two silver cups from his employer and had them on his person when arrested. Jean claimed that he was drunk because the other workers had given him wine and that he didn't know what he was doing. The Fifth Tribunal ordered him to spend one year in prison. This was overruled on appeal by the First Tribunal, which ordered Jean released to the custody of his parents and told him to be more careful in the future. Unfortunately he had spent ten months in the prison of the Châtelet awaiting trial.

It was an irony of the judicial system that young offenders might be held in regular prisons while awaiting trial but sent to correctional institutions as their punishment. There was a children's section in the Salpetrière where offenders under sixteen were to serve their sentences, but very young offenders were normally sent back to their parents if they had a family.[48] Adults who had encouraged them to crime, however, suffered the full penalty of the law as if they had committed the crime themselves.

Judges sometimes appeared to respond to the pressure of public opinion in their prosecution of a case. Crimes of violence, especially armed robbery, and crimes that threatened society as a whole, especially counterfeiting, were vigorously prosecuted and heavily punished. Claude Geoffroy,[49] a priest and former assistant to the Bishop of Dijon, was arrested in January 1792 and accused of making and circulating counterfeit money. He denied knowing that it was counterfeit. He had been arrested one day when a young man recognized the money paid to him as false and set up a hue and cry. When the guard arrived, Geoffroy was in fear for his life from the crowd that had gathered. The court discovered from the report of his landlord and neighbors that he had manufactured the counterfeit *assignats*. Having heard of Geoffroy's arrest, they led police to a room in the rue Jean St. Denis (which Geoffroy had not reported to the court) where they found partially burned *assignats* and equipment for their manufacture. Geoffroy claimed in his defense that he traded in *assignats* because he no longer had any money to live on. He was ordered executed in March 1792 by the Second Tribunal. After a quick trial, the sentence was confirmed on appeal by the Third Tribunal on May 5, 1792.

Treatment of public officials who had betrayed their trust was harsh. Adrien Louis Carre, a *commissaire* of the Châtelet, was charged with stealing money from the valise of a deceased man while placing seals on the property, in November 1790. His case was also processed quickly. In May 1791 he was condemned to public disgrace and the galleys in perpetuity. The judgment ordered the following ceremony of disgrace:

> He shall be transported through the streets of Paris in a cart, wearing only a shirt, by the executor of criminal judgments. He shall wear a rope around his neck and carry a candle weighing two pounds [*livres*] in his hands, bearing these words: "Commissaire au cy-devant Châtelet de Paris, prevaricateur dans ses fonctions." At the foot of the stairway of the Palais de Justice he shall kneel, and with head bared declare his crime in a loud voice, repent, and beg pardon of God, the nation, the law, and the king. He shall then spend two hours in the stocks on the Place de Grève, be branded GAL and be sent to the galleys forever. This judgment is to be printed.[50]

His sentence was declared not subject to appeal.

If the accused admitted his crime and claimed that it was indigence that had driven him to it, the judges might be sympathetic and impose a light sentence. This was more often the case if the "misère" was temporary—as with a laborer who had just lost his job—than if it was the result of not having worked for a long time. Leonard le Maigre,[51] a twenty-two-year-old day laborer working with masons, stole some lead from the building where he was working. He confessed to the crime and claimed that it was need that had forced him to steal. He was sentenced to six months of *police correctionnelle* for simple theft in August 1792, instead of being punished for theft by an employee, a crime which required a prison term of four years in the Penal Code.[52]

Legislators working to reform the judicial system of France have left an extensive verbal record of their attitude toward those accused of crimes. Judges have left a record not so much of words as of actions. The accused have also left a record of their attitudes toward the courts; from unselfconscious actions and statements during their trial to rhetorical posturing in their communications with the judges. Most of the accused limited their communication in the courtroom to denials of guilt. They were generally taciturn and humble, although repeat offenders were not so meek and frightened as those arrested for the first time. François Belair,[53] sixteen, a tailor's apprentice, was arrested in March 1791 for stealing a watch while a guest in a friend's room. He escaped from the Conciergerie, where, he said, he had been held in a dungeon with men who had murdered a priest. Four days after his escape, he was arrested for stealing a watch in a tavern in Roule, where he had been drinking with a prostitute. In his first trial he had been taciturn and hostile in his responses during interrogation. In his second trial he admitted his crime readily, showed no remorse, and seemed not to care what happened to him. He signed his interrogation in a beautiful hand, showing that he was probably educated and knew what was happening to him. In April 1792, he was sentenced to eight years in irons by the Fourth Tribunal.

Some of the accused expressed a complete hopelessness about their lives and apparently about their chances to prove their innocence. Anne Blanchard,[54] a cook, also admitted in court that she was a compulsive thief and should probably be punished, although she was accused of stealing more than she had actually stolen. She was sentenced to ten years in prison by the Second Tribunal. Jean Querquin,[55] arrested for theft on July 17, 1791, refused to give his name when questioned in court, saying that he would "just as soon die today as tomorrow." The judges did not press him to explain this remark but only to answer the question, which he did.

Despair is common in the letters to the judges of those awaiting trial, especially when they believed their case was delayed unnecessarily. There are a surprising number of letters from the accused to the judges, usually petitioning for a speedy trial. If one were to believe that the accused wrote them, they would show that prisoners spoke the language of the Revolution as well as legislators. This is unlikely. Professional secretaries probably wrote the letters and humbly beseeched the judges to take notice of their poor despairing clients for they are almost all written in a beautiful hand. The letters are interesting, even if they are of dubious value as a guide to the real attitudes of the poor toward the system of justice.

Nicolas Renaudin, a thirty-six-year-old unemployed shoemaker, was arrested in January 1791 for stealing a basket of fruit in the Market of the Innocents. He wrote to the judges (the letters are never dated) asking them to speed up his trial:

Nicolas Renaudin has the honor of repeating to you his very humble request and prayer. He is detained in the prison of the Châtelet, without any interrogation, contrary to the decrees of the National Assembly sanctioned by the King. He has shown his innocence, his gentle nature, his honest conduct, his irreproachable character. He wishes to show himself a good citizen, always ready to give his last drop of blood for the defense of the Constitution. Look at him now, without cause confined, relegated to a dark prison, mixed in with a multitude of thieves and rascals, . . . his virtuous wife is bathed in tears to find herself deprived not only of the person of her husband but of their meager means of subsistence. . . . From the darkest shadows I lift my weak voice to you, Sir. Please, Sir, rescue a poor unfortunate. . . . Use your power to give him his liberty and in so doing you will render a citizen useful to the State, a husband to his wife, . . .[56]

In fact Nicolas Renaudin waited no longer for his trial than most people: eight months elapsed between his crime and first judgment. The Second Tribunal assigned him a very light penalty, two hours in the stocks in the Market of the Innocents and three *livres* fine, confirmed on appeal by the Third Tribunal in September 1791. It is likely that the public prosecutor appealed the first sentence, rather than that Nicolas did so. A similar case involved Nicolas Fasse, nineteen, also a shoemaker, accused of stealing a watch from an individual walking in the rue du Four in April 1790. He addressed his request for a speedy trial to the public prosecutor:

[I appeal to] your charity, so obliging to the nation submissive to the law. . . . [A]ll of those who have the honor of being protected by you, who make their humble supplication to you, . . . thank heaven for the confidence they have in you, the greatest benefactor and the most dignified protector of all nations . . . I have been in prison for fifteen months. . . . It is this which brings me to implore your mercy and your goodness: that the poor prisoner may appear before your tribunal, that he may receive justice and hear by the mouth of justice what is to happen to him. . . .[57]

Nicolas Fasse was judged in August 1791 by the Sixth Tribunal. He also was sentenced to two hours in the stocks and three *livres* fine. His case also was appealed to the Third Tribunal, which confirmed the sentence. The eloquence of the letters sent from the accused to the court officials may have influenced the outcome of these two cases, but this was not always the case. It is certain in both of these cases that the letters were

written, and probably composed, by professional secretaries: Nicolas
Fasse could not write his name, Nicolas Renaudin wrote very badly. Such
letters, especially if repeated, usually did have the desired effect of speed-
ing up the trial, even is all those who sent them did not receive sentences
as light as these two. The letters are interesting in that they demonstrate
that the accused criminals of the French Revolution did not have to wait
for a Dupaty or a Voltaire to launch an emotional appeal in their defense,
but were quite capable of doing it themselves. The poor and uneducated
could use the rhetoric of the new era as well as Beaumetz or Robespierre.

Had the system of justice changed? Most definitely: its people, procedures, and penalties were all distinct from the old courts. Had the change
been beneficial? Perhaps, although probably not in the eyes of those who
were supposed to benefit from the change: the accused, waiting for their
trials in overcrowded prisons. Was the new system better, more just, more
able to accomplish the goals set for it by reformers? The question is moot.
In September 1792, many of the persons who had come before the six
provisional courts were victims of prison massacres, subjected to a popular
justice that paid no attention to legal procedure or the Penal Code.

Notes

1. Edmond Seligman, *La Justice en France pendant la Révolution,*
vol. 1, p. 252.

2. Ibid., p. 250.

3. This would be a continuing problem for judges in the Revolution.
A legislative body is not capable of dealing with the minute details of im-
plementation of new rules of judicial process, but in the early stages of
the reform of the law many such inquiries were made to the Assembly.
See Jacqueline Lafon, "Recherches sur la Fin des Juridictions d'Ancien
Regime pendant la Révolution: le Châtelet et le Parlement de Paris,"
Book 1, chs. 2-3.

4. For a summary of the activities of the *Tribunal des Dix, see* Lafon,
"Recherches," Book 2, ch. 1. Lafon has calculated the backlog of civil
and criminal cases from the old courts meticulously, and describes
their disposition in detail. One major change in the Revolution was to reduce the backlog considerably. In the Old Regime, the Châtelet judged
as criminal cases "Affaires avec parties civiles." In these cases, complaints
were brought by individuals and the judgment in the case usually involved
a fine paid to the individual lodging the complaint. These cases were, for

the most part, ignored by the Revolutionary courts. The departmental tribunals and the six provisional tribunals judged only those cases brought by the public prosecutor. This reduced the backlog from the Châtelet to 474 cases from 1,238. This is a very significant change in law that was accomplished *de facto* by the courts, but never *de jure*.

5. *Gazette des Nouveaux Tribunaux,* ed. Drouet, 16 vols. (Paris, 1791-1795), vol. 1, pp. 17-18.

6. Archives Nationales, BB^5 356. The prosecutors were concerned not only about justice for the prisoner awaiting trial, but also about their own workload. The prosecutor took the initiative in criminal trials in the six provisional tribunals: he decided if there was grounds for the formal *plainte,* for the order for arrest, and for calling witnesses. He did not question the accused or witnesses in court; this was done by the judge. Nullification of a large number of cases already half-tried would vastly increase the prosecutor's workload. The points of procedure complained about indeed seem trivial, reflecting a very zealous concern by the judges for the precise letter of the law. The prosecutor asked for a decision on the seriousness of the following defects of procedure:

1. If the names of the *notables* were not declared by the judge at the beginning of the hearing, but the *notables* signed the documents to which they were witness, was this grounds for nullity?
2. If the *notables* did not swear the oath required of them that they were not related to the defendant before the hearing began, but in fact they were not related to the defendant, was this grounds for nullity?
3. If the judges did not sign every page of the information but only signed at the end, was this grounds for nullity?

7. Archives Nationales, BB^3 36. Their letter to the Assembly is undated, and is not printed in the records of the Assembly. It may never have reached its destination.

8. Ibid.

9. Archives Nationales, Z^3 116 (cited as Z^3).

10. Archives Nationales, BB^5 356.

11. Lafon, "Recherches," pp. 60, 61. The *notables* were elected officials. Early in the Revolution, their profession was carefully recorded in court records. *Notables* who served the Parlement tended to be jurists and lawyers; those assigned to the Châtelet tended to be businessmen. After the initial period of judicial reform, they tend not to be identified beyond name and address. Seligman, *Justice,* vol. 1, p. 402, also discusses the problems of the *notables.*

12. I have tried to test the effectiveness of the lawyers for the defense by analyzing sentencing patterns given their absence or presence. There are no statistically significant differences in outcome of trials based on the presence of lawyers.

13. Archives Nationales, BB[3] 36.

14. Z[3] 60, 72.

15. The Fourth Provisional Tribunal didn't hand down its first sentence in first instance until July. The other five had managed at least one per month before that, but had judged more cases on appeal in their first three months than they had in first instance.

16. Jacques Godechot, *Les Institutions de la France sous la Révolution et l'Empire,* p. 126. Seligman, *Justice,* vol. 1, pp. 399-400 says the newly elected judges were not "men steeped in the habits of secret procedures" but enthusiastic supporters of the reforms. He does not say whether they were men of legal training or experience.

17. Sigmond Lacroix, ed., *Actes de la Commune de Paris, 1791-1792,* Second series, 8 vols. Collection de Documents Relatifs a l'histoire de Paris pendant la Révolution Française (Paris: Cerf, 1900), vol. 3, pp. 399-405 lists the judges and their Departments. The *Almanach Royal* for 1792 lists only the names of the judges and their addresses in Paris, but gives the additional information that Saladin, from the Second Provisional Tribunal, was a deputy in the Assembly.

18. Lacroix, *Actes,* vol. 3, p. 399.

19. Ibid., pp. 401-02.

20. Ibid., p. 404.

21. These 1,064 cases, by court of original jurisdiction, are as follows:

Original Jurisdiction	No. of Cases	No. of Accused	No. of Cases Already Judged
Old Regime courts	439	704	93
Departmental tribunals (Paris only)	409	611	7
Six provisional tribunals	216	305	
Totals	1,064	1,620	100

Source: Archives Nationales, Series Z[3] 2, 3, 24, 25, 43, 60, 72, 100.

Most of these crimes had occurred in Paris or its immediate vicinity, although the six provisional tribunals were assigned forty-one cases involving ninety-three persons who had committed crimes outside of the Paris area as part of the 439 cases remaining from the Châtelet and the Parlement. I have excluded non-Parisian crimes and criminals from my analyses of patterns of crime in chapter 4, but have included them in patterns of judgments in this chapter, for the sake of a larger sample. All judgments rendered in first instance by Old Regime courts have been excluded from this analysis of the pattern of sentences assigned in first instance, for obvious reasons. In a few cases, judgments from the departmental tribunals appear in the records of the six provisional tribunals. There were seven cases, involving nine persons, judged in first instance by the departmental tribunal and appealed to the provisional tribunals. In addition, thirty-nine cases, involving forty-eight individuals, were judged on appeal by the departmental tribunals, having been judged in first instance by the six provisional tribunals. Crimes, criminals and sentences from the departmental tribunals are included in figures given for the six provisional tribunals.

22. The law of March 14, 1791, establishing the six provisional tribunals, ordered them to process only those crimes committed before January 25, 1791, the date of the installation of the departmental tribunals, giving special attention to those in which the accused was in prison awaiting trial. Most of the 439 cases they took on involved crimes committed in 1789 and 1790, but a few involved crimes committed before then. The oldest were from 1783, but the accused had not been in prison since that time: they were being judged on appeal. In general, crimes committed in 1790 were to be judged in first instance, those from 1789 on appeal.

23. The length of their sentences was as follows:

Perpetuity	26
29 years	1
9 years	8
6 years	1
5 years	5
3 years	12

Source: Archives Nationales, Series Z^3.

Most of these appeals were for serious crimes, carrying heavy penalties. Even if the sentences were changed in form, the new courts could be expected to maintain their severity.

24. Of seventy-four individual sentences decreased on appeal, twenty-nine were orders of PAI changed to acquittals.

25. Porphyre Petrovitch, "Recherches sur la Criminalité à Paris dans la Seconde Moitié du XVIIIe Siècle," pp. 228-29. The number of crimes prosecuted in the Châtelet rose from 252 in 1775 to 326 in 1785. In these years the records of the Châtelet are relatively complete. Speculation about increasing harshness of the judiciary in response to a rising crime rate over the century is tempting but extremely uncertain. Court prosecutions always represent a small part of the total number of crimes committed. Petrovitch suggests that the rising crime rate, and the talk of reform, actually caused judges to become more harsh as social and legal norms came into question in the decade before the Revolution. While this would seem to be supported by the increase in long-term banishments and galley terms, it seems to be contradicted by the decline in the number and percentage of death sentences just before the Revolution. For figures on sentences by year in the Old Regime, *see* Petrovitch, "Recherches," pp. 232-33.

26. Punishments for juveniles were not limited to prison. They could be sentenced to adult penalties, including death by hanging and burning, and could be tortured during trial. *See* Yvonne Bongert, "Délinquance Juvénile et Responsabilité Pénale du Mineur au XVIIIe Siècle" in Andre Abbiateci et al., *Crimes et Criminalité en France 17e-18e Siècles.*

27. Religious buildings were especially tempting, and several were turned into prisons during the Revolution. In May of 1792 the minister of the interior called on the Mayor of Paris for a report on the city's prisons. "The investigation revealed that the conditions were as charged [by the prisoners]. The air was foul and the straw on which most of the prisoners slept was alive with vermin." Shelby T. McCloy, *The Humanitarian Movement in Eighteenth Century France*, p. 160.

28. Gerard Aubry, *La Jurisprudence Criminelle du Châtelet de Paris sous le Regne de Louis XVI*, pp. 178-79, cites at least one case, in 1790, in which a young man was burned at the stake (after being strangled first) for domestic theft. This may have been the last public burning in Paris.

29. I have been unable to find a picture illustrating this punishment and am not certain if the form of public disgrace changed from the Old Regime to the Revolution.

30. Petrovitch, "Recherches," gives no figure on appeals. A chart on pp. 228-29 gives a graphic presentation of the number of sentences carried out, compared to the number ordered in first instance, but does not differentiate those which had been appealed and those which had not. On

p. 231 he says that most sentences were confirmed on appeal but again gives no figures.

31. Petrovitch, "Recherches," pp. 209-33, discusses crimes and penalties in general, using examples but not figures. Aubry, *Châtelet*, makes no attempt to translate a mass of details into statistical tables, but is very useful for the many examples he gives.

32. Z^3 52.

33. $Z^3$72, 100, 110.

34. *Gazette des Nouveaux Tribunaux,* vol. 2, pp. 647-48.

35. $Z^3$43, 51.

36. $Z^3$3, 5.

37. $Z^3$24, 25, 72.

38. $Z^3$24, 33, 60.

39. *See,* for example, the case of Jean Louis Verret, accused of stealing handkerchiefs in the vicinity of the statue of Henry IV. Since no one claimed the goods, he was acquitted by the Second Tribunal on May 3, 1791 ($Z^3$24, 32).

40. *See,* for example, the case of Catherine Collot, arrested for having sold stolen goods. She was declared to have known that the goods were stolen when she bought them and was sentenced to one year of prison by *police correctionnelle,* May 8, 1792, by the Fourth Tribunal, $Z^3$60, 67.

41. $Z^3$25, 35.

42. $Z^3$25, 35.

43. The precise legal meaning of a "false" key is not clear. Apparently any skeleton key would qualify, and seemed to be an object that witnesses would readily recognize. In cases where keys were introduced into evidence, locksmiths were called into court to testify if the key was "valid" or "false." If a key had been visibly altered in some way it was judged to be "false."

44. $Z^3$72, 84.

45. $Z^3$60.

46. $Z^3$60, 67. There is some question whether the marriage was legally sanctioned. Many of the defendants in these courts lived in common-law marriages.

47. $Z^3$2, 72.

48. If their parents had been involved in the crime, they were sent to a relative. Although it was a popular prejudice that beggar's children were trained thieves, this issue never came up in the courtroom. No matter what their family background appeared to be, children were considered "saveable" until the age of fifteen or sixteen.

49. $Z^3$25, 41.

50. $Z^3$43, 50.

51. $Z^3$43.

52. Title II, section 2, article 19, *Code Penal.* In *Collection Général des Lois,* 6, 110-58.

53. $Z^3$60, 66.

54. $Z^3$25, 39.

55. $Z^3$43, 56.

56. $Z^3$24, 29.

57. $Z^3$100, 105.

PATTERNS OF CRIME
AND CRIMINALITY_____4

One night, as I was passing by a prison . . . I
saw an unfortunate man descending from one
of its high towers by a rope, whose end was in
the river. My hair stood on end: "Who could
this be?" I said to myself. "Is it a murderer,
an assassin?" I thought again. "Is it some unfortunate fleeing the oppression of his family
or of some powerful enemy? Ha! I hope he
escapes their tyranny!" I stood quietly. The
man fell into the river. [Restif helped him out,
even gave up his hat to the man since his had
floated away.] I found out later that this man
was a notorious thief and swindler and I regretted
giving him my hat. . . . But who, unless obliged
by official duty, could take it upon himself to
return to the depths of his misery a poor unfortunate who has reached out for the tree of
liberty! . . . Compassion is always laudable,
although we are sometimes deceived.
                        Restif de la Bretonne
                        Les Nuits de Paris[1]

In this brief encounter, Restif captured much of the ambiguity of attitudes
toward the criminal justice system in eighteenth-century France. Restif
had no sympathy for those who broke the law, and in this encounter he
assumed immediately that the escaping prisoner was guilty of the worst
sorts of crimes. Normally he would depend on the judicial system to protect him from such an individual—the murderer clearly deserved to be in

prison. Confronted with a single individual, however, his belief that the system may have been unjust came to dominate his actions: he helped the man escape and regretted his actions afterward.

The dichotomy between crime and the criminal, between justice and the judicial system as it existed, was fundamental to popular attitudes to crime in the eighteenth century. Before examining court records for patterns of crime, it seems appropriate to look at popular perceptions of crime and criminality. In any society there are three levels of crime: There is a "real" crime rate—the number of offenses actually committed, a number that can never be known with certainty. There is "legal" crime— the number of arrests made, or of persons convicted, always a subset of "real" crime. And there is "perceived" crime—what people think is happening, who they suspect of being dangerous. To the extent that people act on what they perceive to be happening, rather than what may be objectively measured, it is important to examine their attitudes. Restif acted on what he thought to be true, as did the National Assembly and the *philosophes*. Little was known about real crime in eighteenth-century France, but much was said about what was thought to exist, and policies were made on that basis.

For all the sympathy for the rights of the accused generated by the movement for reform of the criminal law, crime was perceived as a serious problem in France, at all levels of society. A few criminals were romantic figures, popular heroes, admired for their daring and for their ability to defy the law.[2] They were the exception. The average criminal one could expect to encounter was a thief, amateur or professional, and the normal response of Parisians was to cry "Thief" and expect that those who heard would come running to help make the arrest.

Even when nothing was stolen, persons found in compromising circumstances were taken to the *commissaire* of police if they looked "suspicious" (poor, dirty, a stranger). Restif himself was once arrested under such circumstances. (With his nocturnal habits and his large dark cloak it seems that he must have been arrested more than once.) As part of a discourse on the need for public toilets, Restif relates the events of an evening when he was seized by the inhabitants of a house he had entered to use the common bathroom on the fourth floor.[3] The neighbors arrested him and beat him soundly on the way to the *commissaire*. Justice was done in the end, however, at least according to Restif. His assailants were all charged with false witness; those who had beaten him most energetically were ordered off to prison.

To some extent, encountering a criminal in Paris was a test of one's nerve. Mercier tells the story of a theft in the Arcade St-Jean in his *Tableau de Paris*. The Arcade, he complained, was the only passage from the rue St-Antoine to the Portail Saint-Gervais, and was a natural place for thieves to ambush their victims.

> One thief stopped a man around midnight, thrusting a pistol against his chest and demanding his purse. The thief's hand was shaking, he was no doubt only learning his trade. The victim, fearing that this movement inspired by the man's terror would bring him to harm, reassured the man with the greatest calmness and self-possession; "Do not tremble so, sir, I will give it to you. . . ."[4]

Restif believed that thieves could be intimidated if only their victims showed sufficient determination: One night, as he was walking, a thief struck him and stole his cloak. Restif struck the man in turn and took back his cloak. They confronted each other, eye-to-eye. The thief was intimidated: "He seemed to measure me with his eyes, and seeing the resolution in mine, he fled. I continued on my way contented with myself."[5] Restif seemed to shrug off the incident. Others, less determined than Restif, were probably not so fortunate. These two incidents give some insight into the everyday confrontations between two sectors of society—criminals and their victims. In Paris, such confrontations were clearly a daily occurrence.

Many eighteenth-century Parisians believed that their city had special problems with crime because it was the capital. As a large city, it attracted unemployed workers from the provinces. Failing to find employment, they might have no alternative to staying in the city but turning to crime to support themselves. It was widely believed that a criminal subculture existed, into which these provincials fell easily, and in which they were trained in begging, stealing, and crimes of vice.[6]

Even if a newly arrived provincial did not fall into bad company, the conditions of life in the city might be a corrupting factor. Mercier especially developed the theme of the unhealthy conditions of life in Paris as a contributing factor to crime. He described the foulness of the air in the most crowded quarters from things that were rotting in the streets.[7] If a man lost his health how was he to live but by begging and stealing? The rooms in which provincials were often forced to stay on their arrival in Paris were filthy. If a man were arrested in such a place, no one would question that he was a thief. If a man could not find or could not afford even such a refuge, he was likely to be arrested on suspicion of crime or criminal intent.

The crime rate in Paris was not always a matter of hard luck. Professional thieves were believed to come to the city for the challenges it presented:

> Scoundrels and swindlers of all types, distributed over the different provinces of France, come at least once in their lives to the capital. [Paris] is a vast theater where they may deploy all their talents, gain the biggest prizes, and find the largest number of willing dupes. Polite swindlers come well dressed, stay in good hotels, rent carriages, and have servants. They pay for the goods they order in cash at first, but then begin to buy on credit and disappear. Pickpockets do with their hand what these others do with their tongue. . . . By the time their victim cries out they have passed the object on to an accomplice. They seek out jewels, leaving the theft of handkerchiefs to those miserable men, petty thieves, whom [the police] tolerate at first, in order to use them as spies later. . . .[8]

The problem of crime in Paris then, was a problem of working men versus "dangerous men." By and large, work was the key to social acceptability. Those who did not, could not, or would not work were dangerous.

Laws and police directives on beggars and vagabonds show very clearly the perceived relationship between idleness, begging, and criminality:

> Beggary is the apprenticeship of crime; it begins by creating a love of idleness, which will always and everywhere be the greatest political and moral evil: in this state the beggar, having no principles or at least no habit of honesty, does not resist the temptation to steal very long. Soon, there is no other brake on his ideas of plunder than the fear of punishments due wrongdoers, and as soon as he has acquired enough skill to persuade himself that he will always escape from police investigations, he becomes a thief at the very least on a daily basis and often a professional thief. Among brigands, there are very few who did not become so through this fatal progression of which begging is the first step and indigence the first cause.[9]

Indigence may have been seen as the first cause of beggary, but it was clearly not the only cause:

> The greatest number of beggars, especially healthy and able ones, are nothing but libertines whom the love of idleness has caused to

go around begging rather than seeking work. We have a large number
of Ordinances on this subject, which to the shame of our police are
not being enforced.[10]

The response of the police was to arrest vagabonds, put them in workhouses, or even send them to the galleys. In August the roundups became even more energetic, and the able-bodied sent out to the countryside to work on the harvest.[11] To save oneself from the galleys, the work-
house, or forced labor, it was necessary only to prove recent employment,
no matter how poor the wage.

Many reformers objected to the imprisonment of persons who had
technically committed no crime. Mercier especially opposed punishing
those whose only crime was their poverty and appreciated that even hard
work could not guarantee a living wage:

> One sees arrests of these people, rounded up at night on secret
> orders. Old men, children, and women lose their liberty and are thrown
> into foul prisons. . . . They die there while calling in vain on the law to
> protect them or on the charity of the authorities.
>
> The pretext for this is that indigence is the neighbor of crime, that
> seditions begin with that crowd of men who have nothing to lose. . . .
>
> In general, those who work with their hands are not paid enough,
> considering the difficulty of living in the capital. It is this which plunges
> men into beggary. . . .
>
> The traveller, in his first glance, sees better than we who are accus-
> tomed to all this, that the people of Paris are the hardest-working on
> earth, but the worst nourished and seemingly the saddest. . . . The poor
> Parisian crushed by the weight of labor without respite . . . at the mercy
> of powerful men, crushed like an insect when he tries to raise his voice,
> gains his living with great hardship and does no more than prolong his
> days with a bare subsistence, being totally unable to provide for his old
> age.[12]

It was the low wages of the laboring poor, according to Mercier, which
drove many of them to crime.

> It is hardly possible, in the present situation of our government, that
> there should not be a great number of criminals because there are so
> many poor and needy who live a precarious existence, and for whom
> the first law is that one must live. The terrible inequality of fortunes,

always increasing . . . forces the unfortunate into inevitable disorder.
. . . The distribution of property is protected by the whole system
of criminal law. . . . Those who commit crimes succumbed to temptation in their situation. . . . They would have obeyed if the law had
protected them. Hunger on one side and the atrocious penalties of
the law on the other kept them in suspense. Finally a cruel and im-
perious need drove them to risk their lives. . . . Every poor man who
mounts the scaffold seems to me to accuse a rich man.[13]

Mercier was a most sympathetic observer. In general, Parisians maintained a distinction between the "laboring classes" and the "dangerous
classes." Those who would not work were dangerous, and distinct from
the "true poor," the "honest poor," and the laboring poor, for whom
there was a long tradition of charity. The distinction between indigence
deserving charity and indigence that led to crime was important to maintain. Even the accused were aware of it: brought into court, they were less
likely to claim poverty as a defense than to claim that a "moment of weakness" had led to their act. Crime was not so much a conscious choice as
a temporary loss of self-control, a personal moral failure.

How many Parisians confronted by a thief responded sympathetically?
How many believed the pickpocket's plea of indigence or the shoplifter's
"moment of weakness?" There is no way to know. Court records reveal
only those cases brought to the police. In eighteenth-century Paris there
were many.

Was crime increasing at the end of the Old Regime? Most Parisians
thought so, although court and police records are inconclusive on this
issue.[14] That public and official concern about crime as a social problem
was increasing is clear. In a remarkable but uncompleted work, *Observations sur la Moralité en France,* the Baron de Montyon sought to derive
a scientific table of the causes of crime by studying 10,000 persons who
had appealed their cases to the Parlement of Paris.[15] His work was inter-
rupted by the Revolution, which forced him into exile, but it is significant
as the first of a series of attempts in France to derive uniform criminal
statistics and to find a scientific theory of the causes of and remedies
for crime.[16]

It would be beyond the scope of this work to try to test any of these
theories against the data derived from the Revolutionary courts. Certain
patterns of crime are remarkably consistent over time: the higher crime
rates of urban areas as compared to rural; the concentration of crime in

the center of a city, especially if the center is the oldest and poorest part; the predominance of theft as the typical crime; the predominance of youthful offenders, and of males.

Yet certain larger factors seem to influence criminal statistics: the state of the economy, the wage-price index, the level of unemployment, political uncertainty, social anomie (especially family disorganization), and war or peace. My concern here is the effect of the Revolution on French society. Montyon had observed that most crime emerged from "la classe du peuple," by which he meant not the honest agricultural worker but "merchants, artisans, manual workers, street peddlars and men with no profession."[17] Who committed crimes in Paris? What types of crimes did they commit? Who were the victims? What sections of the city were most dangerous? How did patterns of crime change from the Old Regime to the Revolution? How do patterns of crime revealed in court records compare to the assumptions being made by those who were writing the criminal law? What were the apparent causes of crime?

Comparing the patterns of crime and the collective biographical data of criminals from the records of the Revolutionary courts with the records of the Châtelet gives only one indication of the extent of change in daily life and social patterns from the Old Regime to the Revolution, but it is one of the more vivid and interesting glimpses. In the analysis that follows, I give special attention to crimes committed in 1791 for two reasons. First, given the confusion of the first stages of judicial reorganization, almost all crimes committed in Paris in that year were tried in the six provisional criminal courts. Records are nearly complete, and most are comparable with those of the Old Regime. Second, 1791 was a relatively peaceful year in the Revolution. How early, and how much did the daily life of society change, even in peaceful years? The records of Parisian courts provide some surprising answers.

Patterns of Crime in Paris in the Early Revolution

The single most striking change between court records of the Old Regime and those of the Revolution in Paris is the massive increase in the number of crimes of all types prosecuted in the Revolution. Prosecutions for theft jumped from 190 in 1785 to 445 in 1791; crimes of violence, including murder, jumped from 9 to 37; crimes against the public authority jumped from 0 to 14; and fraud (including swindling and counter-

TABLE 10

Pattern of crimes prosecuted in Paris in the eighteenth century and the early Revolution.

Type of Crime	18th Century*	1785	1789-92*	1791(%)*	Cases
Theft	86.9%	190	79.5%	76.3%	445
Swindling, abuse of confidence, counterfeiting, etc.	5.8%	13	8.9%	11.3%	66
Morals	1.6%	4	1.1%	1.5%	9
Violence	2.4%	5	4.6%	4.8%	28
Homicide	3.1%	4	1.8%	1.5%	9
Crimes against the public authority	.2%	0	1.7%	2.4%	14
Other	0.0%	0	2.4%	2.2%	13
TOTAL	100.0%	216	100.0%	100.0%	584

Sources: Porphyre Petrovitch, "Recherches sur la Criminalité à Paris dans la Seconde Moitié du XVIIIe Siècle," *Crimes et Criminalité en France 17e-18e Siècles*, Cahiers des Annales No. 33 (Paris: Librairie Armand Colin, 1971), p. 208.

Archives Nationales, $Z^3$2, 3, 24, 25, 43, 60, 72, 100.

* Percentages refer to the ratio of the specific crime to all crimes for the eighteenth century as a whole, for the first three years of the Revolution as a whole, and for 1791. Numbers refer to the number of offenses of each type in 1785 and 1791.

feit money) rose from 13 to 66. Overall, the number of offenses prosecuted increased from 216 to 584.[18]

What had happened? There are at least three possible explanations. First, of course, is the increased capacity of the criminal courts of Paris: six chambers that devoted their full attention to criminal affairs instead of one. But this seems an insufficient explanation by itself. The six courts were created to deal with a situation already in existence—the terrible backlog of cases in the Châtelet and Parlement, with the resultant overcrowding of prisons in Paris.

More than increased court capacity, the changes in methods of policing the city may have affected the crime rate in Paris. The royal police force, under the lieutenant-general of police since 1667, had become a force roughly comparable to modern urban police by 1789. Men in uniform patrolled the streets and kept guard posts throughout the city; police inspectors sought to track down those suspected of crime.[19] After the fall of the Bastille, the lieutenant-general turned over his authority for policing the city to the municipality. The National Guard became the effective peacekeeping force of Paris, supplemented by citizen and section patrols. In 1790, as part of the reorganization of municipal authority, the office of *commissaire* of police was made a two-year elective local position. The *commissaire,* along with the justice of the peace, heard the first report of a crime and the first defense of the accused. His ability to pursue offenders was limited, however. While there were "peace officers" and "inspectors" there was no regular centrally controlled force as in the Old Regime. In 1791 the "Law of Correctional Police" increased the duties of *commissaires* and justices of the peace to maintain public order, and established a special court for petty crimes and misdemeanors, but without adding additional personnel to enforce the law.[20]

The Revolutionary experiment in democratic police was not very successful. Prostitution became a highly visible activity all over Paris. Gambling, begging, and vagabondage increased. Crime in general increased. There were those, both before and during the Revolution, who believed that only strict police surveillance of the population could control the dangerous instincts of the criminal elements of society. Restif, writing after the Revolution began but describing the events of 1788, said that he had observed the people of Paris, and they were "Savage, ferocious, and ignorant." They must be kept under control: "The sacred authority of the state, like the sacred authority of the father, must be maintained."[21] Did the disappearance of the police unleash the criminal instincts of society, causing the increase in crime? Disorganization of public authority may have had an effect, but this alone does not seem to account for the doubling and tripling of crime in Paris.

The most probable explanation for the increase, and the one that emerges most frequently from the testimony of the accused in court, is that the Revolution disrupted the lives of the poor to such an extent that they were increasingly forced to steal in order to live. Those who came before the six provisional criminal courts were not professional thieves or hardened criminals. In the eyes of the law, at least, they were almost always first offenders. Of 1,527 persons tried by the new courts, only 69 (5 percent) were found to have the mark of the thief or galley-convict on their right shoulder when visited by the court-appointed surgeon.

Contrary to common opinion—held by police, judges, and the general public alike—they were not members of organized bands of thieves operating in the city. Most crimes in Paris, in the Old Regime and the Revolution, were the work of individuals, acting alone, often spontaneously. Less than a third of the crimes prosecuted in both periods involved accomplices. Of these, the most common grouping was a pair of thieves, usually a man and a woman. Larger groups tended to be all male—young men in the same trade cooperating to carry out acts which none would have attempted alone. While less than a third of all crimes involved accomplices, over half of all the accused acted in groups, including 50 percent of the men and almost 60 percent of the women. Their patterns of cooperation and the size of groups are very consistent throughout the century. Their most common offense was theft, usually without violence.

Theft, not accompanied by violence to either persons or property, was the single most frequently committed crime in Paris, in the eighteenth century and in the Revolution. Almost anything could be stolen, but linens—including sheets from lodging houses, shirts from the laundress's drying line, and handkerchiefs from prosperous pockets on the place de Grève—were most common.[22] Unlike the English, French law punished the fact of theft independent of the value of the object stolen. In the Revolution, at least, it appears that the simpler the crime the more likely it was to come to trail. There are more petty thefts in the 445 cases tried in 1791 than there are robberies on a grand scale. Occasional dossiers of unsolved cases in the court records show that there were large-scale thefts from noble houses—perhaps the work of professional burglars. Most of these remained unsolved, however, while more petty thefts were successfully prosecuted.

The courts differentiated between theft, suspected theft, and attempted theft. A person charged with suspected theft might have been arrested walking down the road carrying a suspicious object—an iron bar, a piece of lead, a package of linens—or might have been reported to the police by a neighbor It was not necessary for the owner to claim the "stolen" object for the case to be prosecuted, although this was necessary for conviction on the charge. Persons charged with suspected theft generally had been arrested in compromising circumstances—in someone else's room, for instance—but not always in the act of actually taking something. The line between theft and attempted theft was not so clear as between theft and suspected theft; attempted theft was difficult to distinguish from catching someone in the act. In 1791, 67 percent of all crimes were thefts in which the accused had carried the object away; an additional 7 percent were suspected, and 3 percent attempted thefts.

French law emphasized the circumstances of an offense rather than the value of the object stolen in determining punishment. Highway robbery was severely punished because it involved personal violence. Theft at night, especially when it involved breaking and entering, was more severely punished than simple shoplifting. Domestic theft, under any conditions, night or day, with or without destruction of property, was a special type of offense. The judgment of the courts always specified when the offense was "domestic theft," that is, committed by a regularly employed member of a private household, a shop, or a restaurant. A servant, whether his master was bad or good, betrayed a trust in stealing from his employer that a stranger did not break. The assumption that all domestics would steal if given the chance was widespread. If a bottle of wine was missing from the cellar or if all the household linens had been stolen in the master's absence, servants were the first to be suspected—both those currently employed and those recently dismissed. Whether or not the case came to trial depended on the temperament of the employer and the luck of the servant. In general, the nobility tended to avoid the publicity that prosecution brought, while the middle classes tended to take their servants to court.

Most of the thefts which reached the Châtelet were committed in public places in broad daylight,[23] a trend that appears to reverse itself during the Revolution. In the year 1791, 54 percent of all thefts were from private places—domestic thefts, thefts by breaking and entering, thefts from rooms or houses—and 46 percent were thefts in public places (not including suspected and attempted thefts). There are two possible explanations for this, both of which may be partially responsible. First, it appears that the absolute number of crimes in private places increased. Second, it appears that the public was generally more vigilant in catching this type of thief than had been the case in the Old Regime. The Paris police of the eighteenth century had depended heavily on informers and "spies" to catch criminals.[24] As part of the new procedural guarantees of the rights of the defense, the public prosecutors of the six provisional tribunals were required to specify the name of any informers in a case. They generally stated that there were none. The records of arrests of suspects show a pattern of popular action rather than investigative police work: the victim and his neighbors or a crowd in the street generally arrested the suspect and called the guard, or they brought the unfortunate suspect to the *commissaire*. In those cases carried over from the Châtelet and completed by the new courts, the informer is sometimes identified as such, and sometimes is obvious by his reappearance in several cases, named but not otherwise identified as to profession, residence, or relationship with the accused.[25] The disappearance of informers from criminal trials does not appear to be based so much on the new law, however, as on changes in the climate of opinion. General public rejection of the police practice of using "spies," the replacement of royal police with a more community-based structure, and the principles of the new judicial officials combined to change policy without a formal change in law. The general ineffectiveness of spies may also have helped: persons denounced as thieves were rarely convicted because necessary evidence was lacking.

While theft remained the most common crime in Revolutionary Paris, other types of offenses increased, both in absolute numbers and as a percentage of all crimes prosecuted. There was a marked increase in crimes of fraud: swindling, abuse of confidence, using counterfeit money or forged legal papers. It is difficult to compare the Revolution and the eighteenth century in this regard for two reasons: first, the figures on these crimes for the eighteenth century are not available separately, although swindling was a very different offense than passing counterfeit money; and second, neither the Châtelet nor the six provisional tribunals had exclusive jurisdiction over these cases. (Counterfeit money in the Old Regime was handled by the Cour des Monnaies; in the Revolution the Tribunal of the First Arrondissment was assigned all these cases, beginning in January, 1792.)[26] For the period 1789 to 1792, 4.2 percent of all crimes were charges of swindling and 4.7 percent were counterfeiting. In 1791 alone, 4.4 percent of all crimes were swindling and 6.5 percent involved counterfeit money. The introduction of *assignats* into the monetary system in August of 1790 increased the incidence of counterfeiting and swindling (some cases of swindling involved an exchange of *assignats* for coin), a pattern that would continue, and even accelerate, later in the Revolution. The popular passion against counterfeiters was more intense than against thieves, since the crime required more subtlety to detect.[27] Curiously, many of the cases involving counterfeit *assignats* show that their chief source was the prisons of Paris. Precisely how they were manufactured there is not clear, but they were distributed by visitors to prisons, merchants, tavern keepers, and families of prisoners.

Crimes of violence increased in the Revolution, but homicide remained relatively rare. Despite the popular association of crime with violence, the records of the criminal courts of Paris show that the likelihood of suffering physical injury or death at the hands of a stranger—even during robbery—was small.[28] The chances of being injured by a friend or acquaintance, however, were considerably higher and posed a major problem for the courts. The life of the poor was normally marked by a high level of violence: a street-fight between workers, a brawl among drinking companions, a fight between soldiers with too much time on their hands, a fight between husbands and wives. Half the cases of "violence" brought to trial in the Revolution were declared not to be crimes at all, simply street-fights. The accused were acquitted or freed with a warning not to repeat the offense.

Violence became homicide if the victim died of his wounds. Cases of homicide were rare in the Revolution, only half as common as they had been in the Old Regime. When a homicide did come to trial, it was more likely a case of personal rivalry or dispute than of armed robbery or premeditated murder. Prostitutes seem to have led especially violent lives: they appear as the accused, the victim, or the cause of the dispute in several murder trials.[29]

Although libertinage was a continuing concern of the authorities, both in the Old Regime and the Revolution, few morals offenses appeared in criminal court. Not all acts currently classified as morals crimes were prosecuted in the French Revolution. Prostitution, for example, was a problem of police and public order, but was not a crime in itself. *Attentats aux moeurs,* as far as the courts were concerned, were limited to the sexual knowledge of young children. Only rape, prostitution of young girls, and sodomy with young boys were tried as crimes against morals in the Revolution. It is clear from reading the works of Restif de la Bretonne, Mercier, and others that rape and sexual molestation were not unknown, nor were they limited to children; yet the state took no responsibility for punishing sexual acts if the victim was more than ten years old. The most unusual morals case in the court records is a charge of sodomy tried in the First Tribunal. In 1791, Jean Baptiste Chapelet, a priest, was accused by his young male pupils of forcing them to commit sexual acts. The case, brought by the children's fathers, was an anticlerical's dream as the boys testified to the priest's immorality. At its conclusion, however, the priest was acquitted and his accusers—the boys and their fathers—charged with false witness against him.[30]

Offenses against the public authority also were rarely prosecuted in criminal courts but more frequently in the Revolution than they had been in the Old Regime. Most cases involved rioting or resisting the guard. Offenses were not always political: they also included debtors who refused to pay when the guard was sent to collect a debt and instead attacked the guard physically. Occasionally, a speaker arrested in the Palais Royal for making seditious statements appeared in court. How many of these cases there might have been cannot be known: under a general amnesty declared September 15, 1791, all charges "arising out of the Revolution" whether presently in process of trial or already judged, were dismissed. In the first two years of the Revolution, at least, offenses against the public authority were taken more seriously than in the Old Regime. Charges that were evidently not serious in 1785—verbal insult to, or physical assault on, members of the uniformed police and guards—were brought to trial in 1791.

What general conclusions can be drawn from the court records? It seems clear that crime in Paris increased, was double or even triple what it had been in the Old Regime. Within this increase, patterns of crime changed, with offenses other than theft forming a larger percentage of all crimes prosecuted. The greatest increase was in fraud, especially counterfeiting and forgery, crimes that grew at least in part directly out of Revolutionary legislation. Violent crimes increased but were still rare during the Revolution: Paris was not a city without violence, but by and large Parisians did not need to fear death at the hands of a stranger. The general public became more involved in the control of crime during the Revolution, although it is difficult to tell if the problem of criminality generated the same public interest—and fear—as it would in the nineteenth century. Some widely held popular beliefs about crime are not substantiated by court records: the fear of murderers, armed robbers, and professional bands of thieves seems unfounded, as was the fear of kidnappers and child molesters.[31] Crime was, for the most part, a mundane affair, an action whose rewards could be very small and whose penalties could be very great. Nevertheless, people were driven to commit crimes in ever greater numbers. Who were these people? What caused them to commit crimes? Was the increase in crime a product of an influx of immigrants, lost in the city? Or were the accused of the Revolution the same kinds of people as in the Old Regime? Up to this point, "the criminal" has been a somewhat abstract figure in this study, as he was to so many eighteenth-century reformers. In the rest of this chapter and the next, I will try first to describe some characteristics of Parisian criminals—to compose a sort of group portrait—and then consider the individual differences which made each case different, if not unique.

Portrait of the Accused

The most striking feature of the collective portrait of the accused in the Revolution and in the Old Regime, is the predominance of men. Crime was overwhelmingly a male activity: four out of five of the accused (80 percent) in the Old Regime, and slightly more in the Revolution (84 percent) were men. This is not only striking and consistent over time, it is also difficult to explain. If, as the reformers argued, it was economic necessity that drove men to crime, why did it not drive women in equal numbers? Women's professions, by and large, paid less than a living wage. Women were often abandoned with children to support and little means of doing so. Widows and orphans were, traditionally, most deserving of charity in France.[32] In the Revolution when many traditional charitable institutions disappeared, why did they not appear in greater numbers in court? There are two possible explanations, although neither is really sufficient.

First, women were afforded special protection and special consideration in law, in charity, in the family, that gave them a more "sheltered" life than men. While in many areas of French law they were treated as minors, in the criminal law they were held responsible for their actions, although they often received special consideration. Women were judged to have a diminished responsibility for their actions if they had acted on the orders of a man, especially a husband, or if they had been part of a mixed group, whose leaders were assumed to be men. They were not subject to the same harsh penalties as men: no woman was ever broken on the wheel, sent to the galleys, or sentenced to life imprisonment. The less rigorous treatment of women in the courts was in part a product of

TABLE 11

Distribution of crimes by sex: 1765, 1791, and overall.

Year/Sex	Thefts	Swindling, Counterfeiting	Violence, Homicide	Morals	Other
1765					
Number of men	173	13	8	4	17
Percentage of men	80+	6+	4−	2−	8
Number of women	81	3	0	1	4
Percentage of women	91+	3+	0	1+	4+
1791					
Number of men	539	79	46	7	39
Percentage of men	76.1	11.2	6.5	1	5.2
Number of women	106	14	6	4	5
Percentage of women	78.6	10.3	4.4	3	3.7
Overall					
Number of men	1001	120	83	9	66
Percentage of men	78.3	9.4	6.5	.7	5.1
Number of women	192	22	8	4	14
Percentage of women	79.9	9.2	3.4	1.7	5.8

Sources: Porphyre Petrovitch, "Recherches sur la Criminalité à Paris dans la Seconde Moitié du XVIIIe Siècle," *Crimes et Criminalité en France 17e-18e Siècles,* Cahiers des Annales No. 33 (Paris: Librairie Armand Colin, 1971), p. 235.

Archives Nationales, $Z^3$2, 3, 24, 25, 43, 60, 72, 100.

their legal and social status—considered physically and mentally inferior to men, they required special protection in the law[33]—but it was also a product of the fact that they tended to commit less socially dangerous offenses.

Violent crimes, crimes against persons, and crimes on a grand scale were the monopoly of men in the eighteenth century. Women tended to simple thefts, receiving stolen goods, and to prostitution, which was not a criminal offense but was often associated with gambling and petty crime. The nature of women's offenses is a possible, though not sufficient, explanation for their less frequent appearances in court: a woman, even when caught, might not be arrested because her act was considered less dangerous. If women had a higher level of tolerated illegality than men, it was social custom that determined it, not the law. There is no way to document this tolerance from court records.[34]

The change in the ratio of men to women among the accused in the Revolution is puzzling but is not of such a magnitude that it needs detailed examination. Women in the French Revolution were not becoming less active in pursuing their occupations, their social and political demands, or their everyday needs. If anything, the Revolution was a time when they became exceptionally aggressive and vocal about getting what they wanted.[35] While fewer may have been charged with crime in comparison with men, those who were changed their traditional patterns more than men did.

Table 11 summarizes the distribution of crimes by sex of the accused for one year of the Old Regime (1785) and for the new Revolutionary courts. During the Revolution both men and women tended to commit crimes other than theft more frequently than they had in the Old Regime, although theft was still the largest single category of offense for both sexes. Traditional patterns of sex differences tended to be maintained: Women tended to domestic thefts and thefts from private places—rooms, houses, shops; men tended to commit thefts in public places—in the streets, in markets, and in public squares.[36]

Swindling and counterfeiting had tended to be a man's province in the Old Regime, but during the Revolution women increased their participation in crimes of fraud, most frequently in passing counterfeit money. Many women, when arrested for counterfeit, claimed not to be able to tell good money from bad because they were unable to read. Since the literacy rate among women in this group of Parisian criminals was very low (15 percent of women as compared to 45 percent of men) this is a plausible explanation, but it was not always grounds for acquittal. While women were often arrested for passing counterfeit money, they were never prosecuted for manufacturing it—they received it as shopkeepers or street vendors for the most part, although a few were given the money by family or friends in prison.

During the Revolution, violence and homicide were not so exclusively men's crimes as they had been in the Old Regime, although because of the small number of persons of either sex charged with these crimes it is difficult to draw any conclusions concerning changes in patterns of crime. Overall, in the records of the six provisional tribunals, men committed 82 percent of homicides and women 18 percent. In the one year, 1791, men committed 73 percent and women 27 percent. Most women who became involved in violent crimes (they were more often victims than offenders) were prostitutes, whose lives were often very violent. Prostitutes were also the only women charged with morals offenses, in cases where they were accused of procuring young children for their clients. While men were charged with morals offenses for rape and sodomy, they were not prosecuted for being the client of a procuress.

After the differing participation of the two sexes in Parisian crime, the most striking characteristic of the collective portrait of the accused is their youth. Crime in eighteenth-century Paris was the province of the young adult, whether male or female. The courts demanded the age of every person who came before them for trial as an important piece of identification, as well as name, birthplace, profession, and residence. In the case of adolescents, it could determine whether a person was to be held responsible for his actions, and the court might demand written proof (usually a baptismal certificate, ordered from the appropriate parish) before passing judgment. The age of persons tried by the Châtelet in the eighteenth century varied from eleven to seventy-seven years.[37] In the Revolution the age range was from eleven to sixty-five years. Only the lower extreme is relevant; the upper extreme was more a matter of chance and likely to change from year to year, whereas the lower extreme was set by the courts. How old did a person have to be to stand trial for an offense? The youngest accused were always males, who could be made to stand trial at age eleven: girls did not stand trial before the age of thirteen. It was not unusual for the accused person not to know his or her precise age. Apparently this was not a piece of information very important

TABLE 12

Age-group distribution of Parisian criminals by sex: 1,130 Men; 209 Women

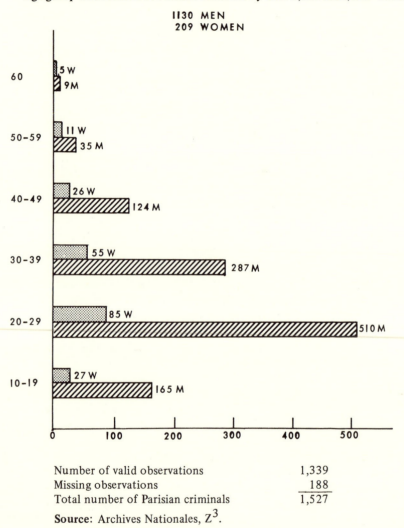

Number of valid observations	1,339
Missing observations	188
Total number of Parisian criminals	1,527

Source: Archives Nationales, Z^3.

in everyday affairs; the accused often stated his age adding "*ou environ*" (or thereabouts). In the eighteenth century, fully one-third of the accused had not reached the age of legal majority, twenty-five years.[38] In the Revolution, this figure rose to 40 percent. The traditional explanation for the high crime rate of youths centered on their lack of attachment to a job or a family, the disappointed hopes of young provincials coming to the capital to make their living, the great physical and psychic energy of youth, and their liking for actions that required elements of skill and of risk.[39] Restif de la Bretonne gave a perceptive portrait of a young delinquent, (reformed by the time he talked with Restif):

> At the age when I was beginning to develop reason I harmed those who had raised me. I foreswore religion and laughed at the laws, I knew no restraint. My self-interest was my supreme law; I did an infinity of reprehensible and evil things. I feared nothing. I paid attention to nothing but hiding myself and my actions. I stole. . . .[40]

The patterns of age at arrest established for the Old Regime appear to remain consistent for the Revolution. Men tended to commit crimes at a younger age than women. As the age of both groups increased, the ratio of men to women became smaller, perhaps because women suffered worse social displacement as they grew older than men did. Many of the older women declared that they were widows.

Crime was the province of the young, but it was also assumed to be largely committed by outsiders, people not native-born Parisians. The courts inquired into the birthplace of each defendant but unfortunately did not inquire how long they had been in Paris. Popular prejudice held that people born in different regions had different personality characteristics, as they had different accents, and that since people from the same province clustered together in Paris, they shared the same occupations and the same criminal activities.[41] In the nineteenth century, the influx of provincials into Paris was one of the strongest factors influencing the rising crime rate in the city.[42] Without knowing the numbers of provincials in Paris, compared to Parisians, and how the number changed from year to year, it is difficult to make the same assertion for the eighteenth century. The records of the six provisional tribunals do show, however, that the number of provincials arrested for crimes was higher in the early Revolution than it had been in the Old Regime. In good years and

TABLE 13

Birthplace of persons accused of crime in Paris in the early Revolution.

Birthplace	1775 (Number of Accused)	Early Revolution (Number of Accused)	Percent
Paris	118	323	26.0
Ile-de-France	64	171	13.8
Normandy	6	108	8.7
Champagne, Sedan	20	88	7.1
Lorraine, Barrois	25	57	4.6
Burgundy	24	69	5.6
Picardy	10	34	2.2
Val de Loire, Berry	13	12	.8
Franche-Comté	8	66	5.3
Auvergne	14	48	3.9
Flanders, Artois	7	20	1.6
Limousin, Marche	4	8	.6
Lyonnais	8	22	1.8
Brittany	5	22	1.8
Dauphine	5	9	.7
Alsace	1	18	1.4
Languedoc	1	10	.8
Gascony, Guyenne, Perigord	3	9	.7
Poitou, Angoumois, Saintonge	1	10	.8
Bourbonnais, Nivernais	1	15	1.2

Provence	1	2	.2
Bearn	0	4	.3
Roussilon	0	2	.1
Orléannais	0	33	2.7
Maine and Anjou	0	21	1.7
Tourain	0	3	.2
Savoy	4	14	1.1
Low Countries	6	10	.8
Empire	3	8	.6
Jew (no nationality)	0	2	.2
Luxembourg	1	4	.3
Austria	1	2	.2
Switzerland	1	8	.6
Geneva	1	3	.2
Piedmont	1	3	.2
Ireland	0	1	.1
England	0	2	.1
Russia	0	1	.1
Other	3	0	—
	359	1242	

Sources: Porphyre Petrovitch, "Recherches sur la Criminalité à Paris dans la Seconde Moitié du XVIIIe Siècle," *Crimes et Criminalité en France 17e-18e Siècles*, Cahiers des Annales No. 33 (Paris: Librairie Armand Colin, 1971), p. 239.

Archives Nationales, Z^3.

bad, during the eighteenth century one-third of those arrested for crimes in Paris were from the city itself, including the Faubourgs, and one-sixth were from the Ile-de-France. (There were never more than a few foreigners.)[43] In the Revolution, the number of Parisian-born criminals declined to 26 percent of those declaring a birthplace, with an additional 13.8 percent from the Ile-de-France. Foreigners made up 4.5 percent of the accused. Table 13 summarizes the geographic origin of those accused of crimes in 1775, and in the early Revolution overall, who stated a birthplace to the judges of the Châtelet or the six provisional tribunals.[44]

The greatest number of provincials arrested for crimes in Paris came from the north of France, especially Normandy, Champagne/Sedan, Burgundy, Lorraine, and Picardy, reflecting the normal predominance of persons from the northern provinces among all provincials living in Paris. The most dramatic increases in provincials arrested were those from Normandy, Champagne/Sedan, Franche Comté, Auvergne, Brittany, and from the Orléannais. The number of foreign-born arrested increased from twenty-one to fifty-nine. There do not appear to be significant differences between men and women as to birthplace. More of the men than of the women arrested had been born in Paris: 27 percent as compared to 21 percent. But more of the women arrested had come from the Ile-de-France: 18 percent as compared to 13 percent of the men. No significant patterns of male or female migration from one province appear in the court records. Even among foreigners, a category where one might expect men to dominate since they traveled more freely than women, crimes are divided between the sexes roughly in the same proportion as for the sex distribution of the accused as a group: 88 percent of the foreign-born were men and 12 percent were women. Jews were an identifiable group, sometimes foreign born and sometimes native born but still foreign. Jews arrested for crimes were exclusively male: no woman ever identified herself or was identified as a Jewess.

I have tried to test the relationship between crime and birthplace by isolating those persons declaring provincial birth from the group as a whole, to see if any patterns of residence or activity stand out as distinctly "provincial."[45] Some of the factors cited as reasons for the high crime rate of youth—lack of family contact, unemployment, lack of education or special skills—were assumed to be aggravated by the fact of provincial origin. I have tried to test some of these assumptions by isolating the provincials as a group and examining the types of crimes they committed, the object of the crime, the number of accomplices, the location of the crime, the relationship between the criminal and his victim, and by examining those provincials arrested for crime as to profession, employment, literacy, and residence. As I discuss each of these areas for the group as a whole I will take special note of the provincials as a subgroup.

The pattern of crimes committed by provincials, including type of crime committed, the object of the crime, and the number of accomplices is not significantly different from the pattern of crimes for the group as a whole. Provincials showed a slight tendency to act alone more often than the group as a whole: 50.9 percent of provincials acted alone while 48 percent of the group as a whole did so. Table 14 shows that the types of crimes committed by provincials were consistent with the patterns of the group as a whole.

The judges of the six provisional tribunals were aware that lack of family, lack of fixed residence, unemployment, and lack of skills might increase an individual's propensity to commit crime and sometimes inquired about these, demanding, "How long have you been in Paris?" "How long since you last worked?" "How do you support yourself with no work?" "Do your parents know where you are?" A fixed residence, stable employment, and an established family situation were all factors which might soften the rigors of the judicial system. Instead of waiting in prison for trial, the accused could be released to the custody of parents or employer or even on his own recognizance if fixed domicile could be established. In fact, this rarely worked as it was supposed to: 92 percent of all the accused were held in prison while awaiting trial and only 5 percent were released on their own recognizance, with a slight tendency for women to be favored in this category over men. (The remaining 3 percent were never taken into custody.)

Although it was widely believed that lack of work was a major cause of crime, few of the accused admitted to being unemployed when brought to trial. Of 1,395 accused who stated a profession, only 296 stated that they were unemployed at the time of their arrest. This figure of 20 percent probably does not represent the real rate of unemployment. Many persons who counted themselves employed were marginally so: secondhand dealers (usually without shops, carrying their goods in a sack), errand boys, prostitutes, shoeshine boys, or street vendors. Some declared themselves to have taken up one of these marginal livelihoods "since the Revolution." Of those admitting unemployment, 90 percent were men while only 10 percent

TABLE 14

Crimes committed by non-Parisian born persons compared with crimes committed overall in Paris in the early Revolution.*

Type of Crime	Number of Accused Overall	Percent	Number of non-Parisians Accused	Percent
Domestic theft	45	2.9	28	3.7
Theft in a private place	512	33.6	243	32.5
Theft in a public place	422	27.7	205	27.4
Suspected theft	168	11.0	90	12.0
Attempted theft	49	3.2	20	2.7
Thefts of all types	1,196	78.4	586	78.3
Swindling	71	4.6	32	4.3
Counterfeiting	75	4.9	39	5.2
Morals	13	.9	6	.8
Violence	69	4.5	38	5.1
Homicide	22	1.4	13	1.7
Crimes against the public authority	42	2.7	18	2.4
Other	39	2.6	16	2.2
	1,527	100.0	748	100.0

Source: Archives Nationales, Z^3.

*The table is stated in terms of the numbers of individuals accused, not the number of crimes. Numbers refer to individuals accused; percentages represent the proportion of crimes as a whole, within each group.

were women. (This represented an unemployment rate of 23 percent among men and 13 among women.) Unemployment was highest among semiskilled laborers (craft apprentices), domestics, unskilled laborers, and provincials. While only 20 percent of the group as a whole admitted to being unemployed 25.5 percent of provincials as a subgroup admitted to it. Of the 296 persons declaring unemployment, 186 (63 percent) were provincials. This would seem to support the popular belief that the crime rate in Paris was inflated by migrants unable to find work in the city.

Unemployment does not seem to correlate with lack of education, as indicated by literacy. The number of unemployed accused who could sign their names was exactly the same as the number who were unemployed but could not sign: 130, or 22 percent. This is approximately the same proportion of the accused as a group who were able to sign their names. In 20.4 percent of all cases, there is no indication of the ability of the accused to read or write; they were not asked to sign anything by the court. This happened most frequently when the accused were acquitted, especially when this was the result of the Châtelet proceedings being declared null. In some of these cases there is no signature, because the accused had escaped from prison or had never been arrested. The number of persons who declared they could not sign their names was greater than the number who could: 41.0 percent could not sign, while 38.6 percent did sign. The men accused of crimes were more literate than the women: 44.6 percent of all the men could sign their names, while only 14.8 percent of the women could do so. (The number not asked to sign was almost identical: 17.8 percent of the men and 17 percent of the women.) There is no apparent explanation for this; the disparity is greater than it had been traditionally. In the Old Regime, 52 percent of all the accused had been able to sign their names, including 61 percent of the men and 33 percent of the women. Figures for the year 1785 showed a decline in the literacy rate to only 48 percent of the accused, including 45 percent of the men and 31 percent of the women.[46] The literacy rate does not seem to have been depressed by large numbers of uneducated provincials flooding into Paris, although it was lower for provincials than it was for the group as a whole: with 12.3 percent of provincials not asked to sign, 40.4 percent could sign their names and 47.7 percent could not.

The drop in the literacy rate of Parisian criminals in the Revolution appears to be a function of age, rather than birthplace. In the group of accused from eleven to twenty-six years old, there are consistently more persons who cannot sign than persons who can. From the ages of twenty-seven to fifty-one this pattern is reversed; there are more who sign than who say they cannot. It is not clear why young people were not receiving the education that had been available to their elders.

It is difficult to measure family background from the records of the Revolutionary courts although this would be highly desirable. The mention of family was often incidental to the main point on which the defendant was speaking. The judges did not always ask the defendant about his family situation, although they frequently asked very young offenders. The rhetoric of the Revolution idealized the middle-class idea of the family:

TABLE 15

Professions of Parisian criminals in the early Revolution.

Profession	Overall Number of Accused	Percent	Provincials Number of Accused	Percent
Nobles	0	0.0	0	0.0
Clergy	4	.3	2	.3
Bourgeois, businessman shopkeeper master artisan	15	1.0	8	1.1
Restaurant, tavern or lodging-house keeper	82	5.7	47	6.3
Arts and liberal professions	30	2.1	10	1.3
Semiskilled workers				
building trades	128	8.9	67	9.0
producing trades	159	11.0	72	9.6
clothing trades	74	5.1	38	5.1
launderers	35	2.4	15	2.0
other	139	9.6	66	8.8
Street vendors				
secondhand dealers (brocanteurs)	74	5.1	52	7.0
used-clothing dealers	20	1.4	9	1.2
food sellers	33	2.3	16	2.1
other	44	3.0	22	2.9
Domestics (home)	87	6.0	55	7.4
(shop)	66	4.6	41	5.1
Unskilled day laborers	221	15.3	113	15.1
Agricultural workers	43	3.0	14	1.9
Soldiers	28	1.9	14	1.9
Prostitutes	32	2.2	22	2.9
Other	56	3.9	34	4.8
No profession stated	75	5.2	31	4.2

Source: Archives Nationales, Z^3.

father, mother, and children all living together. This was difficult to achieve in Paris where housing was in short supply and normal living quarters were rarely large enough to provide any privacy for a family with no children. Among the laboring poor, all members of the family were expected to work and the children—at least the sons—were often sent away from the home as soon as possible.[47] For this study, "evidence of family" was defined as evidence that the accused was living with at least one person related by blood or marriage: wife with husband, son with father or mother, brother with brother, even niece with aunt. Only 16 percent of the accused gave any evidence of living in a family situation. The father living with his wife and supporting the children was the least frequent of these. A higher percentage of all women than of all men showed evidence of living with their family: 26 percent of all women, but only 13 percent of all men. The pattern of paternal desertion in poor families is apparent in the cases of women left alone with small children when the father became unemployed. The pressure of small living quarters is apparent in the statements of young boys that they were forced to leave home because there were too many children, or because their father or mother remarried. The definition of "family" is complicated by the preference of the laboring poor for common-law rather than registered marriages. (I have counted a couple as married if one or the other claims to be so. It sometimes happened that one affirmed the marriage and the other denied it; nor was it always the woman who claimed to be married and the man who denied it.) Family life among those accused of crime appears to have been very unstable and may have been a factor contributing to the crime rate.

Lack of family support, unemployment, low wages, all of these could lead to what the French call "la misère," a word that is not fully translated in the English concepts of poverty or indigence. "La misère" was commonly believed to be a cause, and perhaps a justification, for crime.[49] While it is impossible to derive a scale of poverty or need from the information contained in court records, I have paid attention to the plea of "la misère" on the part of the defendant as an excuse for his actions. Only 3 percent of the accused claimed need as defense for their actions (45 out of 1,527).[50] Drunkenness was a more common excuse, although most of the accused simply denied their guilt. Men and women pleaded poverty at an equal rate, 3 percent of each group. Suprisingly, few provincials sought to claim hardship in court (only 2.7 percent). In no case did the simple plea of need appear to have any effect on the judges, on the way the case was handled, on the time it took to process, or on the sentence. In many of these 45 cases the accused pleaded necessity to those persons making the arrest. It is impossible to tell how effective their plea was at that level, although it appears that it sometimes led those making the arrest to try to help instead.[51]

Indigence might describe those who worked for low wages as well as those who were without work. Crime was thought to be the province not only of those without work but also those who lacked the skills to make a living wage. The records of the six provisional courts show that both of these assumptions may have been wrong: 80 percent of the accused claimed to be employed and more of them claimed to possess some skill than admitted to being unskilled. In the Old Regime, those who claimed to work with some element of skill or wit formed the largest group of the accused, more than half.[52] The second-largest group was made up of small proprietors: shopkeepers, master artisans, lodging-house keepers, restaurant and tavern keepers. The unskilled were the third-largest group, followed by domestics. Table 15 summarizes the distribution of the accused by profession in the early Revolution, including the group of accused overall and provincials as a subgroup.

Semiskilled workers still formed the largest group of the accused: 535, or 37.0 percent. Unskilled workers formed the second largest group; 264 unskilled and agricultural workers, or 18.3 percent. Street vendors accounted for 171 of the accused, 11.8 percent. Domestics were a large group, counting those in the home and those in taverns, restaurants, and shops: 153 or 10.6 percent. The most notable changes from the Old Regime to the Revolution were the increase in the number of unskilled workers, from 8 percent in 1785 to 18.3 percent in the Revolution; and the decrease in the number of small proprietors such as shopkeepers, lodging-house keepers, and master artisans from 14 percent to 6 percent. Persons of provincial birth did not cluster in any one profession. It seems significant that no member of the nobility was arrested for crime in the early Revolution. Their absence from the Châtelet records may have been based on the privilege of having errant sons and daughters corrected by a separate system of justice. When privileges were removed from the judicial system, the old nobility still did not become involved in ordinary crime.

This collective portrait of the accused shows that one of the most fundamental social attitudes toward crime was not completely accurate: crime was not the exclusive province of those who would not work. Rather it seems to have been part of the life of Parisian workers, especially young male workers. The accused did not present themselves as destitute persons being driven to their actions by misery or necessity, but rather as honest workers who committed a foolish action in a moment of weakness, or who were being falsely accused. The Parisian criminals of the French Revolution were similar to those of the Old Regime, with some specific differences: crime tended to be more exclusively a male phenomenon; there were more provincials arrested as compared to Parisians; the accused were slightly younger as a group than they had been previously; they were less literate, with the highest rates of illiteracy among the young and among women; and they were more likely to be unskilled workers and less likely to be small proprietors than before the Revolution. Some of these changes are products of the Revolution, like the numbers of provincials coming to Paris looking for work. Others are obviously the result of long-term developments in French society, for example, the decreased education available to the poor and to women.

The collective portrait of the accused suggests that during the Revolution, the normal lives of Parisian workers were disrupted, bringing about an increase in the number of crimes committed and the number of workers prosecuted for crimes. The increase in crime is not explained by any massive change in the types of persons being arrested for crime: there was no flood of beggars, of unemployed provincials, or of professional thieves apparent in the court records. But numbers do not reveal everything. The accused seemingly tried to hide in court what may have been the chief cause of the increase in crime: economic and family dislocation resulting in high unemployment and no alternate means of subsistence. (These conclusions are tentative, although more evidence to support them will be presented in chapter 5, because they are inferred from reading the individual dossiers of the accused as well as from analyzing their collective demographic characteristics.)

Conclusions about the causes of crime, or its place in society, or about the meaning to be attributed to the collective portrait of the accused, must always be modified by the highly individual nature of each crime and each of the accused. Despite the consistency with which types of people appear in criminal statistics, each crime is a product of individual circumstances. Despite the fact that we may draw tentative conclusions about the overall reasons for crime, nothing in the collective portrait of the accused tends

TABLE 16

Number of crimes committed in Paris sections, 1789 to 1792, prosecuted in the six provisional tribunals.

Section	Number of Crimes	Percent of Crimes
Roule	13	1.6
Champs Elysée	12	1.5
Place Vendôme	21	2.6
Tuileries	30	3.8
Grange Batelière	13	1.7
Palais Royal	47	6.0
Bibliothèque	15	1.9
Fbg. Montmartre	7	.9
Poissonnière	5	.6
Fontaine Montmorency	10	1.3
Postes	18	2.3
Place Louis XIV	14	1.8
Oratoire	16	2.3
Louvre	20	2.6
Marche des Innocents	24	3.1
Halle au Blé	11	1.4
Fbg. St. Denis	8	1.0
Bondy	13	1.7
Bonne Nouvelle	11	1.4
Mauconseil	11	1.4
Ponceau	23	2.9
Gravilliers	20	2.6
Lombards	21	3.8
Temple	30	3.8
Beaubourg	13	1.7
Enfants Rouges	10	1.3
Roi de Sicile	10	1.3
Arcis	25	3.2
Place Royale	11	1.4
Popincourt	3	.4
Rue de Montreuil	13	1.7
Quinze Vingts	11	1.4
Ile St. Louis	7	.9
Hôtel de Ville	27	3.5
Notre Dame	35	4.5

TABLE 16 (cont.)

Section	Number of Crimes		Percent of Crimes
Arsenal	8	1.0	
Quatre Nations	20	2.6	
Croix Rouge	14	1.8	
Invalides	7	.9	
Fontaine de Grenelle	6	.8	
Luxembourg	7	.8	
Theatre Français	14	1.8	
Thermes de Julien	24	3.1	
Henri Quatre	5	.6	
St. Geneviève	42	5.4	
Gobelins	16	2.0	
Jardin des Plantes	24	3.1	
Observatoire	17	2.2	

Source: Archives Nationales, Z^3.

to explain the causes of crime at the individual level—why some persons
but not others committed crimes or were arrested for crime. To most
eighteenth-century Frenchmen, crime was a matter of individual choice.
Legally, this was certainly the case. Yet a few observers had begun to ap-
preciate the ways in which the environment of the city could influence
individuals. Examining the geography of crime in Paris in the Revolution
makes it clear that there were differences within the city—some sections
were more dangerous than others. Were there factors beyond the individual
that led to crime? It certainly seems so.

The Geography of Parisian Crime

The consistently high crime rates of certain areas of cities and the
tendency of large numbers of the accused to declare residence in these
areas, year after year, has led criminologists to refer to "crime-producing
zones" within cities.[53] The criminal population of a large city tends to
concentrate in certain types of neighborhoods: older areas, usually in the
center of the city, usually run down, and generally densely populated.
This is generally true in Paris in the eighteenth century[54] and in the Revolution. Crimes tended to be committed in the center of the city, on the right
bank of the Seine especially, and in the area of the Hôtel de Ville above all.

TABLE 17

Crime rate in Paris in 1791, by section

Section	Total Number of Crimes 1791	Number of Crimes per 10,000 population (Population:1792)[1]	Population density in 1800: Inhabitants per 4000 sq. meters.[2]
Tuileries	27	21.42	74
Notre Dame	21	17.82	310
Palais Royal	33	16.17	251
Hôtel de Ville	17	15.13	304
Arcis	18	15.00	580
Thermes de Julien	18	12.42	325
Lombards	15	11.95	438
Gravilliers	13	11.81	364
Ponceau	16	11.72	360
Postes	11	11.14	330
Oratoire	7	10.58	444
Temple	25	10.00	48
Halle au Blé	7	9.98	294
Grange Batelière	11	9.50	39
Louvre	11	9.32	259
St. Geneviève	21	9.27	320
Marche des Innocents	13	8.83	555
Champs Elysée	7	8.75	11
Place Vendôme	12	8.57	75
Bibliothèque	11	8.47	147
Beaubourg	9	8.17	315
Jardin des Plantes	13	8.12	60
Gobelins	10	7.84	35
Enfants Rouges	7	7.80	132
Ile St. Louis	4	7.60	204
Quinze Vingts	8	6.37	27
Croix Rouge	11	6.25	67
Roule	8	6.22	23
Place Royal	9	6.20	123
Place Louis XIV	8	6.15	266
Observatoire	12	6.02	32
Bondy	8	6.00	32
Theatre Français	9	5.42	275
Rue de Montreuil	8	5.33	45

TABLE 17 (cont.)

Section	Total Number of Crimes 1791	Number of Crimes per 10,000 population (Population: 1792)[1]	Population density in 1800: Inhabitants per 4000 sq. meters.[2]
Bonne Nouvelle	5	5.02	360
Fontaine Montmorency	6	4.81	224
Marche St. Jean	5	4.76	239
Fbg. St. Denis	6	4.30	62
Quatre Nations	9	4.18	204
Poissonnière	5	4.16	43
Mauconseil	4	3.63	388
Arsenal	6	2.85	82
Henri Quatre	1	2.79	297
Fontaine de Grenelle	3	2.75	86
Invalides	3	2.72	17
Popincourt	3	2.18	17
Luxembourg	3	1.76	52
Fbg. Montmartre	2	1.44	51

Sources: George Rude, *The Crowd in the French Revolution* (London: Oxford University Press, 1959), pp. 242-43.

Archives Nationales, Z^3.

[1] George Rude, *The Crowd in the French Revolution* (London: Oxford University Press, 1959), pp. 242-43.
[2] Ibid.

Crime rates were high in densely populated areas (like the Arcis section) and in areas with large populations (like the Temple section), but also in sections with areas of concentrated public activity, like the Palais Royal. No section of Paris was completely free of crime. Table 16 summarizes the number of crimes committed in each section of Paris during the early Revolution.[55]

Simple frequency, however, is not a true measure of the rate of crimes, which is affected by such factors as size of area and density of population. Table 17 and map 1 summarize the crime rate for Paris sections in 1791. (Crime rate is defined as the number of crimes committed in the section per 10,000 population. Sections are listed in order, from highest crime rate to lowest.)[56] Sections with the highest crime rates were not necessarily those with the greatest number of crimes overall. They were, generally,

MAP 1. High crime areas of Paris, 1791

Over 10 crimes per 10,000 population

8-9.9 crimes per 10,000 population

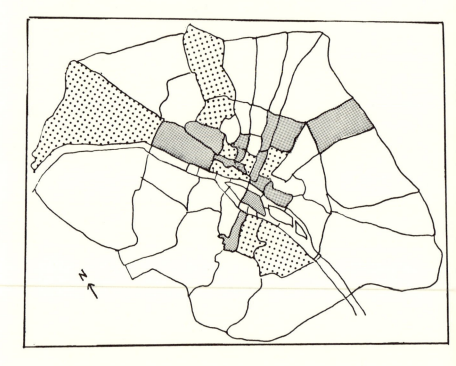

in the center of Paris: Tuileries, Notre Dame, Palais Royal, Hôtel de Ville, Arcis, Thermes de Julien, and Lombards. They were densely populated sections (with the exception of Tuileries) or areas of public congregation for business (the markets, city hall) or pleasure (Palais Royal). Sections with the lowest crime rates were on the edges of the city, generally not densely populated: the Faubourg Montmartre, Luxembourg, Popincourt, and Invalides.[57]

The pattern of criminal residences was not the same as the pattern of crimes. While the location of crimes can be explained, at least in part, as a function of opportunity, no simple explanation appears for the pattern of criminal residences in Paris. Just as no section of the city was completely free of crime, no section was without at least one resident accused of crime. Table 18 summarizes the frequency with which the accused declared residence in the various sections of Paris from 1789 to 1792.[58]

The residences of the accused tended to concentrate not only in the center of the city, especially in the area immediately around the Hotel de Ville, but also in the Faubourg St. Antoine, the Faubourg St. Marcel, and the Faubourg St. Victor. Table 19 and map 2 summarize the concentration of accused declaring residence, by section, for 1791. (Concentration is measured by the number of accused declaring residence per 10,000 population.)

It was in the Arcis quarter above all that the accused tended to congregate: in the run-down lodging houses of the rue de la Vannerie, du Tannerie, the rue Jean de l'Epine, de la Tisseranderie, Jean Pain Mollet, and Verrerie. Here they lived in furnished rooms, as many to a room as in a barracks. Such an arrangement was not conducive to a stable home situation. Family life would be impossible; indeed such rooms were often shared by young men who had been forced to leave their families, in Paris or the provinces, for lack of space or lack of money. The inhabitants of furnished rooms were forced to spend a great deal of time away from home. When they were not working they sought out cheap restaurants, taverns, cafés, or the diversions of the life in the streets of Paris, all of which increased their opportunities for crime. The residences of the accused tended to be on the edges of Paris to a greater degree than the patterns of crimes would indicate. The accused were often a long way from home when they stole. Crime was thought to be committed by a "floating population" in Paris, those with no fixed residence.[59] Even when the accused were able to declare a residence they might still be part of the "floating population." Unable to do much more than sleep in their rooms, they were constantly moving around not only their own section, but the whole city of Paris. The housing conditions of Paris in the Revolution thus appear to have been a contributing factor to the crime rate, as they had been in the eighteenth century and would continue to be in the nineteenth.

It appears that the number of crimes committed and the number of accused declaring residence is higher in several sections because of the presence of non-Parisians in those sections. Provincials seem to have favored the center of the city and the right bank of the Seine for both residence and crime. However no firm statements can be made about their influence on

TABLE 18

Number of accused criminals declaring residence in Paris,
by sections, 1789 to 1792.

Section	Number of Accused Declaring Residence	Percent of All Accused
Roule	21	2.0
Champs Elysée	3	.3
Place Vendôme	17	1.7
Tuileries	14	1.4
Grange Batelière	20	1.9
Palais Royal	19	1.9
Bibliothèque	7	.6
Fbg. Montmartre	27	2.6
Poissonnière	9	.9
Fontaine Montmorency	15	1.5
Postes	6	.6
Place Louis XIV	16	1.6
Oratoire	32	3.1
Louvre	30	2.9
Marche des Innocents	15	1.5
Halle au Blé	15	1.5
Fbg. St. Denis	16	1.6
Bondy	15	1.5
Bonne Nouvelle	19	1.9
Mauconseil	18	1.8
Ponceau	29	2.8
Gravilliers	39	3.8
Lombards	24	2.3
Temple	21	2.0
Beaubourg	40	3.9
Enfants Rouges	10	1.0
Roi de Sicile	16	1.6
Arcis	77	7.5
Place Royale	17	1.7
Popincourt	6	.6
Rue de Montreuil	50	3.8
Quinze Vingts	24	2.3
Ile St. Louis	10	1.0
Hôtel de Ville	10	2.9
Notre Dame	23	2.2
Arsenal	18	1.8

TABLE 18 (cont.)

Section	Number of Accused Declaring Residence	Percent of All Accused
Quatre Nations	24	2.3
Croix Rouge	18	1.8
Invalides	5	.5
Fontaine de Grenelle	11	1.1
Luxembourg	15	1.5
Theatre Français	13	1.3
Thermes de Julien	24	2.3
Henri Quatre	2	.2
St. Geneviève	65	6.3
Gobelins	30	2.9
Jardin des Plantes	34	3.3
Observatoire	15	1.5
TOTAL	1024	100.0

Source: Archives Nationales, Z^3.

TABLE 19

Concentrations of criminal residences in Paris 1791, by sections.

Section	Total No. of Accused per Section, 1791	No. of Accused/ 10,000 Population (pop. 1792)	Population Density in 1800: Inhabitants per 4000 sq. meters
Arcis	46	38.33	580
Oratoire	19	28.73	444
Gravilliers	29	26.36	364
Beaubourg	26	23.60	315
Rue de Montreuil	32	21.33	45
Gobelins	24	18.83	35
Hôtel de Ville	21	18.69	304
St. Geneviève	34	15.01	320
Ponceau	20	14.65	360
Bonne Nouvelle	13	13.06	360
Quinze Vingts	16	12.74	27
Marche St. Jean	13	12.38	239
Jardin des Plantes	19	11.87	60
Thermes de Julien	17	11.73	325

TABLE 19 (cont.)

Section	Total No. of Accused per Section, 1791	No. of Accused/ 10,000 Population (pop. 1792)	Population Density in 1800: Inhabitants per 4000 sq. meters
Roule	15	11.67	23
Fbg. Montmartre	16	11.59	51
Notre Dame	13	11.03	310
Louvre	13	11.01	259
Lombards	13	10.35	438
Fontaine Montmorency	12	9.62	224
Tuileries	12	9.52	74
Place Louis XIV	12	9.23	266
Halle au Blé	6	8.55	294
Place Royal	12	8.27	123
Bondy	11	8.26	32
Mauconseil	9	8.18	388
Marche des Innocents	12	8.15	555
Grange Batelière	9	7.77	39
Fontaine de Grenelle	8	7.35	86
Luxembourg	11	6.47	52
Palais Royal	13	6.37	251
Arsenal	13	6.19	82
Theatre Français	10	6.02	275
Fbg. St. Denis	8	5.78	62
Ile St. Louis	3	5.70	204
Henri Quatre	2	5.58	297
Enfants Rouges	5	5.57	132
Temple	13	5.20	48
Croix Rouge	9	5.11	67
Observatoire	10	5.02	32
Poissonnière	6	5.00	43
Quatre Nations	10	4.64	204
Bibliothèque	6	4.62	147
Champs Elysée	3	3.75	11
Place Vendôme	5	3.57	75
Popincourt	4	2.90	17
Invalides	3	2.72	17
Postes	2	2.02	330

Sources: Archives Nationales, Z^3.
George Rudé, *The Crowd in the French Revolution* (London: Oxford University Press, 1959), pp. 242-43.

patterns of crime in any one section without knowing the number residing in each section of the city. Provincials seem to have favored the center of the city and the right bank of the Seine for both residences and crimes.

The geography of crime in Paris in the early Revolution shows several clearly defined patterns: Crimes tended to be committed in the densely populated center of Paris and in areas of frequent public activity; opportunity for crime was greatest in sections where a large resident population was increased by an influx of nonresidents attending to business or pleasure. At any given moment there were large numbers of persons forced into public places—restaurants, taverns, cafés, promenades—by the inadequate housing conditions in Paris. Persons able to declare a residence were frequently unable actually to live there, in the sense of feeding and entertaining themselves, but were forced into areas where the opportunities and temptations to crime were great. This seems to be the case especially with taverns, which were not only the scenes of many crimes but were also responsible for the drunkenness which the accused often pleaded as a justification for their actions.

The pattern of residences of the accused differed from the pattern of locations of crimes, showing that the pressure of overcrowding considered by itself was not solely responsible for high crime. While large numbers of the accused lived in densely populated sections, such as Arcis, large numbers also lived in uncrowded areas, such as Montreuil and Gobelins. But, while no section of Paris was free of crime completely, certain "crime-producing zones" seemed to exist. These were crowded areas, especially those with poor housing conditions and large numbers of taverns, restaurants, and public services or public spectacles. It seems clear that a significant part of the working population of Paris were forced or drawn out of their "homes" and into situations where the temptation to crime was great because the opportunity was high. There was a distinct "geography" of Parisian crime, and several environmental factors appear to have contributed significantly to individual involvement.

The Victims of Crime in the Revolution

Information on the victims of crime is less complete than information on the individual accused. While every witness in a criminal trial stated age, profession, and residence, the victim of the crime was not always among the witnesses. If the victim were wealthy or aristocratic, he would certainly have no part in the trial: the servants of the house were likely to

MAP 2. Concentration of residences of the accused in Paris, 1791

Over 20 accused per 10,000 section residents

10-19.9 accused per 10,000 section residents

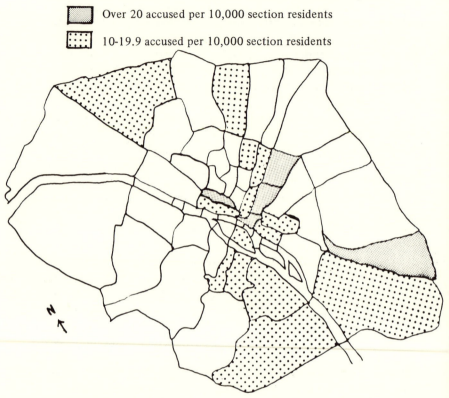

have discovered the crime and they would testify in court. While it is usually possible to find the profession of the victim, the relationship—if any—between the accused and the victim is not always stated but must frequently be inferred.

Crime was popularly believed to strike more frequently at the upper classes than at the lower classes:

> Since the most frequent crime was theft, it was necessary that the victims have more than the accused in order for the latter to rob the former. The social scale of the victims will thus necessarily be high; the poorest groups of society will not be the most frequently represented.[60]

However, the victims would probably not be of the highest social classes; for the second factor in theft (the most common crime), besides the desirability of the object to be stolen, is its availability. In fact, the group most frequently victimized in the eighteenth century was not the upper class but the middle class: the shopkeeper rather than the aristocrat.[61]

In the Revolution the middle class continued to be the primary victims of crime. Table 20 summarizes the professions of the victims of crimes

TABLE 20

Professions of victims of crime in Paris in the early Revolution.

Profession	Number of Victims	Percent of all Victims
Nobles	6	.6
Clergy	17	1.7
Bourgeois, businessman, shop-keeper, master artisan	63	6.2
Restaurant, tavern or lodging-house keeper	351	34.1
Arts and liberal professions	4	.4
Semiskilled workers		
building trades	26	2.5
producing trades	17	1.7
clothing trades	15	1.5
launderers	33	3.2
other	14	1.4
Street vendors		
secondhand dealers		
(*brocanteurs* and		
revendeuses)	17	1.7
food sellers	10	1.0
other	4	.4
Domestics	14	1.4
Unskilled day laborers	30	2.9
Agricultural workers	19	1.9
Soldiers	35	3.5
Prostitutes	2	.2
Other	4	.4
Unknown	347	33.3

Source: Archives Nationales, Z^3.

prosecuted by the six provisional tribunals, for the period as a whole. Shopkeepers, master artisans, restauranteurs, and lodging-house keepers were the largest single group of victims. Unfortunately, a very large number of victims' professions are unknown. The second-largest group of victims, but much smaller than the first, were semiskilled workers. This group appears to have been declining in importance as victims of crime in the eighteenth century;[62] a trend which continued in the Revolution. (I have included the launderers within this group, as one of the primary groups who were the target of theft. The goods stolen from them generally did not belong to them, but it is impossible to tell to which group the stolen goods did belong.) Unskilled laborers and domestics formed almost as large a group of victims as semiskilled laborers. This group was more frequently victimized than the upper-middle class, businessmen and professionals. Street merchants were a surprisingly small number of all victims. Their merchandise was more accessible than that of shopkeepers, it would seem, but perhaps less desirable. (Secondhand dealers may also have been hesitant to report thefts of goods which they themselves might believe to have been stolen when they bought them.)

Considering the large numbers of the accused who committed their crimes away from their home section, one might expect that there would frequently be no relationship between the victim and the accused, but there is a great deal of missing information in this area. In the Old Regime, the accused was known to the victim at least by sight in 60 percent[63] of all cases, but in the Revolution there was no visible relationship between the two in 73.5 percent of all cases. While this may indicate a rise in the number of anonymous crimes, and thus a very real change in the nature of crime from the Old Regime to the Revolution, there is too much missing information to assert this conclusion in any but the most tentative fashion. The single most frequent visible relationship between victim and accused was that of tavern keeper or lodging-house keeper, with 9.5 percent of the accused choosing victims in this category. These people were victimized while providing a service to the accused. The second most frequent relationship was that of employer and employee, with 7.1 percent of the accused in this category. Roommates and neighbors were chosen as victims by 4.6 percent of the accused. Friends and relatives were infrequently victims: only 2.9 percent of the accused committed crimes on persons close to them by blood or friendship. The government was a victim in 2.2 percent of cases, generally thefts or destruction of government property. There is little evidence here of crime as class consciousness or protest against social inequality, a conclusion that is reinforced in reading the dossiers of individual crimes.

An examination of the patterns of interaction between victims and accused, one-to-one, produces a different perspective than the comparison of the two groups; it indicates the interaction between them more clearly. There were few crimes committed against the nobility; these were normally committed by their domestics. The upper-middle class were also the victims of their domestics. However, the visibly rich bourgeois was also a frequent victim of the semiskilled laborer: the shoemaker who attempted to steal his watch in the Palais Royal. Merchants, lodging-house keepers, and tavern keepers were victimized more frequently by semiskilled workers and unskilled workers than by their own domestic help. Semiskilled workers were victimized by those in their own profession above all, by workers at their own level but in another trade, and by unskilled workers and prostitutes with whom they associated in taverns or shared their lodgings. Launderers, whom I have singled out as a significant single group of victims, were victimized by semiskilled and unskilled people. Unskilled workers were the victims of those in their own occupation or at their own economic level more frequently than of any other group. To a lesser extent, they were the victims of semiskilled workers. Thus crime seems to be a product of opportunity as much as of the potential value of the object to be gained: each individual tended to victimize the person most accessible at a higher economic level, or the person most accessible at the same socio-professional level.

The oysterseller robbed the shopkeeper, the shoemaker's apprentice robbed the tavernkeeper, the footman stole his master's silver. What does this aspect of the collective portrait of the accused that emerges from court records show? That the rationale underlying the Penal Code (the assumption that crime was a conscious choice of those who would not work and that the penal system should inspire men and women with a love of honest labor) had little relationship to the realities of everyday crime in Paris. The life of the Parisian criminal was, by and large, the life of the laboring poor with all its problems and opportunities for surviving under increasingly difficult circumstances. "Ignorance of the criminal law" was not the cause of crime, and knowledge of the law would not be likely to have much effect. But changing the criminal law was more easily accomplished than changing the physical and economic environment in Paris which contributed to the increase in crime in the Revolution. Until these were changed, however, the new law would have the effect of more harsh repression of crime, but would not serve as the instrument of social reform its designers hoped it would be.

Notes

1. Nicolas Edme Restif de la Bretonne, *Les Nuits de Paris,* vol. 1, pp. 395-96.

2. Jeffry Kaplow, *The Names of Kings,* pp. 138-41, and ch. 6, *passim.*

3. Restif, *Nuits,* vol. 4, pp. 1761-66.

4. Louis Sebastien Mercier, *Tableau de Paris,* vol. 6, pp. 71-72.

5. Restif, *Nuits,* vol. 2, p. 566.

6. Olwen Hufton, *The Poor of Eighteenth-Century France,* pp. 245-57, asserts that such criminal fraternities existed and describes the conditions under which they might be created, but without giving specific examples of such a "band of thieves" from court or police records. Restif developed this theme into several successful novels about peasants who came to Paris and were corrupted, although their corruption is as much sexual as criminal, and Restif's books were often pornographic.

7. Mercier, *Tableau,* vol. 1, pp. 126-35, 140-47, 147-50. Alan Williams, *The Police of Paris 1718-1789,* pp. 272-73, gives a graphic example of how foul the air might be. The Cemetery of the Innocents, in the quarter of Les Halles, served twenty parishes in Paris, as well as the Hôtel-Dieu and the Châtelet. "Each year workers cast two thousand bodies—more than five a day—into the large open pits. . . . Enclosing the cemetery on three sides were rows of five- and six-story dwellings in which perhaps two thousand persons made their homes." In 1730, the smell was so bad that residents complained to the canons of Saint-Germain l'Auxerrois, who owned and administered the cemetery, but to no effect. During the summer "inhabitants of the area abandoned verbal protest and rioted in the streets." The canons claimed it was not the bodies that caused the stench but the fact that inhabitants of the area dumped excrement and urine into the cemetery, not wanting to climb to the fifth floor to use the common vats into which they were supposed to empty chamber pots. The dispute, though violent, was apparently never resolved.

8. Mercier, *Tableau,* vol. 1, pp. 90-98.

9. Kaplow, *The Names of Kings,* p. 134, quoting Caillard d'Allieres, president of the Bureau du District de Mamers (Sarthe) in March, 1789.

10. Edme de Freminville, *Dictionnaire ou Traité de la Police* (Paris, 1775), p. 474.

11. Williams, *The Police,* p. 284.

12. Mercier, *Tableau,* vol. 3, pp. 216-17. Mercier also condemns able-

bodied beggars who refuse to work, but his sympathy is greater than his anger.

13. Mercier, *Tableau*, vol. 3, p. 225.

A similar opinion was expressed by Lenoir, lieutenant-general of police in Paris (August 1774 to May 1775 and June 1776 to August 1785):

> Begging seems to be the transition between the working classes and the criminal classes; the various regions expel the beggars incessantly, driving them from one to another by police regulations which are becoming more and more restrictive. It is easy to foresee the moment when, if the present policies on begging in the various countries of Europe do not change and become more coordinated, we will be forced to allow beggars to multiply without interference or to massacre them without pity. It is doubtless in the interests of the general and individual security to repress and prevent begging. But the individual interest of the truly poor must never be forgotten. Our laws on this subject leave much to be desired, and all good men should turn their attention to them. The poor man is a member of the great family of man; we plunge him into despair and perhaps barbarism when we leave him abandoned with no resources. Public charity has fallen into a poor state when crime finds recruits among such men." He also observed that it seemed that machines (water power) were putting people out of work (Jacques Peuchet, *Memoires Tirés des Archives de la Police de Paris pour servir à l'histoire de la morale et de la police, depuis Louis XIV jusqu'a nos jours* 6 vols, [Paris: A Levasseur, 1838], vol. 3, pp. 65-67).

14. Kaplow, *The Names of Kings*, pp. 146-47, says that the middleclass diarists of Paris believed that this was so, although he found no evidence that it was. The Baron de Montyon began his study of 10,000 convicted criminals appealing to the Parlement because he believed that crime was increasing. Jean Lecuir, "Criminalité et 'Moralité' : Montyon, Statisticien du Parlement de Paris" *Revue d'Histoire Moderne et Contemporaine* 21 (July-September 1974): 445-93, examines the Baron's studies, concludes that crime was increasing, and sees it as a sign of increasing social tension. Arlette Farge, *Le Vol d'Aliments à Paris au XVIIIᵉ Siècle* (Paris: Plon, 1974) states that the increase in food thefts after 1762 showed "a growing disposition to crime among the population of Paris" caused by their declining economic situation and that this was a sign of "the rupture of the upper and lower classes." Michel Foucault, *Discipline and Punish*, pp. 83-89, discusses the increase in crime and changes in "forms of tolerated

illegality." (As property crime increased, he argues, it was less tolerated by the increasingly powerful bourgeois.) Olwen Hufton, *The Poor*, states that the massive economic disruptions of the 1780s increased migration, vagrancy, begging, and crime in France generally. Studies by Chaunu's students on provincial crime also show that crime was increasing: Bernadette Boutelet "Étude par Sondage de la Criminalité du Bailliage de Pont-de-l'Arche (XVIIe-XVIIIe siècle); Jean-Claude Gégot, "Étude par Sondage de la Criminalité dans la Bailliage de Falaise (XVIIe-XVIIIe siècle).

The two chief dissenters to the observation of a rising crime rate are Alan Williams, *The Police*, who does not mention any concern for an increase in crime in official police documents of the end of the Old Regime. While this may be oversight, editing, or lack of space to discuss everything that concerned police, it is striking in its absence. Porphyre Petrovitch, "Recherches sur la Criminalité à Paris dans la Seconde Moitié du XVIIIe Siècle," shows no marked increase in crime in the last decades of the Old Regime; in fact, the Châtelet tried only 216 cases in 1785, as compared to 276 in 1755. The Petrovitch figures are the most useful for this study since they have similar bases. The major problem of trying to establish whether the crime rate was increasing, based on the variety of studies that have been done, is the noncomparability of data bases. Lecuir, (p. 482), attempts to put together figures on theft as a percentage of crimes from ten different studies of crime ranging from the seventeenth to the nineteenth centuries. This attempt shows the problems of incompatible data bases, as it includes rural and urban areas, periods as short as one year or as great as fifty-five years. The figures would seem to indicate that property crime, considered a distinctly "modern" form of crime, was greater just before the French Revolution than it was four decades later (87 percent of all crimes in 1785; 67.6 percent from 1825 to 1830).

15. Lecuir, "Criminalité et Moralité." Unfortunately, it is sometimes difficult to tell Montyon's observations and conclusions from Lecuir's.

16. For an excellent, brief discussion of the beginnings of criminology, see Leon Radzinowicz, *Ideology and Crime* (New York: Columbia University Press, 1966), ch. 2. Césare Lombroso's theory of the "born" criminal was the product of a study of prisoners rather than of criminal statistics. Studies done with statistics by Adolph Quetelet and A. M. Guerry stressed social causation. Their work stressed environmental factors responsible for crime. For a summary of their work *see* Terence Morris, "Some Ecological Studies of the 19th Century," in *Ecology, Crime and Delinquency*, eds. Harwin L. Voss and David M. Petersen (New York: Appleton-Century-Crofts, 1971), pp. 65-76.

17. Lecuir, "Criminalité et Moralité," p. 476.

18. Throughout this chapter, I will use the figures from the Petrovitch

data that are the most complete and/or the most relevant for comparison. For the period of the Revolution, I will generally give a figure for "overall" cases, referring to the 1,527 individuals tried by the six provisional courts. A few (21) committed their offense before the Revolution but are included for the sake of a larger sample. In addition I will give the figures for 1791 as the general standard of comparison with a single year of the Old Regime.

19. The best study of the pre-Revolutionary police is Williams, *The Police*, but *see also* Henry Buisson, *La Police: Son Histoire*.

20. There are no adequate studies of the Paris police in the Revolution, but for a good introduction *see* Philip John Stead, *The Police of Paris*, ch. 4, as well as Buisson. Georges Garrigues, *Les Districts Parisiens pendant la Révolution Francaise* (Paris, n.p. n.d.), pp. 53-72, describes the involvement of section leaders in police activity.

21. Restif de la Bretonne, *Nuits,* vol. 7, pp. 3355-59.

22. The frequency with which various objects were stolen is:

Linens (including handkerchiefs)	20.5%
Money	17.4%
Unknown	10.1%
Watches/jewels/precious metals	10.1%
Food and drink	3.5%
Silverware	3.3%
Animals	3.0%
Mixed objects, other	32.1%

Source: Archives Nationales, Z^3.

One explanation for the frequent theft of linens might be that pickpockets, stealing handkerchiefs, were really in search of money. Those who did not have a purse frequently kept their coins tied up in their handkerchiefs. The low incidence of food thefts is notable, given the popular image of the starving man stealing a loaf of bread in desperation. Food thefts were relatively infrequent in the eighteenth century as well. Arlette Farge, *Les Vols Alimentaires* has found only 107 such thefts in the records of the Châtelet from 1750 to 1790. This was not based on an examination of every case tried by the Châtelet but by sampling one month out of three. Therefore the total number could be four times that high. Those who stole claimed that it was need which had driven them to their act in 18 percent of the cases. Most simply denied the theft. The thefts were generally petty: a piece of bacon, a basket of cherries, a piece of bread. The chief differences between food thieves and other thieves was a higher rate of illiteracy (74 percent of food thieves, 52 percent of all Parisian criminals) and of recidivism (15 percent had been in prison before, compared to 6 to 7 percent of all Parisian criminals). Farge, *Les Vols Alimentaires*, pp. 10, 301-17, 176. Petrovitch "Recherches," pp. 248, 225.

23. Petrovitch, "Recherches," p. 209, states this as a fact, but gives no figures.

24. Williams, *The Police*, pp. 104-11. Unfortunately, the French word commonly used in court, *dénonciateur*, does not differentiate between unpaid informants and paid informers.

25. Petrovitch, "Recherches," pp. 194-95 takes note of a group of a dozen women, dealers in secondhand goods, who informed the police regularly of suspect goods they received in 1765. They testified in trials, which was highly unusual; police "spies" often sought anonymity.

26. The subject of counterfeiting in the Revolution has been explored in depth by Jean Bouchary, *Les Faux-Monnayeurs sous la Révolution Francaise* (Paris: Marcel Riviere, 1946).

27. *See* the case of Claude Geoffroy in chapter 3.

28. Petrovitch, "Recherches," pp. 216-21. Kaplow, *The Names of Kings*, p. 105, states the common belief that violence was used only by professional criminals. The violent nature of working-class life, not murder but daily fights and beatings, as well as riot, is perhaps best captured in Richard Cobb's works. *See The Police and the People*, parts one and two; and *Reactions to the French Revolution*.

29. *See* chapter 5 for specific examples. The violent nature of the life of a prostitute in eighteenth-century Paris is documented by many social observers, but especially in the works of Restif de la Bretonne. *See* Antoinette Wills, "Prostitution in Old Regime France," paper given to the Third Berkshire Conference on the History of Women, June 1976.

30. Archives Nationales, Z^3 2, 9.

31. Kaplow, *The Names of Kings*, pp. 24-25, describes the fear of kidnapping.

32. Olwen Hufton is particularly eloquent in describing the plight of women economically in *The Poor of Eighteenth-Century France*, chapters 3-4. If migration to find work was a solution for men, it was rarely so for women. Male migration frequently turned into desertion. Hufton observes that when divorce became legal in the Revolution, many of the petitions filed by women showed the pattern of paternal desertion in the bad years before the Revolution. "Women in Revolution 1789-1796," *Past and Present* no. 52 (November 1971): 90-108.

33. The best survey of women's status in the eighteenth century is Leon Abensour, *La Femme et le Feminisme avant la Révolution Francaise* (Paris, 1923).

34. The lesser participation of women in criminal activity is still strik-

ing, both in France and in the United States in the twentieth century. Several attempts have been made to explain the phenomenon, the best of which is Rita James Simon, *Women and Crime* (Lexington, Mass: D. C. Heath & Co., 1975). Her thesis is that women commit crime as opportunity permits, that is, their crimes are related to their occupation. When they stay at home, their crime rate is less. In the same working environment as men, their crimes increase. This seems borne out by the pattern of women's crimes in the Revolution, related to their occupations as domestics, street vendors, dealers in secondhand goods, and prostitutes. *See* Antoinette Wills, "Moll à la Francaise: Female Criminality in Eighteenth-Century Paris," paper presented to the Society for Eighteenth-Century Studies, May, 1977.

35. Hufton, "Women in Revolution," pp. 95-108.

36. The distribution of thefts by sex in 1791 was:

	Domestic Theft	Private Place	Public Place	Suspected Theft	Attempted Theft
Number of men	24	212	208	75	20
Percent of men*	3.4	29.9	29.4	10.6	2.8
Number of women	10	51	29	14	2
Percent of women	7.4	37.8	21.5	10.4	1.5

Source: Archives Nationales, $Z^3$2, 3, 24, 25, 43, 60, 72, 100.

*Percentages refer to the total number of offenses by each sex, not just theft.

37. Petrovitch, "Recherches," pp. 235-41.

38. Petrovitch, "Recherches," p. 237. For a discussion of age as a factor in criminal responsibility see Gerard Aubry, *La Jurisprudence Criminelle,* p. 226-30.

39. Petrovitch, "Recherches," p. 237.

40. Restif de la Bretonne, *Nuits,* vol. 3, pp. 1114-16.

41. This belief appears in a great many places. See Mercier, *Tableau de Paris,* vol. 5, p. 11, "The Savoyards are shoe-shine boys, janitors, and wood-cutters; the Auvergnats are almost always water carriers; the Limousins are builders; the Normans are stone-cutters, pavers, and thread merchants." It would be interesting to find all of these descriptions and compare them. Olwen Hufton believed that the grouping was slightly different. In her study, "Begging, Vagrancy, Vagabondage and the Law," *European Studies Review* 11 (April 1972): 91-124, she states that "There existed a myth in favor of the Auvergnat, of the hardness of his life, his thrift, his sobriety, devotion to his family. . . ." He was usually a pedlar but was preferred by builders for his habits of hard work and honesty (pp. 104-105).

The "Savoyard did not have a virtuous reputation but a romantic image— somewhat ironic in view of the fact that his personal filth was unsurpassed; he was a story teller, a musician, fiddler, or organ grinder, a fortune teller, popular with women and with an easy tongue. . . ." (p. 105). Richard Cobb, *The Police and the People,* pp. 228-30 also speaks to this point, associating the personal filthiness of the Savoyards with their occupation as cleaners and chimney sweeps, declaring that the Normans dominnated horse trading and that doormen were Swiss.

42. Louis Chevalier, *Classes Laborieuses et Classes Dangereuses.*

43. Petrovitch, "Recherches," pp. 238-39.

44. Ibid. There are evidently a large number of missing observations, even though the information for 1775 is the most complete. Petrovitch gives 359 birthplaces but there were 432 accused in 1775.

45. These conclusions are tentative because a large number of the accused did not declare a birthplace: 285 persons out of 1,527 arrested for crimes in Paris, or 18.6 percent. Of the remaining 81.4 percent, 49 percent declared non-Parisian birth and 32.4 percent had been born in Paris or the Ile-de-France.

46. Petrovitch, "Recherches," pp. 248-49.

47. Kaplow, *The Names of Kings,* attempts to discuss family life, pp. 62 ff. The large numbers of children abandoned in Paris in the eighteenth century may be taken as indicative of the difficulty of keeping a family together. Kaplow estimates that one-fourth of all children born in Paris were abandoned. Petrovitch, "Recherches," p. 242 shows that few of the accused in the eighteenth century lived with their parents (nineteen in 1755; twelve in 1765; twenty-five in 1775; nineteen in 1785).

48. Kaplow cites an interesting case in regard to this question of the influence of the family on crime. The problem for the parents would be not only how to support the children and how to find housing, but also how to control a rebellious teenager. In December of 1777, Louis Pirouel and his wife, Marie Jeanne Prevot, both domestics, asked the lieutenant-general of police to lock up their fifteen-year-old daughter because she could not keep a job, stayed out late at night, and was a suspected thief. She was setting a bad example for the other children. Kaplow, *The Names of Kings,* p. 64.

49. In a study of crime in modern Paris, this attitude has been found to persist as the reason and the justification the poor give for young people turning to crime. See V. V. Stanciu, *La Criminalité à Paris* (Paris: Centre National de la Recherche Scientifique, 1968), pp. 179-244. He speaks of crime-producing zones in Paris, where people were badly housed and had little money, where family life was unstable and the young were often in-

volved in crime. He interviewed the residents of the area and found that they thought the causes of crime lay in the lack of control of parents over their children and in hunger and need on the part of the children. They generally believed that if a child were hungry he would steal food: while this did not make the act legal it was a "justification."

50. They were as follows: twenty semiskilled workers, *compagnons* and apprentices; ten unskilled and agricultural workers; nine domestics; and six others.

51. *See* chapter 5, case of Marie Marian, the widow Jacob.

52. Petrovitch, "Recherches," pp. 246 and 253, provides two different groupings of the occupations of the accused. Neither is directly comparable to the scheme I have adopted. In trying to analyze the criminal population in comparison to the population of Paris as a whole, on p. 246, Petrovitch has used François Furet and Adeleine Daumard, *Structures et Relations Sociales à Paris au Milieu du XVIIIe Siècle* Cahiers des Annales, No. 18 (Paris: Librairie Armand Colin, 1961). Since this study is based primarily on marriage contracts and the people in my sample did not often sign marriage contracts, it seems that the value of the comparison is limited. On p. 253 Petrovitch uses a different socio-professional distribution, which suffers from a large number of missing observations (82 out of 432 missing in 1775; 79 out of 532 missing in 1785). The division is as follows:

Profession	Percent of Accused 1775	Percent of Accused 1785
Ecclesiastics, nobility	0	0
Bourgeois, liberal professions, businessmen	4.85	9.00
Shopkeepers, master artisans, lodging-house keepers	15.40	14.00
Domestics	8.00	7.00
Compagnons, shop assistants, secondhand dealers	54.21	53.00
Day laborers, errand boys	10.28	8.00
Other	15.18	9.00

53. See V. V. Stanciu, *La Criminalité à Paris,* pp. 179-82.

54. Petrovitch, "Recherches," map insert between pp. 248-49. It is not possible to make precise comparisons because of the nature of the map, which locates the residences of the accused by street. No listing is made of residences of the accused or location of crimes.

55. The courts tried 782 crimes committed inside Paris and 178 out-

side the city proper. I have not tried to represent the latter, but confined my analysis to the city itself. An additional 85 crimes could not be precisely located from court records.

56. I have tried to test the effect of population density on crime rate by including in Table 17 a figure of approximate density: the population per 4,000 square meters in 1800.

57. There were exceptions: densely populated areas with low crime rates (e.g., Henri Quatre, Mauconseil). In one case, that of Henri Quatre, this may be explained by the number of guards in the area, which included the Palais de Justice.

58. In addition to the 1,024 declaring residence in Paris, 130 declared that they had no fixed residence; 162 declared residence in the area outside Paris proper, and 211 did not declare residence or their residence could not be located with certainty.

59. The Revolution made fixed residence extremely important; section committees were supposed to be aware of the conditions of life of all the residents in their section, for purposes of police and for purposes of welfare and relief. The law of Municipal Police of July 22, 1791, had ordered the police to take a census of all Parisians at regular intervals. Those without stable employment or fixed residence were to be registered as "suspicious persons."

60. Petrovitch, "Recherches," p. 252.

61. Ibid., p. 253.

62. As in the case of the professions of the accused, I have adopted a different socio-professional organization from Petrovitch. The distribution of professions of the victims (Petrovitch, "Recherches," p. 253) is as follows:

Profession	Percent of Victims 1775	Percent of Victims 1785
Ecclesiastics, nobility	2.08	9.00
Bourgeois, liberal professions, businessmen	13.75	12.00
Shopkeepers, master artisans, lodging-house keepers	37.90	37.00
Domestics	8.75	7.00
Compagnons, shop assistants, secondhand dealers	25.41	11.00
Day laborers, errand boys	3.33	2.00
Other	8.78	22.00

63. Petrovitch, "Recherches," p. 255.

CRIMINAL LIFE
DURING THE REVOLUTION_____5

The records of the six provisional courts contain a great deal of information about the lives of the people of Paris which does not translate into
numbers. In this chapter I will examine some of this information for the
insights it provides into the life of the laboring poor, the nature and
causes of crime, the lives of the accused, and public attitudes towards
crime and criminals. I have tried, as far as possible, to let the court
records speak for themselves, summarizing individual cases within
themes that emerge repeatedly in trial testimony. I have paid special
attention to the problem of political awareness and class consciousness
because the political involvement of "le peuple"—as Montyon called them—
has been of such interest to historians.[1] Was crime an expression of class
consciousness or social protest?[2] How did the poor view the Revolution?
What changes affected their lives? What did they think of what was happening to them? Some of these questions have been touched on before,
but I hope to explore them more fully in what follows by looking at
individual cases in greater detail and above all, by letting those most
directly involved speak for themselves.

The "Floating" Population of Paris in the Revolution

A significant portion of the Parisian population was "floating" at all
times in the eighteenth century, especially during the French Revolution.
While this term ordinarily refers only to the problem of domicile,[3] the
records of criminal courts show that "floating" was characteristic of
many of the social relationships of the poor: marriages were by consent
or habit rather than contract; friendships arose without either party inquiring the name or business of the other; stable employment was dif-

ficult to find and marginal employments had to be sought in the interim (selling secondhand goods, running errands, sweeping out taverns); a bottle of wine was to be shared with anyone willing to pay for it. Women were as likely to be "floating" as men, Parisians as likely as provincials.

The case of Marie Joseph Boulogne,[4] a mackerel seller arrested "for entering another person's room with intent to do wrong," demonstrates the phenomenon of "floating," and how it could lead to arrest for crime. While the case is typical of many other arrests for "suspicion" or "attempted theft," it is unusual for the amount of information it gives about the accused, who was not afraid to speak her mind in court.

On May 27, 1791, two members of the National Guard appeared before the police commissioner of the section Roule, leading a young woman, followed by an older woman and several of her neighbors. The group reported the following series of events: Mme. Racine, the victim, had gone out on an errand. When she returned to her room she found it locked from the inside and raised the cry of "Thief!" Her upstairs neighbors, M. Mascon and M. Bouilly, had come running to help her; M. Bouilly had brought along his pistol. Breaking into the room, they arrested a young woman who said her name was Marie. She insisted that one M. Baptiste, a merchant, had told her to wait there, that it was his room, and that he would soon return. Mme. Racine, noticing that things were not in place, accused the young woman of being a thief and searched her. In Marie's purse she found a piece of lace and some money. Thinking that Marie had gotten in by a false key, M. Mascon searched the room and found a key buried in the ashes in the fireplace. Mme. Racine went to call the guard while the men held Marie at gunpoint. After the testimony, the *commissaire* questioned the suspect who identified herself as Marie Joseph Boulogne, called Marie, twenty-five years old, native of Paris, parish of St. Germain l'Auxerrois, mackerel seller. The *commissaire* asked her what she did when there were no mackerel to sell. She responded that she sold the bones and that it was silly to ask such a question. She said that she lived with a wigmaker, but she did not know his name or the number of the house. She said that her mother and sister lived in the rue Froidmanteau but that she did not go there as she did not like her brother-in-law. When she fought with her wigmaker, she went to live with two other girls and each paid 100 *sous* every three months for their room. This morning, having had a fight with them, she was looking for a place to go and met a young man whom she knew by sight from the markets. He had invited her for a drink, had led her to his room, given her the piece of lace, and gone out for another bottle of wine. She was very surprised when Mme. Racine and her neighbors broke into the room and accused her of being a thief.

The police commissioner did not believe Marie's story. He ordered her held in La Force prison to await trial. The judges also said they did not believe her, although she never changed her story and even produced a note from Baptiste that said that he had tricked her into thinking she was in his room, knowing that she would be arrested, and that he did it to get revenge on her because she had refused to come to live with him for so long. The public prosecutor of the First Tribunal requested that she be sentenced to six years in prison for theft with false keys, but the court ordered her to serve two years in prison by the law of *police correctionnelle*. She could not sign her name and did not appeal.[5]

Although Marie was "floating" in many ways, she found it necessary always to have a roof over her head. Few women arrested claimed to be completely without domicile, but men seemed to have more difficulty finding housing.[6] Men tended to share rooms, and to do so in larger groups than women did. These sharing arrangements existed not just for young men, or for those who had just arrived from the provinces to look for work. Joseph Mathieu, seventeen, native of Saint-Prix, a builder's helper, living in the lodging-house owned by M. Bordier near the place de Grève (rue de la Vannerie), was arrested December 15, 1791, for stealing money from his roommates. Five of them lived in the tiny room, including a seventy-two-year-old water carrier. Mathieu was sentenced to eight years in irons on July 31, 1792, by the Fourth Tribunal.[7]

Overcrowded but cheap lodgings were readily available around the place de Grève, along the rue Mouffetard, in the Faubourg Montmartre and the Faubourg St. Marcel, around the markets and around the tavern centers, such as the Porcherons. The names of certain innkeepers and lodging-house keepers reappear as witnesses in criminal trials. Madame Galland, who kept a lodging-house near the Porcherons, maintained her reputation for lodging petty thieves from year to year.[8] All persons keeping lodging-houses were required to report the names of their tenants to the police, although there is no evidence in the court records that they acted as informers to the police, spying on their tenants.

Those who could not find or could not afford housing often slept in the streets of Paris, summer or winter. Pierre Marais, twenty-one, an apprentice wigmaker, native of Vincennes, said that he slept in different lodging-houses for three *sous* a night, whenever he could afford it, or in the streets when he could not. Arrested for stealing handkerchiefs on the place de Grève during an execution, he died in prison before he could be sentenced.[9] Jean Baptiste Sainville, twenty-three, a tailor, arrested for stealing sheets from the drying line of a laundress, said that he had no fixed residence but that he slept with different people, whose names he could not remember, and sometimes paid up to twelve *sous* a night.[10] Jean Massotte, twenty-three, native of Rongeux (province of Champagne), errand boy, had been sleeping for the past month "around the silversmith's ovens in Montmartre" when arrested for stealing eggs and bread in March 1791. He had been unable to find work and had stolen the food, he said, because he was hungry.[11]

It is not surprising that lodging-house keepers, tavern keepers, and owners of inexpensive restaurants were the primary victims of thefts: their clientele walked out with the sheets hidden under their clothing, with the napkins in their pocket, and with the silverware if it appeared at all valuable. Innkeepers were suspicious of persons who appeared disreputable. Jacques Malherbe, forty, a clothing merchant, was arrested for stealing three sheets from an inn in Bondy. When searched, his sack of goods was found to be full of straw. He explained that he was afraid the innkeeper would not have let him stay if he did not look sufficiently prosperous.[12] Sheets were stolen from charitable institutions, especially the Hôtel Dieu. Louise Geneviève Mariage, twenty-four, a seamstress, received as a charity patient at the Hôtel Dieu, attempted to steal half a sheet when she left, "to make it into shirts to start earning a living again." Stopped by the guard at the gate, she pleaded poverty as her only defense—as did many persons with no fixed residence—but was sentenced to one year in prison for theft.[13]

The poor attempted to help each other through times of crisis. An unemployed shoemaker could count on some friends to let him sleep in their room at least for a while. Marie Marian, widow of Jean Claude Jacob, a tailor (she does not give her own profession but was probably a seamstress), had been without work or a place to live for six months when she was arrested in October 1791 for trying to steal a sheet from the Hôtel Dieu. Having been refused admission there, she said that she was desperate. She had been able to survive for six months because friends had helped her out but were no longer able to do so.[14] Family members could be counted on for food now and then, even if they could not offer an unemployed son or brother a place to sleep. They could rarely be counted on for money.

The Problem of Drunkenness

The single most frequently recurring problem the poor cited as the cause of their involvement in crime was not housing, or even work. Rather it was the problem of drink, of the effects of too much red wine. "Wine was the great consoler of the poor; and in periods of anxiety or dearth, they would drink more and eat less. There was more drunkenness in the year III than in the year II and consequently much more popular violence."[15] Drink brought people together in casual relationships that often led to crime: the drunken man sleeping in the cabaret or in the gutter was an easy target for a thief. Drink loosened men's tongues, so that they talked too much and even boasted of committing crimes—whether they really had done so or not. Cabarets and taverns were believed to be the favorite meeting places of gangs of thieves.

The bad housing situation in Paris affected the drinking patterns of the poor in profound ways. Many rented rooms were adequate only for sleeping and had no cooking facilities. The poor could have hot food sent up to their rooms, but it was much more usual to go to a *traiteur*.[16] Even if the meal were only bread and cheese, it was often eaten in a tavern, brought in from outside by those seeking a place that was warm and sociable to eat their supper. Entertainment was sought in cafés and taverns, especially those clustered around places of public spectacle—like the Palais Royal and the place de Grève—which provided "free" entertainment. Business was transacted over a bottle of wine.

Many of the accused came before the police commissioners in a drunken state. Catherine LeNoir, sixty-five, laundress, arrested in the Palais Royal for stealing the watch of a man with whom she was drinking, was very drunk when she was brought before the police commissioner of the Palais Royal. Since questioning her was obviously futile, she was searched. The watch was found in the sleeve of her dress; still she claimed not to know how it got there, having been drunk at the time. She insisted that the man with her in the cabaret was trying to get her drunk "so that he could do as he desired with me." Nevertheless, she was sentenced to two years in prison by *police correctionnelle* for stealing the watch.[17]

The accused sometimes claimed to have been doing a "favor" to a drunken friend by keeping valuables overnight. The judges tended not to believe these stories. The case of Jean Claude Dessertains illustrates the way in which "floating" relationships and drink often led to crime. On August 20, 1791, Jean Claude Dessertains, thirty-eight, a member of the National Guard in the first division (a troop assigned to the center-city area), was brought before the police commissioner of the section Tuileries, accused of stealing the wallet of Claude Robin, fifty-three, a valet living in Versailles. The day before, Robin had entered a tavern on the place de la Carousel. Seeing a guard there, and being a guard himself at Versailles, he engaged him in conversation. From four in the afternoon until eleven at night the two had talked. Various other persons had drunk with them, drifting in and out; all testified that Robin had paid consistently and had seemed to have a lot of money. Anne Fleury, who had come to the tavern to find her husband—another guard—and had dined with him there, had warned Robin of thieves and said he should hide his money. Dessertains had courteously offered Robin a place to sleep in the barracks, but Robin had been determined to return to Versailles and the two had set off together. The last thing Robin remembered was seeing a group of prostitutes near the tavern and contemplating that opportunity. When he woke in the morning, on the Quai du Louvre, all his papers were gone, his money and watch as well. He set off in search of Dessertains, enlisting the aid of other guards of the first division. Dessertains was found to have the wallet and was brought to the police commissioner by his sergeant.

Despite the plea of drunkenness and the declaration of lack of malicious intent by Dessertains, he was sentenced to two years in prison by *police correctionnelle* by the First Tribunal on March 20, 1792.[18]

In some cases the plea of drunkenness and lack of ill intentions was accepted. Catherine Gillais, thirty-two, a prostitute, native of the province of Berry, was accused of stealing money from one of her drinking companions at lunch. She claimed to know the victim only from having spent the night with him; the other man in the party was an old acquaintance of hers from Passy. They had eaten soup, salad, and radishes and had drunk nine bottles of wine, according to her testimony. This did not strike her as an extraordinary amount of wine, although she was quite drunk. The friend had promised to pay, she said, and she was only taking money out of his pocket to pay the bill. The tavern keeper had stopped her from actually taking the money from the man asleep on the table, and this appears to be the reason she was acquitted of the charge.[19] His vigilance could be expected in her case, for any woman of her profession would be thought to steal as much as possible under similar conditions.

In cases involving drunkenness, the judges—if not the law—had to distinguish between misunderstandings and crimes. Philippe Geoffroy, fifty-three, was arrested for trying to rob a friend of seventy-five *livres*. The friend had just bought a violin from Geoffroy, but neither had the correct change; they had decided to split the difference in wine in a nearby tavern. Six bottles of wine later both were "dead drunk" and neither could remember exactly what had happened. Geoffroy was sentenced to *blâme* and warned to be more careful in the future.[20]

Drunkenness led men to do things they would not do when sober. Gaspard Guerin, twenty-five, had left his family in Ligny (in the Barrois region) three months before he was arrested in Paris in October 1790. He had not found steady work in Paris. One afternoon he was left in charge of a store in the rue du Vert Bois by a friend of his who owned the store. Becoming drunk while on duty, he had sold the merchandise to continue buying food and drink. The friend had first demanded an exorbitant sum in repayment and then had had Guerin jailed. The charges were eventually dropped, but only after Guerin had spent a year in prison while the case moved from the Châtelet to the Third Provisional Tribunal.[21]

Violence as well as theft was the result of too much drink. Jacques Antoine Lecoq, twenty-eight, a mason, went drinking with his friend Nicolas Amable Thevenet, twenty-five, a carpenter. Being drunk, they insulted another carpenter's wife on the boulevard des Invalides and got into a fight with her husband and a bystander who came to her aid. When blood began to flow the guard was called. The Sixth Tribunal ordered the young men to spend two hours in the public stocks with a sign proclaiming them to be "libertines who insulted an honest woman on the public promenades," and then to spend two years in Bicêtre prison. This sentence was reduced on appeal to the First Tribunal to *blâme* and they were warned to be more careful in the future. They had probably learned the lesson already, having spent a year in prison awaiting trial.[22]

A city man who decided to have some fun with the country people in Villejuif (near Paris) was lucky to escape his imprudence with only a prison term. François Michel Millet, twenty-nine, a harness maker in Paris, became drunk in an inn in Villejuif and began boasting that he was part of a band of professional thieves operating in the area, that he had robbed farmers and broken into churches, and that the inn would be attacked that night. When two strangers walked in, one carrying a pistol, all three were arrested by the local guard. They were lucky not to have been set upon by the crowd instead. It took five months to process the case. Millet was ordered to serve one month in prison for his indiscretion; the other two were acquitted.[23]

Finding the Accused: Men the Police Looked For

The belief in professional "bands of thieves" was strong in Paris, as well as in the countryside. Several dossiers of cases brought before the Revolutionary courts show that the basis of arrest was the suspicion of a tavern keeper or of the guard that a group of people looked dangerous. The arrest and prosecution of these people gives a very clear idea of "the men to look for"[24] as seen by the police. Most persons arrested under such circumstances were eventually acquitted, but not before the police and the judges went through a set list of questions and a search for the telltale signs of the professional criminal. The case of Marie Briola and Jacques Louis Clabaud is typical of this kind of arrest. The record of the arrest made by the police commissioner shows police methods and assumptions in detail.

On April 12, 1791, fourteen people were brought before the police commissioner of the section Champs Elysée. The guards accompanying them said that they had been arrested in a cabaret "in response to the public clamor that they were thieves holding a suspicious meeting." The persons under arrest were questioned as follows:

> Marie Briola, wife of Joachim Clabaud, master shoemaker, living in the rue du Faubourg St. Honoré No. 86, said she was in the cabaret on the demand of a man who wanted some shoes; she had not even had time to have a glass of wine when the guard arrived and she was arrested. The only other person in the group known to her was her laundress. Asked if she were really married to Clabaud she admitted that she was not. [This question was asked to help determine the moral character of the suspect.]
>
> Marianne Davon, twenty-eight, a laundress, living in the rue St. Florentin and owning her own furniture (a sign of stable residence), said she was in the cabaret with Marie Briola. She volunteered to have other laundresses testify to her good character.

Françoise Sauterot, twenty-two, native of Berci (in Burgundy), said that she had lived in Paris for two years and made her living by selling secondhand clothing. She was having a drink in the cabaret with Jean LeClerc, who lived in her building. Asked if she had her *livre de vente* (a book in which she was to record purchases and sales) as the law required, she admitted she did not. Shown a set of false keys and asked if she recognized them, she said that she did not. When searched she was found to have twenty-four *sous* and a piece of paper with a name and address written on it. (Although she said she found the paper on the street, the person named on the paper would be questioned later and perhaps arrested.)

Madame Oblet (no biographical information), seamstress, said that she had been given some pieces of cloth and some very fine shirts by Marie Briola that morning. (She suspected that they had been stolen and may have denounced Marie to the guard, but this is not specified.)

Pierre Lemaire, called Gerard, thirty-eight, native of Nemours, living with Marianne Davonne for the past two months, had gone to Marie Briola's to get some shoes and then had gone to the cabaret with her. When searched, he was found to have a mark on his shoulder but said it was an old hunting wound. He claimed not to have any money but some was found hidden in his vest.

Jean Louis Yvon, twenty-six, a butcher by training, said that he had been out of work for six months and was living with his brother in the rue du Temple. (He had lost his certificate from his former employer, however, and could not prove that he had been employed.) He was in the area visiting another brother when arrested. Asked what he did for money he answered that he ate and drank at his brothers' expense. Asked why he wore rags even though he had money, he answered that he didn't want to wear out his good clothes. When searched, he was found to have a considerable amount of money and also to be wearing silk stockings, a silk cravat, and clean, new linens.

Victor LeClerc, thirty-six, a secondhand dealer, said that he had lost his *livre de vente* when asked to produce it. When searched, he was found to be branded *GAL*, to have money, and to be wearing new linens. The guard became angry that a branded man was wearing the national jacket (it is not clear what sort of jacket this was) and tore off the collar and the buttons. LeClerc was ordered to submit a letter to the police commissioner, giving his criminal record.

Antoine Latour, native of Mareuse, a carter, said that he had been in Paris only two weeks, looking for work. He was in the area with LeClerc, from whom he bought a jacket. They were sealing the bargain with a glass of wine when arrested. Nothing suspicious was found on him when he was searched.

Charles Louis Gausse, twenty-nine, a mason, living at the lodging-house of the Dame Galand near the Porcherons, said that he had been without work for two years. Not having any money, he had entered the cabaret with "a group of people" who had invited him for a drink. When searched, he was not found to have anything suspicious; his linens were full of holes.

Jean Nicolet, twenty-two, native of Paris, living in the rue des Vertus, without work, said he ran errands for a living. Asked about his family, he said that his mother was still alive but too poor to have two beds and thus he had been forced to leave home. He had been looking for a friend and had stepped into the cabaret to have a drink when arrested. His linens were very new, very white, and of very good quality.

Four more people were interviewed: a carter, an errand boy, a second-hand dealer, and Jacques Louis Clabaud, called Flamant. He had been called from his shoemaker's shop on the arrest of his "wife" but denied knowing anything about her business, saying that everything in the house was hers except the shoes, and that he was a respectable man with his own shop and five employees. Compiling the record of the arrest—interviewing and searching all the accused—had taken five days. Only two of the group were allowed to leave immediately: the Dame Oblet and François Jamain, a thirty-two-year-old carter.

On January 4, 1791, a large theft had been reported by the servants of M. de Beauvais, living in the section Roule but absent in the country at the time of the theft. On hearing that such a large band of thieves had been arrested, the servants demanded that a search be made for their employer's stolen goods. They were found to be in the possession of Marie Briola. The first judgment in the case was handed down on May 22, 1792, more than a year after the arrest. The First Tribunal ordered that the case be retried because of irregularities in the original record of the arrest. Marie Briola was to be held in prison while this was done, but Jacques Louis Clabaud was to go free. Most of those arrested with Marie had been released in

May 1791, except Victor LeClerc, who was held in the Conciergerie prison because he had been branded. Ultimately all the accused were acquitted; no link could be established between them and the crime other than Marie Briola's possession of the stolen goods and her inability to explain where she got them.[25]

The spring of 1791 seems to have been a time of special concern about bands of thieves in Paris. Eight people were arrested in a tavern near the Marché des Innocents when the owner decided that they had stolen goods. Such judgments must have been difficult to make: two of the men arrested were secondhand dealers who had aroused suspicion by the quantity of goods they were carrying but who were apparently engaged in a normal business transaction. One of them wrote to the court to argue his case:

> The writer of this letter has been in Paris six months or so, and taken up the trade of dealing in second-hand clothing and goods. As this trade obliged him to travel round the city every day, going to the markets, . . . he made the acquaintance of another man carrying clothing and other goods under his arm, as second-hand dealers usually do, last May 23.
>
> At the corner of the Rue au Lard there was a wine-merchants shop. And as is usual with men in this profession, who never contract any exchange without drinking a glass of wine, the other individual invited the writer to enter the shop to examine the merchandise while drinking.

It was so dark inside the shop, however, that he went to ask the owner for a candle, at which point he was arrested. Because the tavern was so dark, he said that he could not identify any of the persons arrested with him.[26] (The excuse of darkness must have struck the judges as peculiar, since the shop had been chosen for examination of goods and a business transaction.) The arrest of these eight persons led to prison terms for three of them, an abnormally high number for such a group arrest. The two secondhand dealers were acquitted.

"Bands of thieves" arrested in taverns, cafés, inns, and wine shops were rarely convicted of specific crimes but were usually acquitted for lack of specific charges against them or of evidence linking them to known thefts. Such cases took a long time to process, however, and the entire group was often held in prison awaiting trial. The two examples cited show that the groups were usually made up of random people, a few of whom might know each other. The groups usually included women, who lived in a sexual rather than a criminal relationship with the men accused of being leaders of the group, either as prostitutes or in long- or short-term cohabitation. Such women were thought to be an integral part of any "band of thieves."[27]

The police were looking for suspicious individuals as well as groups. Louis Bucher and Jean Baptiste Allain were "observed trying to hide themselves on the Place Louis Quinze." When the guard ordered them to halt, they ran; when he shot at them, they hid themselves behind a pile of stones. Finally arrested, they were found to have false keys (which they had thrown on the ground) and wax in their pockets that matched the form of the keys. Arrested in July 1791, protesting that they did not know each other and were walking home from an evening of drinking, they were acquitted of the charge in June 1792, because there was no evidence of any kind against them except the pieces of wax. They had spent almost a year in prison.[28]

False keys in a pocket—especially a hidden pocket—were one of the signs of a thief the police looked for. Antoine Blin, arrested in the courtyard of a house in the rue de la Grande in June 1790, allegedly trying to break into a shop, had pockets full of the professional thief's equipment: he had several keys (certified false by a locksmith), a pair of scissors, some wax, a piece of metal, and a knife. He was acquitted in May 1791, having protested throughout his trial that he was in the courtyard looking for a place to relieve himself after drinking all evening.[29]

Fleury Mure and Augustin Clairau were arrested in June 1791, by a guard who reported that he had heard someone calling for a guard and had seen them running down the street at the same time. They claimed that they had locked themselves out of their room and so had decided to walk the streets all night. Unfortunately for them, a package of stolen goods was found in a garden near the spot where they were arrested. They were held in prison until March 1792, and then released on a six-months PAI.[30]

When persons who were very suspect were acquitted, the judges would sometimes add the admonition that the municipality was to be notified that they were "suspicious persons" and the police were "to survey their activities as much as the law allows." When suspects found to have been previously branded were acquitted, this notification was automatic.[31]

Arrests made on the basis of denunciations by informers, whether professional or amateur, were rarely prosecuted successfully.[32] While the practice of basing criminal charges on information provided by informers declined during the Revolution, it did not cease entirely. The prison spy, the pickpocket who promised to testify against others whose criminal activities were known to him, the person carrying out an act of personal vengeance by reporting others to the police, did not disappear.

One of the most interesting cases involving an informer is that of seven people who were reported to be a gang of thieves by Bernard l'Aubi, a secondhand dealer and former ditchdigger. His motives for reporting the seven were never clear. His story was fantastic and lurid: it reveals what seems to have been the ordinary man's idea of the world of the professional criminal. It was certainly a story the police wanted to hear in detail. The secretary's report of l'Aubi's original testimony runs to more than 100 handwritten pages.

On April 9, 1791, Bernard l'Aubi[33] appeared before the police commissioner of the section Arcis. He reported that a few days earlier, as he was walking along the rue St. Honoré near the Oratoire, at about three in the afternoon, a man had tapped him on the shoulder, a friend he used to work with, and asked how he was doing. The friend said he could help him get a better job if Bernard would meet him at a certain wine merchant's shop. They were joined there by two men and a woman "with the gross manners of the countryside." The woman "was a shameless prostitute" and offered to do things for them that Bernard thought too shameful to repeat. They told him that they were part of a secret society and that he could join them for forty-eight *livres* if he were a man of courage and stout heart. To prove that they did not want him only for his money, they showed him fistfuls of *assignats.*

Bernard's description of the exploits they allegedly described to him showed a lively imagination: the secretary became so excited in taking down the story that it is written without any punctuation. There was much blasphemy, not only the repetition of the phrase "Sacre nom de Dieu," but also a description of robbing a church:

> You should see the candlesticks we've got! Pure silver! It's easy to rob
> a church: just break in, post a guard outside with two good pistols,
> kill anyone who comes along. No-one is ever hanged anymore. We
> will never be hanged because if one of us is captured he will never
> reveal his comrades. They never hang people anymore except people
> who don't deserve it. When you are with us six months you will have
> two gold watches and a fistful of money besides.

Bernard reported that they went on to describe their past achievements and their plans for the future:

> I have robbed a coal merchant of 1,000 *livres* and made him think his servant did it. But it was no profit to me; within two weeks I had eaten it all. There is a coal merchant from my region making a trip next Monday with 21,000 *livres* in *assignats* in his pocket. We will ask to travel with him in his coach and then shoot him. Another merchant I know has asked me to find someone to buy wine he wishes to bring to Paris. You will dress up like the merchant and we will rob him. . . . The woman, as less suspect, will carry the stolen goods across the customs barriers.

The police investigated these allegations. They began by questioning the landlord of the building where the thieves were supposed to live. How long had they been there? What were their professions? Two men were arrested and questioned; the maid who cleaned their room was also questioned. The room was searched so thoroughly that straw was pulled out of the mattresses and ashes from the fire sifted.

The room contained pistols, knives, gold watches, false keys, clothing, and a few *livres* in *assignats*. The police also found several pieces of paper with names and addresses on them. They sought out the woman who was involved in the first meeting with l'Aubi. The police commissioner of the section Champs Elysée was called in on the case because some of the addresses were in his territory. The conclusion of the investigation was that Bernard l'Aubi had indeed discovered a gang of thieves posing as second-hand dealers. The group had many people marginally attached to it, mostly unemployed people who traded secondhand goods but who did not appear to be thieves. The trial took a full year. In April 1792, the First Tribunal declared that the charges made against the group were impossible to prove, that none of the goods found in their rooms had been claimed as stolen property, and that there were no witnesses against them except l'Aubi. They were all acquitted but the municipality was informed that they were suspicious persons.

Plea-bargaining was not unknown in the Revolution, although instances of information given in hopes of a lighter sentence are rare in the records of the six provisional tribunals. One such case involved Etienne Toussaint, arrested as a handkerchief thief and brought before the police commissioner of the section Oratoire. Etienne was eighteen, a native of Burgundy in Paris only six months, and a tailor by profession who worked and lived with an aunt in the rue Serpillon. Although the evidence against him was not substantial, he decided to bargain with the court and promised to inform on other thieves whom he knew if the police commissioner would let him go. He led them to a rooming house in the rue de la Vannerie at 2 A.M. (Such an early morning raid was a standard police tactic to find the accused.) In a room on the fourth floor they found two men, each in bed with a woman, and another woman in the room but not in bed. Much time was taken up initially with trying to establish the identities and relationships of the women: the landlord said that they were wives, while the women claimed to be prostitutes. Nine false keys were found on one of the windowsills, but nothing else suspicious was found in the room. The two men were unemployed artisans, which led the police commissioner to ask how they could afford to have the women sleep with them. They knew their accuser from having lived in the same building.

In the time that it took—that morning and later at the section headquarters—for the commissioner to question the accused and to establish their identities, the original thief and informer left, apparently unnoticed. The nine false keys found on the windowsill were critical, however, The five persons found in the room at 2 A.M. stayed in prison one year before they were acquitted.[34]

Those already convicted of crimes and serving a sentence might also try to bargain by informing: prisoners informed on other prisoners in hopes of getting their sentences reduced. Edme Jomard tried to reduce his sentence of sixteen years in the galleys by denouncing seven men he met in prison as a gang of thieves who had broken into a church and stolen the sacred vessels. Once again sufficient evidence to convict the accused was lacking: two were acquitted, two were ordered PAI three months, in prison, and three were ordered PAI three months, at liberty. The dossier gives no indication of what happened to Jomard, nor is the nature of his crime ever revealed.[35]

Finding the Accused: Public Attitudes Toward Crime

Successful prosecution of a criminal charge required a body of evidence, preferably the stolen object found in the possession of the accused, and witnesses to the crime. Public outcry, public arrests, and private individuals searching out the suspect resulted in successful prosecution more often than denunciation supplied by informers. The abundant street activity of Revolutionary Paris was at once the criminal's greatest asset and his greatest problem. Crowds provided opportunities for theft and the chance of escaping into the anonymity of the crowd. When the theft was observed, however, the thief was often pursued by a crowd that seemed intent on punishing the action on the spot. The number of people in the streets at all times increased the possible numbers of witnesses to crimes, even those in private places. The person who came back to his room and discovered that he had been robbed would likely ask around to see if anyone had seen anything suspicious before calling the guard. Most frequently the victim would inquire of the local errand boy or of prostitutes, who tended to station themselves at one spot regularly and wait until their business came to them. They were very aware of strangers in the neighborhood. Girard Tournier and Antoine Berry were found out in this fashion. A watchmaker returning to his room on the first floor of a house in the rue des Poulies found that he had been robbed. He inquired around the neighborhood if anyone had seen the thief in his room and was told by three women (in all probability they were prostitutes) that they had seen "a groom in a blue vest" and an errand boy who had been stationed the previous year at the corner of the street. The errand boy had given a package to the groom, telling him to be careful because the contents were fragile.

The prostitutes knew the name of the errand boy—Girard—but were uncertain where he lived. The local errand boy was consulted and led them to Girard's room. The guard was informed, and the room raided at midnight. Girard was there with a woman who said she was a prostitute. The police commissioner making the arrest questioned the woman before he questioned Girard; he seemed as interested in the morality of the accused as in the details of the theft, asking the two why they didn't get married. (Both answered that they intended to do so eventually.)[36]

Errand boys appeared frequently in criminal cases as witnesses but also as participants. They were not supposed to help transport any goods they believed to be suspicious. In one case a domestic tried to steal her employer's silver by giving it to an errand boy to carry away, but he became suspicious and refused. He did not report her to the police but did testify against her in her trial. An errand boy caught helping to load furniture into a hand cart at night was fortunate not to be judged an accomplice in the theft; he was admonished to adhere to the rules more strictly in the future and to avoid suspicious circumstances.[37]

If the identity of the suspect were known there were specific places one could go to look for the person if he could not be located in the neighborhood. Runaway employees, especially domestics, could often be found at the public spectacles passing their newly found leisure time or even wearing their newly stolen fine clothing. The Palais Royal was one of the first places to seek them out; there they were often apprehended spending their new wealth on food and drink for their friends, on gambling, and on women.

The Palais Royal was also a place to look for runaway, lost, and abducted children, especially daughters. There was a popular belief that children were kidnapped by procuresses or were tempted to leave home voluntarily by promises of food and candy.[38] Adolescent girls who ran away from home often became prostitutes, a trade which centered in the Palais Royal.

Victims of crime, or the police, might also inquire among the city's secondhand dealers, among the silver- and gold-smiths, or even at the state-owned pawnshop, the *Mont de Pieté*. The state's pawnbrokers were kept informed on a daily basis of objects reported stolen so that they might watch out for them. Secondhand dealers, jewelers, and silversmiths were supposed to report any suspicious items to the police and often appeared in court to testify in criminal trials. The Palais Royal was a popular gathering place for these merchants and thus thieves trying to sell their stolen goods to them: one young man was so unfortunate as to attempt to sell a silver buckle to a secondhand dealer who had just purchased its mate from the victim.[39] The young man was sentenced to eighteen years in irons because he had stolen the buckle at night, on the open highway, with violence to the victim.

Other signs recognized by the police and the general public enabled them to identify suspicious persons, even if they had not seen a crime committed. It was widely believed that a person who had just committed a crime gave physical evidence of the fact by turning pale or trembling. Victoire Montigny was found on the second floor of a house when the cry of thief was raised in the street. When one of the inhabitants of the house questioned her, she claimed to be looking for the toilet, but she also paled. The man took this as a sign of her guilt, searched the area, found a suspicious package, and had her arrested.[40] Bernard Maubert, accused of being an accomplice to a theft in the rue du Bussi, protested that it was all a misunderstanding. He was having lunch with his wife, he said, but the meal was so terrible that he had gone into an alley and had become ill. When he heard the cry of thief, he came to see what was happening. Seeing him pale and trembling, the crowd arrested him. He was acquitted of the charge.[41]

In general, the public attitude toward crime was characterized by vigilance and cooperation with the victim, to the extent of physical violence to the person of the suspect. In several cases the suspect welcomed the arrival of the guard who found the victim and his friends beating the accused with fists and canes, or threatening to hang, shoot, or otherwise punish him on the spot. Antoine Sabatier and Jean Ontra[42] objected to the testimony of the witnesses at their trial, saying the testimony should not be allowed because the witnesses had tried to kill them after they were caught stealing linens from a room in the rue de Viarmes. The court declared the objections irrelevant and sentenced Jean to twelve years in prison; Antoine had died in prison while awaiting trial, perhaps of the wounds he received in the beating. The beating had been more severe since Jean Ontra had been found to be branded as a thief when the crowd tore his coat off at the time of his arrest.

The public often made false arrests, especially when the thief was not arrested in the act of stealing but when a witness notified an unsuspecting victim after the fact. The victim often chased after the thief and arrested anyone who was running, was pale, or had been standing near him earlier.

A person caught in the act of crime could beg for mercy from his accusers; it was necessity that made him steal, it was a moment of weakness. In many cases this was not effective. Dominique Toussaint Charles Grosjean, twenty-two, native of Paris, a shoemaker, stole a handkerchief from the pocket of Etienne DuFour, sixty-four, a watchmaker, while the two were standing on the square in front of Notre Dame watching a military exercise on July 7, 1791. DuFour seized the thief's hand and recovered his handkerchief. Grosjean began to cry and to plead with the victim not to arrest him, saying that he had been out of work for two months and only stole to eat. DuFour told the court that he was willing to let the young man go since he had recovered his property. Other persons in the area were not so generous; Grosjean was brought to the police commissioner of the section Notre Dame by the victim, an innkeeper, and a wine merchant who had witnessed the crime. The innkeeper testified that he had insisted on bringing Grosjean to the commissioner "because the tears and pleadings of thieves are not touching to me."[43] Grosjean was sentenced to one year of prison by *police correctionnelle* on January 31, 1792.

The police themselves were sometimes more sympathetic to the accused than the public. Frederic Hyacinth Langlet, twenty-two, native of Picardy, a waiter in a tavern, was accused of stealing a watch from one of his roommates, an apprentice carpenter. When his roommates brought him to the police commissioner, he admitted his crime, said it was need that had made him commit his act in a moment of weakness, that he had sold the watch and bought himself some shoes and a shirt. He was so humble and contrite that the police commissioner recommended that the court allow him to return to his home in Picardy and provide him with work there. The Penal Code did not allow for such a resolution to a crime in which the facts were so clearly established; Langlet was sentenced to eight years at hard labor.[44]

The charity of the public and of the police was not always rewarded. Jacques Velmont was arrested by a section patrol in July 1791, for wandering around suspiciously at night. Released the next day, he complained to the guards that he could find no work in his profession—he was a tailor. They took pity on him and set him to work mending uniforms and let him stay in the barracks. When the wife of one of the guards brought him food the next day, he was gone, as were a number of uniforms. Brought to trial, he was acquitted of the charge because the uniforms were never found. He had spent ten months in prison awaiting trial, however.[45]

Violence and Murder

If the public and the authorities were sometimes sympathetic to thieves, this sympathy never extended to crimes involving violence. The court records show, however, that occasionally the neighbors of the accused were less willing to become involved in aiding the victims of violent crime—and arresting a violent person—than in helping to arrest a thief. The case of Jacques Haas provides a vivid depiction of a violent crime which took place in an overcrowded boarding house and of the various reactions of the neighbors to the crime.

Jacques Haas, twenty-five, an unemployed domestic, earning a living as a money changer, had dinner with a friend from his home province, Louis Dubu. Dubu owed him 800 *livres,* he claimed. They returned to Dubu's room in the rue St. Jacques after dinner, but Haas was unable to sleep because the neighbors were making so much noise. Dubu also slept lightly, waking at five in the morning. He was surprised to see Haas awake and sitting up but went back to sleep. At seven he was awakened by a blow on the right side of his head and then was shot. Haas fled, wearing only his shirt, crying out that his friend had been murdered.

The first people to hear the noise were M. and Mme. LeBrun who had the room next to Dubu. Hearing the pistol shot, Mme. LeBrun told her husband to go see what was happening, but he told her to be quiet and not to get involved. They stayed in bed until the police commissioner arrived.

Antoine LaPorte, an innkeeper, was passing by the house when he heard the shot and saw Haas run out into the courtyard naked and screaming for help. He helped other persons coming out of the house to lead Haas back to the room where Dubu lay wounded. Jean Pierre Gabriel Eurin, a baker's helper, was returning to the house after an appointment with his hairdresser. When he discovered what had happened he went down into the courtyard and recovered the pistol.

It is not certain who called the police; the commissioner arrived shortly after the shooting, accompanied by a surgeon and two *notables,* one of whom acted as the secretary. They found the wounded Dubu in his bed and Haas standing in the corner of the room. Dubu was questioned on what had happened before he was taken to the Hôtel Dieu, despite the fact that he was bleeding badly. The neighbors were then questioned, including the LeBruns who said they knew nothing. Haas was questioned last, having stood in a corner of the room all the while. He protested that someone else had broken open the door, shot Dubu, and escaped.

There was no apparent motive for the crime; Dubu's money was still in his wallet. Nor was there any sign that the door had been broken open; Dubu swore that he had locked it. Haas was condemned to die for the shooting.[46]

Crimes of violence were judged on several factors: the amount of evidence in the case, the number of witnesses, and especially the question of intent. The penalties for violence varied. In some cases the victim dropped the charge and the court could acquit the accused at its own discretion. Violence as part of theft was punished seriously; under the Penal Code the death sentence was mandatory even if the victim did not die but was seriously wounded. The victim could sue for a monetary indemnity instead of a prison term for the accused.[47]

Violence was not only frequent, it was accepted as inevitable by many of the poor. Murders went unsolved, even when the victim did not die before help arrived but simply refused to name the assailant. The death of the Femme Richard is one of the most poignant and tragic stories in a series filled with tragic stories. On December 19, 1791, the police commissioner of the section Grange Batelière was called to a room on the fourth floor of a house in the rue du Faubourg Montmartre where a woman lay dead following an attack the previous night. He questioned the dead woman's friends who were gathered around her. The first to speak was Thérèse Herard, oyster vendor. She had known the victim— Marie Roblot—for years; they sold oysters together. Marie was the wife of a soldier named Richard but they had been separated for six years. The previous Saturday she had seen Marie drinking with a young man named Bourgignon, whom she knew to be her lover. Later the same evening she saw Fichet de La Roze, who lived with Marie, looking for her; he had locked himself out of their room and needed the key. On Sunday morning she was on her way to pick up Marie and to go to La Halle to buy oysters for the day when she saw La Roze coming to get her. He said that Marie had been badly wounded and he needed her help. When they arrived, she asked Marie if it was Bourgignon who had done this to her, but Marie said that it was not. She had left him in the Faubourg St. Denis and come home by the rue de l'Echiquier when this happened. Thérèse asked if the prostitutes in that street had beaten and robbed her, but Marie said no, that she fell.

The surgeon reported that the cause of death was not a fall but a bullet in the stomach, evidently from a small pistol. The police searched the room and examined the clothing Marie had been wearing, which was bloody and badly torn. She had been attacked with considerable violence. They questioned Bourgignon as the prime suspect. He stated that his real name was Joseph Fromageot, that he was a coachman but was presently unemployed. He had known Marie for three years but "had never taken any liberties with her." They had spent Saturday afternoon drinking; when she became very drunk the wine merchant refused to serve her any more. She punched the wine merchant, a woman, and they left. He had left her because she was so drunk and had gone home by himself. Thérèse had sent the police for him when she heard what had happened but Marie herself had denied that he had injured her.

Marie was found, after she had been wounded, by Fichet de La Roze. When she hadn't come home on Saturday night he had gone to sleep at a friend's place. He came home at five in the morning and found her in the courtyard, bareheaded, in her slip, her corset torn, only one stocking, her skirt at her feet. He assumed she was drunk; but while taking her up to their room he had noticed that she was wounded. She had called him endearing names all the time that it took to carry her upstairs and get a locksmith to open the door.

The police questioned the neighbors; only one woman had heard anything unusual. At two in the morning she had been awakened by a voice from the courtyard calling the name of La Roze. She had leaned out her window, said that he lived on the fourth floor and told the caller to be quiet.

The murder was never solved; Bourgignon was the only suspect arrested, and he was held only a few hours. In June 1792, the First Tribunal officially declared the case closed because there was no clue to the identity of the attacker. The motive of the crime had probably been theft—although Marie had no money—and possibly rape. The reason Marie kept the identity of her attacker secret was unknown.[48]

Crimes of violence and murders which appear in the records of the six provisional tribunals were more often cases of personal discord between people who knew each other than cases of random violence. Frequent instances of family violence almost certainly went unreported, although there is evidence of some such attacks in the records of other crimes. Michel Marie LeMoine, twenty-eight, a ditch digger, living in the rue des Vertus, was denounced to the police by his landlady for a beating he gave her. She said that he beat the woman he lived with so often that she had asked him to leave, and he had responded by beating her. She admitted that she had hit him first with her umbrella. He had been drunk at the time, and she received a severe beating in return. The court declared that no crime existed, and he was acquitted without even paying damages.[49]

Personal quarrels that led to violence and even murder were judged leniently, but attacks carried out in situations of trust were dealt with very severely. Antoine Bangelet, a tapestry maker, and Andre Dupont, a day laborer, were accused of beating and robbing a vinegar merchant from Dijon who had asked them for directions. After leading him around for an hour they had hit him over the heat and taken fifteen *livres* from his pocket. They were sentenced to be hanged.[50]

The number of women involved in violence and homicide during the

Revolution was greater than it had been in the Old Regime. Some of the women charged with violence, and many who were its victims, were prostitutes. During the eighteenth century prostitution was a police matter, more a problem of public tranquility than of morals. The best protection from arrest for a prostitute was silence. If she complained of being beaten there was a higher probability that she would be sent to prison for prostitution than that her attacker would be sent there for the beating. During the Revolution, prostitution *per se* was no longer a matter of police; it was not specifically declared illegal. Women openly identified themselves as prostitutes in court, whether they were the accused or the witness, and brought suit when they were the injured victim.[51] They were arrested for murdering their lovers, but not their clients.

Prostitutes and Prostitution

Not all women who were prostitutes identified themselves as such in court but thirty-two of the accused did so. Of these, twenty-five were accused or suspected of theft, two accused of murder, one of violence, two of debauching a young girl, and one of counterfeiting. (In one case no crime was specified.)[52]

Prostitutes were arrested for thefts carried out in cabarets or in their rooms, and were usually charged with having taking advantage of their client's drunkenness in order to rob him. Louise Colin, a twenty-seven-year-old prostitute, from the province of Maine, living in the rue des Filles Dieu, stole a gold watch from a marble worker with whom she was drinking near the place de Grève. The victim claimed that she had cut his culotte and stolen the watch. She denied it; the watch was not found. She was subjected to an outburst of abuse by the police commissioner of the section Arcis:

It is necessary to punish shameless public women who take advantage of the weakness of men to swindle and rob them every day. Yet such women are never found to have stolen goods when they are searched because they are so practiced at their art that they find ways to pass them on and divide the spoils among themselves.

Therefore, even without evidence, he ordered her to be detained at La Force prison, although he knew that when she came to trial the evidence would not be sufficient to convict her.[53]

The Palais Royal was the center of Parisian prostitution, of gambling, of public spectacles, and of café and tavern life. There prostitutes stole watches, money, and business letters from their drunken clients. Marguerite Gilson, a nineteen-year-old-prostitute, native of Paris, living on the rue de la Cossonnerie, accosted a young man outside the Palais Royal and asked if he would buy her a glass of wine. In the cabaret he gave her twenty *sous* and began to caress her. While he was doing so, she stole his wallet. He did not notice the theft immediately. She had excused herself to go to the restroom and he became suspicious only when she did not return. She was eventually sentenced to a PAI of one year in prison.[54] It was difficult to convict prostitutes of theft. As the police commissioner of Arcis had observed, they divested themselves of the evidence as soon as possible, selling it to fences or to the owners of the taverns in which they committed the theft, giving it to their lovers to dispose of, or giving it to other prostitutes. Cohn and Gilson acted alone; usually prostitutes acted in groups. They seem to have been very sociable, spent a great deal of time in each other's company even when working, and banded together for mutual protection against the authorities.

On Sunday, October 3, 1790, Joseph Girard, a surgeon, complained to the police that he had been robbed of his wallet and his watch. The night before he had gone to the Palais Royal and being somewhat drunk he had gone with a woman who solicited him. They went to the room of Louise la Parisienne. Although there were three other women there, he amused himself with her, paid her three *livres* and fell asleep. When he awoke in the morning he was alone, his watch and his wallet were gone. The police investigated his complaint, asking around the Palais Royal for the woman known as Louise. She admitted drinking with the man and bringing him to her room; she identified the other women who were there as "Chouchou" and "La Grosse Julie," and she said that it was Julie who had stolen the things and sold them. Julie was never arrested; Louise waited for a year in prison for her case to come to trial and was sentenced to a PAI of three months, at liberty.[55]

Prostitutes acting alone tended to commit small thefts, spontaneously seizing an opportunity. When they were involved in larger thefts they were usually acting in partnership with men; the men appeared to be the leaders of the group. Every group of professional thieves was believed to have at least one member who was a prostitute. Catherine Verdal, a twenty-two-year-old prostitute, stole 5,400 *livres* from a man in a cabaret in the

Rue Vivienne with the help of two men. Nevertheless, she was the only one sentenced to prison because she was the one seen picking his pocket.[56] Louise le Grande was accused of stealing 520 *livres* in *assignats* and various other goods after breaking into a room in the Rue Philippeaux with the help of Antoine Barthelemy. Both were sentenced to fourteen years in prison.[57]

Most prostitutes were already acquainted with prison. While few had previously been convicted of crimes, most stated that they had been in prison because of their profession. They were very much *en marge* in Parisian society in the eighteenth century and the Revolution. They frequently could find no other means of support; they were often not very bright and were generally brutalized by their life style and by their clients.

Louise Villequier, a twenty-six-year-old woman who had come to Paris from Besançon, said she had been forced to become a prostitute because she could not find work and that she had no fixed residence but stayed one or two days here and there. The last two days she had been in a lodging-house in the rue de la Tannerie, whose name she did not know. She was arrested for stealing three forks from a wine merchant in the rue Feydeau. She was not very bright; she had taken a young girl who was not a prostitute with her to the shop, and the girl had reported her to the police. The forks were not found, however, and Louise Villequier was acquitted of the charge.[59]

Just as the women moved from one furnished room to another, sometimes on a daily basis, men with no fixed residence often said that they had stayed with prostitutes for lack of alternative lodging. Prostitutes were part of a "demi-monde" which was not only sexual but often criminal. They lived in areas of high crime: around the Palais Royal, the Tuileries, and the place de Grève, near the markets, and in the Faubourg Saint Germain. They lived on the rue Jean Saint-Denis, the rue de la Mortellerie, the rue des Vertus, the rue de la Tannerie, and the rue de la Vannerie in cheap, furnished rooms and in brothels.[60]

The lives of prostitutes were frequently violent, in the eighteenth century and in the Revolution. They were the victims of their lovers and their clients and occasionally committed violent acts. On January 27, 1792, Pierre Loiseau shot Marie Philippine Minique in her room in the rue Saint-Honoré, near the Palais Royal. She was not killed but only wounded and brought civil and criminal charges against him. She reported that she had met him in the Palais Royal, that he had solicited her to take him to her room, that she had felt repugnance towards him but had agreed. In the room he had offered her forty *sous* (a ridiculously small price) and she had refused to sleep with him. He had shot her immediately, without any argument first. The public prosecutor recommended that she be paid 300 *livres* indemnity since she was now unable to continue in her profession, but the court awarded her only 150 *livres*.[61]

Prostitutes usually had a male "friend" with whom they formed an attachment that was very proprietary. These men felt that they "owned" their women and received sexual favors and money on demand.[62] Once established they were not easily dismissed. They appear to have been petty, small-minded men, easily offended and easily incited to violence. The case of Rosalie Cabot and Jean Baptiste St. Villiers shows how this type of relationship led to violence. On August 27, 1791, St. Villiers, a teacher from Cambrai, fought Nicolas Desmoulins, a soldier of the National Guard, over the favors of Rosalie Cabot, a prostitute living in the Palais Royal. Desmoulins had been her "friend" for some time but she had decided to establish St. Villiers in this position instead. Desmoulins had forbidden her to see him and on several occasions had threatened them both with violence. Having found them eating lunch together one day in the Palais Royal, he had beaten them both; they armed themselves with pistols in anticipation of the next encounter.

On August 27, St. Villiers had come to say goodbye to Rosalie before returning to Cambrai. While they were in her room, Desmoulins entered and attacked him. St. Villiers lost an eye in the ensuing fight; Desmoulins was shot in the stomach and died a few days later. St. Villiers and Rosalie Cabot were eventually absolved of the charge of homicide by a letter of remission from the king in January, 1792.[63]

In a similar case, Jeanne Adelaide Duquet, a twenty-year-old bookbinder and former prostitute, was accused of murdering her former lover, a soldier named Montenot, by throwing him out of the window of her house on the rue Percée. She had lived with him for five years, during which time she admitted that she had been a prostitute but had given up both the relationship and the profession and had been living with a printer named Rigolet for the last three months. On December 3, 1791, Rigolet had come to her room to have dinner with her: she was ill in bed, recovering from a beating Montenot had given her the week before. Rigolet testified that Montenot had been very upset when she had refused to live with him any longer and had held her by the hair and beaten her head against the wall. They heard a noise in the street. Montenot was lying in the gutter, having fallen from the window of a house.

All the neighbors testified in defense of the accused: Montenot had been upset that she had left him and had often talked of killing himself, although no one had actually seen him jump. On April 23, 1792, she was released from custody while the investigation was continued, a sentence tantamount to acquittal.[64]

Despite the fear of child molesters and kidnappers, only one case of procurement of young children for prostitution was successfully prosecuted in the Revolution. Louise Bertrand, widow of Jean Desbleds, twenty-six years old, was accused of procuring a twelve-year-old girl, the daughter of a locksmith, for purposes of prostitution in May 1790. The girl had been sent on an errand from her home in the rue Aubry le Boucher on a Saturday morning. When she did not return, her mother looked for her and reported her missing to the police on Monday. Since they refused to help, saying that she would have to find her daughter by herself, she went to the Palais Royal to ask if anyone there had seen her daughter. Three young women whom she met near the Café de Foi said that they knew of a young girl who "was recently debauched by a woman in the rue Froidmanteau," and offered to take her there. She found the address, but the woman had gone. Testimony from the neighbors that the girl had been there and that a young man had visited her and that she had complained to neighbors that he had hurt her was sufficient to involve the police in the search, but since they simply repeated what the mother had already done, they were completely ineffective. On June 10, the father of the girl finally located the widow Desbleds and brought her to the police for questioning. She did not deny that she knew the girl; she claimed instead that the girl went begging with her (Desbleds was a day laborer and beggar by profession, she said), was always hungry, and complained that her parents beat her. The little girl was also found, although she was no longer with the widow Desbleds. She testified that she had been prostituted many times, that she was given twelve to twenty-four *sous* each time, and that she was told that if she went home and told her parents what had happened they would beat her and send her to the Hôpital. Since she had developed venereal disease, she was afraid that this was true and had not tried to return home. The girl's story was believed, the woman Desbleds was sentenced to the traditional punishment for procuresses: being led through the streets seated backwards on a mule with a sign proclaiming her crime, branding with a *fleur de lys,* three years of prison, and perpetual banishment from Paris.[65]

The world of Parisian prostitutes had undergone one profound change from the Old Regime to the Revolution: prostitution *per se* was no longer illegal. Women were more honest about admitting they were professional prostitutes; they became more visible and probably more aggressive about soliciting customers. Other aspects of their lives did not change: the root-lessness, the desperate desire to get money while still young, the concentration in certain areas of the city, the life of drinking cheap wine in taverns, the violence to which they were subjected by "friends" and clients, and the connections between prostitution and crime.

Revolutionary and Class Consciousness

The extent to which the poor were conscious of and active in the political events of the French Revolution has been a matter of debate among historians. There are only a few references to the Revolution scattered throughout the records of the six provisional tribunals; the questions at hand, after all, did not focus on the political opinions of the accused but how many people had seen him steal the watch from the old man's pocket. Court documents provide only a rough sketch of the Revolutionary awareness of the poor, of how they saw the Revolution affecting their lives, and of whether they saw themselves involved in a struggle between classes or between workers and their employers.

The most outstanding fact about the Revolution in the minds of the laboring poor, was that it had disrupted the "system" of the Old Regime, to which they had become adjusted. Traditional patterns of employment and of charity were disrupted, people were out of work and had no place to seek relief. The Revolution had brought trouble to the poor, as they told the judges repeatedly. A woman accused of theft was asked if she was in the habit of coming and going from her room at odd hours of the night. "She responded that she had developed that habit since the Revolution; that she had become a prostitute because she could no longer make a living as a seamstress."[66] A young man arrested for theft said that he "is presently a second-hand dealer, formerly a cabinet-maker, unable to find work since the Revolution."[67]

A young locksmith arrested for theft said "that since the Revolution he had had a great deal of trouble, without ever thinking of doing anything wrong." But since he had been unable to find steady work he had finally taken to stealing.[68] Domestics and unemployed provincials who had come to Paris expecting to be hired as domestics were also aware that the Revolution had caused their unemployment.

Unemployment and need had always been part of the lives of the laboring poor. Had the Revolution created any sense of class consciousness, any sense that their poverty was somehow unjust? There is little evidence of class consciousness among the men and women tried by the six provisional tribunals. One thief arrested for highway robbery was supposed to have inquired of his victim's social status before he demanded his money, asking if he were an aristocrat. The victim testified to this; the accused denied it. Pierre Aube, a twenty-six-year-old domestic, stole a fur vest and told the judges he believed he was justified because he was out of work and did not have a *sou* and the man from whom he stole the vest was wealthy. He was sentenced to one year in prison.[69]

Jean Pierre Boinet, twenty-one years old, an unemployed lawyer's aide, wrote a letter to his judges while awaiting trial for theft that spoke of poverty and social justice from the viewpoint of the poor. He had been arrested in June 1791, for stealing a sheet from the Hôpital Saint-Gervais. At the time of his arrest he had told the police commissioner that his poverty was brought on by the Revolution. When questioned about the reason for his act he responded:

> It was the most pressing need that forced him to it. Since the Revolution he had lost two positions (names his employers) and not being able to count on his family who had also been paralysed by the Revolution, he had come to Paris to seek a means of subsistence. . . . Not having succeeded in finding stable work he had lived as a vagabond, without a place to live and without work.

He had lost or sold all of his possessions and entered the Hôpital. In November 1791, he wrote to the judges saying that poverty such as he had known was such a degrading state that it was a punishment without a crime. Poverty had been his only crime; stealing the sheet was its inevitable result. The poor were degraded every day, he said, especially by charity. Every morning at the Hôpital the sheets were counted. If one was found to be missing the guard was called and everyone forced to undress. Eventually he had accepted society's opinion of him and taken the sheet. He was sentenced to one year in Bicêtre for the theft.[70]

Much more serious sentences were handed down in cases of employees trying to achieve a just wage settlement from their employers by taking the matter into their own hands. Madeleine Begasse, fifty-three years old, a hatmaker, complained that she earned only five *sous* a day and had not been paid in so long that she was owed twenty *livres*. She had told her employer that she was going to take a pile of rabbit skins and sell them if he did not pay her. When she did so, he had her arrested. She was sentenced to eight years in prison, as required by the Penal Code; the sentence confirmed on appeal.[71] Pierre Perrie, a forty-one-year-old gardener, stole two watering cans from his employer for the same reason and received the same sentence.[72]

The six provisional tribunals did not deal with political questions as often as they dealt with crimes against persons and property. A few cases of "speaking against the government in the Palais Royal" were ordered prosecuted as criminal cases, but all the accused were acquitted under the amnesty of November 1791. These cases do show a level of political consciousness but they rarely involved the poor. Antoine Chapuis, a thirty-nine-year-old lawyer, and Pierre Retir, a nineteen-year-old medical student, were rescued by the guard from an angry crowd in the Palais Royal who accused them of speaking against the Revolution. Their case was typical of those involving crimes of political opinion; the testimony of the witnesses is revealing about political consciousness in everyday life. Jean Marie Solle, a wine merchant, testified that he was there because he had heard several people say that "the aristocrats" were going in a crowd to the Palais Royal. He went there as well, stopping at home first to eat some soup and fetch his saber, and heard "infamous things being said about the National Assembly." He testified that Chapuis had said, "Your law is being made by scoundrels and brigands" and had refused to fight a duel for the honor of the nation to which Solle had challenged him on the spot. Louis Etienne Robert L'Heritier (no profession given) was in a nearby café when a guardsman came in and said that people were speaking against the Constitution in the Café du Foi. Louis said that he went there "with a group of patriots" to argue with the speakers. Pierre Crosnier, "French citizen," Marie Pierre Chesnie, musician, and Pierre Laing, a locksmith, testified to the same statements by the accused.

Antoine Chapuis defended himself by saying that he was having a scholarly discussion with his friend Pierre Retir, comparing the present Revolution with the English Revolution under Henry VIII, and had said that both revolutions were the result of faction and villainy (*sceleratesse*). At these words a group of drunken men had jumped on him and tried to slit his throat. Retir claimed that he had never met Chapuis before that day and that he hadn't even been listening to what he was saying. They were released from prison within a month of their arrest, because no crime existed of which they were accused.[73]

Political consciousness was low among the poor on the fine points of faction, ideology, and ideas. Jean Duchesne was arrested in a tavern with two other men as a gang of swindlers. He denied that he knew the two men; he had seen them reading a newspaper called the *Père Duchesne,* and since that was his name he had gone to their table to talk to them when they were all arrested.[74]

The courts were conscious of political opinions and affiliations. A man or woman awaiting trial could have a speedy trial and a good chance of being acquitted if someone in the family was a proven patriot, a citizen active in section politics. Jean Pisson, sixty-five years old, a stablehand at the École militaire, was arrested in December 1791 for using counterfeit money. His brother, "a curé who had taken the oath," wrote to the court asking that his brother be released because he could not have committed the crime knowingly. He was released, partly on the strength of his brother's letter.[75]

The Revolution produced changes in attitudes toward the Catholic church. Women insulted other women, especially nuns, trying to enter churches; church property was destroyed by crowds and the clergy subjected to public humiliation. It is not possible to say what part attitudes played in these incidents, nor what those attitudes were precisely; the persons accused in these cases denied the charges against them rather than explaining their actions.[76]

From these few cases, it seems that the poor were aware of political events insofar as they affected their everyday lives. They perceived that they were suffering from unemployment, from hunger, and from social displacement that seemed to stem from political events; but they did not seem to be aware that they now possessed the rights of man and citizen, or that anything had been done to improve their lives. In the area of crime and criminal justice their lives had been seriously disturbed by the Revolution. Larger numbers of people were being arrested and held longer in prison both before and after trial than in the Old Regime. The nature of life in prison changed from the Old Regime to the Revolution. Prisons became seriously overcrowded, creating unmanageable police problems for the municipal authorities and a threat to the internal security of the state.

Life in Prison

Antoine Chapuis, an educated young man making a career for himself as a lawyer, was shocked at what happened to him at La Force prison in three weeks he spent there between his arrest and his release:

> I have been robbed of four *ecus* of six *livres,* of most of my linens— handkerchiefs, socks, collar, even a pair of pants. I had to pay for a bed and pay to save my life from the brigands around me.[77]

He was a member of respectable society thrown into the company of the poor and the criminal. This was unusual. Prisoners and prison accommodations were clearly divided, depending on how much one was willing and able to pay for services rendered by the jailers.

Adelaide Freminot, an eighteen-year-old seamstress, was the cook and probably mistress of M. Bondy, prisoner at the Abbaye. In January 1792, she was accused of having criminal correspondence with the prisoner; he had slipped her a note in a piece of bread.[78] Her defense was that the accusation was absurd, given the free access she had to the prisoner every day. She not only cooked his meals and brought them to him, she stayed in prison the whole day visiting with him and with his friends who came by to see him. Many women were doing exactly as she was doing. M. Bondy bought her housecoats to wear in the prison and gave her a lot of paper money. The life he led in prison, as she described it, was not unpleasant.

Her own imprisonment was not so pleasant. She complained in a letter to her judges that she should not be held in prison while awaiting trial because she was a woman of good morals and she was locked up in the Conciergerie with people of bad morals, with criminals, and with people in bad health. After spending six months in prison, she was released.

The unhealthy state of the prisons was a recurring theme in letters from prisoners to the judges, humbly petitioning that their cases be speeded up so that they might leave the prison. Life in the prisons was not carefully supervised. Prisoners showed up in court too drunk to be questioned and had their trials postponed. Women became pregnant. Prisoners walked out posing as their visitors.

Some persons adjusted well to prison life. When Pierre Griffard, a shoemaker, was sentenced to one year of prison for the theft of a hand-kerchief on the place de Grève, he asked if he might remain at La Force. Having set up shop there, he made shoes for the other prisoners and was afraid that he would not be able to continue doing so if forced to move.[79]

Prisoners were supposed to do work that was useful to the state. Left unsupervised they engaged in activities harmful to the state. Counterfeiting was a flourishing business in prisons throughout Paris; counterfeit *assignats* were produced by the prisoners and distributed by their families and friends. Marie Le Saul, wife of Antoine Maitre, a clothing merchant being held in the Conciergerie prison for theft, was herself arrested for passing counterfeit money. She denied that her husband had given it to her, but her eleven-year-old son admitted to it. The money in question was declared not to be counterfeit by a panel of experts who examined it, and mother and son were both acquitted.[80] Josephine Jumont, a prostitute, was also arrested for passing counterfeit money; she admitted that she obtained it from a friend in the Conciergerie and that there was much more of it readily available from that source.[81]

The police tried to encourage prisoners to inform on the counterfeiters even if they themselves were participants, by offering them acquittal and a monetary reward if their charges led to successful prosecution. François Leonard, a prisoner at La Force, wrote a letter to the judges of the Fifth Tribunal, reminding them that this law existed, in case they had forgotten. He had already earned his release several times over, he said, by exposing a group of counterfeiters at La Force and a group that was planning to escape at the Châtelet. He had not been transferred out of La Force after his denunciation to the police. He wrote to the judges not only to demand his reward but to state that his life was in danger; the other prisoners murdered anyone they believed to be an informer.[82]

There was comradeship among the prisoners, marked by much discussion of crime and courtroom defense strategy. It is obvious from the consistency with which some stories and some excuses appeared in court records—not in the first interrogation of the accused but in the third and fourth interrogations, after they had been in prison for a while—that there was a prison grapevine which circulated information and excuses to be used in court. Nicolas Chapuzot, a twenty-nine-year-old unemployed domestic, arrested for stealing silverware from a wine merchant, showed the effects of the grapevine. At his arrest he had simply denied the theft to the police commissioner who questioned him. When questioned by the judges before final sentencing, he said that he had not been alone when the crime occurred; he had been with a man who offered to buy him something to eat, that after they had eaten he had been sent to ask the wine merchant for something and the other man had escaped and taken the silverware with him. He said that he had been told in prison that this was a very common thing to happen to newcomers to Paris and that there were perhaps fifty people in prison with the same story. He was sentenced to three months PAI, with liberty because he did not have the silverware when arrested, but had already spent six months in prison awaiting trial.[83]

One could learn from the other prisoners what reproaches to make against witnesses. Jean Baptiste DesPres, accused of stealing a gold watch, said that the testimony against him was not valid because the witnesses were men of bad character, thieves, beggars, and police spies. The judges asked how he could say such things because he did not know the men who witnessed against him. He said that he had heard that it was so in prison.[84]

Escaping from prison appears to have been relatively easy. Several dossiers note that after the final judgment was rendered in the case, the accused was sought in prison but was found to have escaped, to have been released on another order some time before, or to have been lost in being transferred from one prison to another. Leonard Bertrand, a clothing merchant imprisoned in La Force, managed to escape but was rearrested for passing counterfeit money. The judges asked how he had escaped. He said that he had found a mason's grey coat in his room, went to the secretary claiming that he could not find the person he had been looking for, gave the name of a prisoner who had been released, and thus was able to walk out of the prison. Having escaped, he returned to where he had lived before he was arrested.[85] Other escaped prisoners when rearrested told of digging their way through the prison walls, a highly improbably means of escape. The many escapes, group departures and individual evasions demonstrate that the overcrowding of the prisons could be turned to the prisoner's advantage as much as it could work against him.

Despite the constant interchange and communication between those inside the prisons and those outside, the popular belief in and fear of prison plots was ever present in the Revolution. The most extreme manifestation of this fear were the massacres of September 1792. After that time the prisons became increasingly political institutions, holding members of opposition political parties as well as petty thieves, all living in fear that another popular attack on the prisons might occur at any time.

Notes

1. Richard Cobb's *Reactions to the French Revolution,* is especially thought-provoking in suggesting how completely detached individuals could be from the political events around them, maintaining their own "private calendars" that had nothing to do with the Revolution.

2. Arlette Farge, *Le Vol d'Aliments à Paris au XVIIIe Siècle*, attributes the increase in food thefts to such a class consciousness, "a growing disposition to crime among the population of Paris," resulting in harsher punishments, which in turn hastened the transformation of crime and potential crime to social insurrection (p. 232). Michel Foucault, *Discipline and Punish*, also sees crime and punishment as a struggle between classes and the cultural values of the bourgeois mentality opposed to the poor. The rise in property crimes changed the "tolerated forms of illegalities" and led to the Revolutionary Penal Code. Jean Lecuir, "Criminalité et 'Moralité': Montyon Statisticien du Parlement de Paris," sees the increase in crime in the eighteenth century, and the Baron de Montyon's concern, as "signs of increasing social tensions." Petrovitch, "Recherches sur la Criminalité à Paris dans la Seconde Moitié du XVIIIe Siècle," notes that more priests and nobles were victims of crime in 1785 than had been in 1755, but does not attribute crime to class consciousness or class struggle to the extent that Farge or Foucault do. My own opinion is that there is surprisingly little evidence of class consciousness or conflict. I expected to find more than I did in the court records and have discussed the few indications of political awareness I did find in more detail below.

3. Jeffry Kaplow, "Sur la Population Flottante de Paris à la Fin de l'Ancien Regime," *Annales Historiques de la Révolution Française* no. 187 (Jan-March 1967), pp. 1-14.

4. Archives Nationales, Z^{3}3, 5.

5. While Baptiste may not have existed in this case, charges of crime were sometimes inspired by personal vengeance. Nicolas la Gris, twenty-two years old and unemployed, stole some clothing from a friend and

claimed that Françoise Fischaux, with whom he was living, had received the stolen goods and paid him for them. He later admitted that she had not been involved in the crime; he had stolen the clothes out of need and had tried to implicate her because she had threatened to leave him and he was angry with her. ($Z^3$60, 70).

6. The problems of housing in Paris are discussed in Cobb, *Reactions*, p. 158, although he describes the problems of the young and those newly arrived in Paris almost exclusively. He observes that women, especially young girls, were likely to be received into institutions and private homes (either by charity or as servants) more readily than men.

7. $Z^3$60, 70.

8. A few examples will show who her lodgers were:

$Z^3$3, 18. Laurent Duchanois, eighteen, unemployed carpenter, was arrested in February 1791 for stealing iron bars from a garden in Roule. Jean Leclerc, twenty-seven, also a carpenter, also unemployed, was arrested with him. Both were from Franche Comté and lived "chez la Dame Galand au Porcherons."

$Z^3$2, 10. Michel La Chaud, twenty-five, a blacksmith, was arrested in January 1791 for stealing iron bars from his employer in the place Vendôme.

$Z^3$3, 21. Antoine Delfour, thirty, errand boy, was arrested in January 1792 for stealing furniture on the Quay du Chaillot.

$Z^3$24, 28. Louis Amand, thirty-one, stone mason, was arrested for stealing money from a gardener's room in the rue des Martyrs, near the Porcherons.

9. $Z^3$60, 68.

10. $Z^3$60, 71.

11. $Z^3$43, 54. He was judged by the Third Tribunal on July 26, 1792. He had been arrested because he was walking down the street with two large loaves of bread and twenty-eight red eggs. He admitted stealing them but was acquitted of the charge because the merchants from whom he said he stole did not claim the food.

12. $Z^3$43, 54.

13. $Z^3$3, 10, 60. Louise was fortunate; the judges were often more harsh than this with persons who had been received in charity and repaid their hosts with crime.

14. $Z^3$83.

15. Cobb, *The Police and the People,* p. 223. In his *Reactions,* p. 171, Cobb lists the sections of Paris with the greatest numbers of taverns: in 1794 there were 1,685 cafés and wine shops in Paris, as compared to 724

bakers' shops. There was a heavy concentration of drinking establishments in the central sections of the right bank, particularly those bordering the river, from the Tuileries to beyond the Hôtel de Ville (especially Lombards, the Palais Royal, Tuileries, Arcis, Temple, Gravilliers, Ponceau, Halle au Bled, and Quinze Vingts.) On the left bank they were most numerous in the sections Croix Rouge, Théâtre Français, Quatre Nations and Saint Geneviève. Most of these also had high crime rates.

16. A *traiteur* was technically the keeper of an eating house, but the word implied that it was inexpensive.

17. $Z^3$3, 14. She was arrested October 31, 1791 and sentenced by the First Tribunal on January 31, 1792. The public prosecutor appealed the sentence. On June 8, 1792, the Sixth Tribunal increased her sentence to eight years in prison.

18. $Z^3$3, 15, 43. The sentence was confirmed on appeal to the Third Tribunal April 28, 1792.

19. $Z^3$3, 18.

20. $Z^3$24, 36. Geoffroy described their condition as "mort yvres."

21. $Z^3$43, 49.

22. $Z^3$3, 100, 105.

23. $Z^3$72, 85.

24. Cobb, *The Police and the People,* pp. 26-37. The men the police looked for when dispelling seditious assemblies, quelling riots, and in cases of violence resembled those they looked for as thieves.

25. $Z^3$25, 35. Only two of these persons figured in the statistical tables of chapter 4 because only two, Marie Briola and Jacques Clabaud, were formally charged.

26. $Z^3$25, 35.

27. Crime was at least in part a moral offense. Those who were immoral enough to commit crimes were believed to disregard rules of accepted sexual morality.

28. $Z^3$3, 18.

29. $Z^3$24, 31.

30. $Z^3$25. No final judgment was rendered in this case.

31. The police had a list of "gens suspects." The law of Municipal Police of July 21-22, 1791, for example, ordered that anyone who refused to co-operate with the police census was to be listed as suspect.

32. Cobb, *The Police and the People,* pp. 5-13, discusses the problem of informers and shows clearly the dilemmas faced by the police in trying to use their information, and the questionable benefits derived from supporting such persons.

33. $Z^3$3, 16.

34. $Z^3$43, 56.

35. $Z^3$72, 77.

36. $Z^3$25, 41. The three women referred to the suspect by his first name; his full name was Girard Tournier; he claimed to be a secondhand dealer. His marriage to the young woman would be delayed by a six-year prison term ordered June 22, 1792, by the Second Tribunal.

37. $Z^3$25, 36; $Z^3$43, 49. I have translated the French *commissionaire* as errand boy. The work was taken up by men as well as boys for lack of other employment. The "errands" could be substantial, as the moving of furniture in this case. "Porter" or "messenger" could also be used to describe this occupation but "errand boy" has wider implications; the term should be understood broadly.

38. There were only two cases of kidnapping in the records of the six provisional tribunals. In one a young wife ran away from her old husband, taking most of the household linens. The young men who aided her escape were charged with kidnapping but were acquitted. In the other, a teenaged daughter ran away from home with the aid of the servants. The servants were acquitted. Procuresses were not charged with kidnapping but with "debauch," a morals offense.

39. $Z^3$43, 55.

40. $Z^3$60, 66.

41. $Z^3$100, 112.

42. $Z^3$25, 37.

43. $Z^3$72, 82. Perhaps the greater vulnerability of the innkeeper and the wine merchant to crime explains their lack of sympathy with the accused.

44. $Z^3$72, 80. Sentenced by the Fifth Tribunal, March 3, 1792. The court does not appear to have considered the police commissioner's request. Since Langlet was of sufficient age to be responsible for his actions there was no way the court could have done so.

45. $Z^3$3, 17.

46. $Z^3$43, 72, 83.

47. A few examples will illustrate this pattern of sentences:

$Z^3$2, 10. Pierre Rene Rayel, twenty-four, a roofer, accused of beating a gardener in Saint-Germain-en-Laye. Acquitted.

$Z^3$60, 69. Charles Choiselat *dit* La Roche, seventeen, domestic and soldier. Wounded a gardener who had killed some of his pet rabbits, almost killing him. He was ordered to pay the victim 200 *livres*.

$Z^3$43, 54, 100. Jean Nicolas Paniel, nineteen, and Louis Pierrot, twenty-two, hairdresser and shop assistant respectively, arrested for duelling. Acquitted on the grounds that this was a *rixe*.

$Z^3$43, 47. François Baille, eighteen, soldier. Killed a man in a quarrel in a tavern. Acquitted.

$Z^3$43, 46. Honoré Marie Mariage, twenty, soldier, and Pierre Fruck, forty, soldier. Arrested for fighting with sabers over a bet on a billiard game. Sentenced to *blâme*.

$Z^3$60, 66, 43. Paul Charroy, twenty-eight, coachman, ran down a man in the rue du Monceau. Restif spoke at length of the violence and recklessness of such coachmen. Charroy was sentenced to one year in Bicêtre by the Fourth Tribunal, reduced on appeal to six months of *police correctionnelle* by the Third.

48. $Z^3$19.

49. $Z^3$43, 55.

50. $Z^3$24, 39.

51. There was one such suit in the records of the six provisional tribunals, the case of Marie Philippine Minique against Pierre Loiseau (*see* below). There may have been others pursued in the departmental tribunal.

52. The number of prostitutes involved in crime was undoubtedly higher than this. The connections between prostitution and crime are noted by Jeffry Kaplow, *The Names of Kings,* p. 149; Cobb, *The Police and the People,* pp. 234-40; Cobb, *Reactions,* pp. 140-48 and *passim;* and Olwen Hufton, *The Poor of Eighteenth Century France.* Prostitution is a product of many of the same social and environmental conditions as crime; *see* Louis Chevalier, *Classes Laborieuses et Classes Dangereuses,* p. 333, and *passim.*

53. $Z^3$43, 53.

54. $Z^3$24, 31.

55. $Z^3$2, 12. A similar case involved Pierre Renaud, a mason, who came to Paris looking for work in September 1791 and was enticed into a prostitute's room on the rue de la Mortellerie. He bought wine for three women and a man who was with them, whom he had met at the Port aux Bleds. They had even taken the money out of his pockets to pay for the drinks, saying that he did not know how to count it. The women offered to sleep with him, "in gratitude" for the wine, a prospect which pleased him greatly, although he was disconcerted by the fact that the man accompanied them back to their room. Once there, they all had some more wine. Pierre was very drunk. The women tore his clothes off and searched for more money, the man stabbed him with a knife when he tried to fight back.

This may not have been typical of a young provincial's first day in Paris but it fits the popular stereotype of the evils of the city. The case of Pierre Renaud's attackers, Jean Antoine Oudard, Claudine Marchand, Elisabeth Martin, and Rosalie Tardeux, is in $Z^3$60, 69. The accused denied that they were prostitutes but the neighbors testified that they were. They were convicted of the theft.

56. $Z^3$24, 30.

57. $Z^3$43, 54.

58. Cobb, *Police and the People,* pp. 234-40. *See also* Antoinette Wills, "Prostitution in Old Regime France."

59. $Z^3$2, 10.

60. Thefts on a large scale sometimes occurred in brothels. For example, a young man on his way to Saint-Germain-en-Laye on business stopped by a brothel in the rue de la Bucherie in October 1790. While he was "amusing himself" with one of the girls, two others stole 6,900 *livres* in *assignats.* They were arrested in a café on the rue de l'Oursine, counting out the money and dividing it between them. It is difficult to say if their action was spontaneous or if this was a house policy; the madame of the house was charged and convicted as an accomplice.($Z^3$72, 76).

61. $Z^3$3, 16. The case was judged by the First Tribunal; sentence was passed April 17, 1792. The public prosecutor had also recommended that Loiseau be sent to prison for three months but the court allowed him to go free. This was a very unusual case. Loiseau's actions were declared not to have constituted a crime because they were not premeditated. He testified that he had only meant to threaten her, not to kill her. The fact that the court upheld her suit for damages showed that the court recognized the legality of her profession. While this seems an important legal precedent, few women appear to have followed her example in suing their more brutal clients for damages.

Forty *sous* was not a fair price for an act of prostitution. The price generally stated, by clients and by prostitutes, was three *livres.* This included staying the night in the woman's room or having her stay in the man's room; in addition, he was expected to buy her drinks in the evening and breakfast in the morning, and all her meals if she stayed several days.

62. This was not a prostitute/pimp relationship since the men did not seek out clients for the woman. It was a monogamous "love" relationship within the context of the woman's profession. Men who ceased to be the chosen "friend" reacted as strongly as any jealous husband.

63. The letter of remission should not have been valid since it was issued January 16, 1792. The Penal Code had formally gone into effect January 1, 1792, and specifically outlawed such letters. The two could have been acquitted on grounds of self-defense but it is not clear that the Penal Code allowed for their situation. The fact that they bought pistols in anticipation of Desmoulin's visit showed that the violence was clearly premeditated.

The case gives much incidental information about the lives of prostitutes. The relationship between St. Villiers and Cabot was not a normal "friend" relationship; he gave her money to sleep with him and did not abuse her physically. This led her to prefer him to Desmoulins. Her landlord was ordered to keep her things while she was in prison awaiting trial. This seems to have been standard procedure. He demanded to know who was going to pay her rent: ninety-six *livres* a month, payable bi-weekly. Many of the witnesses she requested be called in her defense were other prostitutes; they were unfortunately not called; they would have provided an interesting sample of the women who lived in the Palais Royal. If they were like Rosalie Cabot, they evidently made a good income.

64. $Z^3$100, 109. It is obvious that Mlle. Duquet was in no condition to have physically thrown her ex-lover from the window. Rigolet was never charged with the murder, although he would have been physically capable of committing it. He had a friend with him on his visit to Mlle. Duquet who could have helped him.

65. $Z^3$43, 48. Children sometimes did make up stories about being kidnapped when they had in fact run away from home. Marie Marguerite Theodore Poiret, a fifteen-year-old spinner, claimed to have been debauched by a woman running a dry goods store as a front for prostitution. In her case it was determined that she was an habitual runaway and had only made up the story to escape punishment by her parents. She was brought to admit in court that she had lied, hoping to turn the popular belief in procuresses who stole young girls to her own advantage. ($Z^3$100, 108).

66. $Z^3$3, 100, 108.

67. $Z^3$43, 48.

68. $Z^3$72, 81. Not all former employment had been honest. Jerome Balleux and Alexis Pasquier were arrested October 1, 1791, for stealing a silver plate used to produce thirty *sou* pieces from the royal mint in Paris. Balleux had carried out the theft but said that it was Pasquier's idea. Balleux had been Pasquier's servant for some years; before the Revolution he had smuggled contraband liquor across the customs barriers into Paris and made a living that way for both of them. Since the barriers were gone, he had to find other work. He said that it was Pasquier's idea that he should work at the mint. ($Z^3$100, 110).

69. $Z^3$24, 32.

70. $Z^3$60, 68.

71. $Z^3$43, 72, 89.

72. $Z^3$3, 100, 107.

73. $Z^3$3, 16.

74. $Z^3$60, 69.

75. $Z^3$100, 103.

76. The longest such case was tried in the Sixth Tribunal, ($Z^3$100, 103).

It involved sixteen people from the town of Issy, outside of Paris, local people who had attacked the local monastery on December 29-30, 1791. They forced the nuns to ride through the town seated backwards on a mule, threatened the servants with violence, and drank wine from the cellar. It is difficult to tell from the records of the case what happened, what was said, and whether this was an anticlerical demonstration or simply drunken mischief, since everyone denied what he was alleged to have done. There is no record of the case being judged, although the accused were held in prison.

Other cases involved women insulting other women outside of churches around Paris. For example, Jeanne Paret, widow of Quentin Jany, a forty-nine-year-old textile worker, tried to stop a nun going into church with a little girl. She called the nun a procuress and allegedly beat her. She claimed to be part of a crowd all saying similar things, but was sentenced to three months in prison in October 1791, reduced to *blâme* on appeal in December. ($Z^3$24, 72, 81).

Marie Anne Catherine Daudet, wife of Pierre Jerome, thirty-three, (no profession stated), tried to stop persons entering a church by saying "Voilà des Bigottes, il faut fouetter ca." ($Z^3$72, 84). Neither of these women claimed to be drunk at the time, both denied the charges against them.

77. $Z^3$16.

78. $Z^3$100, 110.

79. $Z^3$60, 67.

80. $Z^3$3, 16.

81. $Z^3$67. She died before her trial was completed; the case never came to judgment.

82. $Z^3$115. This carton contains a great many miscellaneous documents, pieces of other dossiers which the archivist was unable to find. Leonard's crime is unknown; his case was evidently not processed by the six provisional tribunals. His situation, it appears, was not uncommon.

Richard Cobb states that prison informers were generally more trustworthy than their counterparts outside of prison. A prison informer was closer to his source of information and had a greater interest in providing accurate information. If the information was good, he would be kept on the treadmill of informing as long as possible. (*The Police and the People*, pp. 8-13.)

83. $Z^3$25, 37.

84. $Z^3$2, 9, 43.

85. $Z^3$72, 86.

CONCLUSION

The reform of the criminal justice system in France achieved its fullest realization in April 1792, when the jury system of criminal trials began to operate. Courtrooms in Paris were packed, although the cases on trial were nothing out of the ordinary: thieves and counterfeiters for the most part, with a few murderers.[1] The blade of the guillotine fell for the first time in that month. In its first descent, the symbol of later Revolutionary Terror severed the head of a convicted thief. But the most important event of the month, the one that would determine the fate of the new system of justice—although no one appreciated it at the time—was the declaration of war against Austria. By September 1792, the advance of the Austrian army on Paris triggered the prison massacres in Paris. While the crowds sought to destroy nobles and priests believed conspiring with the Austrians, they killed more ordinary criminals than they did nobles, and with them went the semblance of an orderly system of justice. The pressures of war would negate "normal" political life for years. The expenses of war would drain away funding for social programs such as new prisons.[2]

Before it had an opportunity to become properly established, then, the experiment in the reform of criminal justice was doomed to failure by forces outside the control of judges or legislators. Some elements of the reform survived. Even during the Terror, Revolutionary tribunals were often meticulous about following proper procedure, although the verdict might have been reached before the trial began.[3] But as time passed, even those who had supported the reform before the Revolution began to see it as a failure, even a disaster. The incidence of crime continued to rise,[4] and the new system of criminal justice was held partly to blame, as in these observations from Mercier in his *Nouveau Paris,* written in 1798:

At the moment when all human passions are overflowing, and at a time when we have been so excited and have fought off our foreign enemies, it is not possible that the mud should not rise to the surface and trouble the pure waters.

Today there are thieves and bands of thieves whose numbers and whose audacity is increasing daily. Huge thefts are carried out, conspiracies form daily; the police look on . . . .

Do you doubt the existence of thieves and scoundrels? Go to the public audiences of our criminal tribunals; there you will see them, sitting still, silent, watching the prosecution and the defense, moving their lips to suggest answers to the accused. It is there that they study our criminal code, turning to their own profit all that perverse naiveté suggested to our too philosophical legislators.

Having been on the criminal jury three times, I have always come away filled with sadness at how the moral instinct has been so completely lost in so many criminals. At that, they are not hypocrites! Vice and crime have their apologists. Their officious defenders by their lack of thought, by their profession, or by the desire to hear themselves speak prettily, have perverted the words which used to express morality. How can they, for a mere monetary reward, whet the knife which can turn against society and against themselves?[5]

Mercier's disillusionment was not universal. During the Directory, the judicial structure of 1791 was restored with departmental tribunals, elected judges, and jury trials. Not until Napoleon were many of the Revolutionary reforms abandoned. The Criminal Code of 1808 reestablished secret procedure (almost identical to the Great Ordinance of 1670); the Penal Code reinstituted the practice of branding convicted criminals with the mark of the thief.[6]

But the clock could not be turned back completely; crime and punishment would never be seen in the same light after the French Revolution as they had been before. The failure of the judicial experiment under extraordinary circumstances did not diminish the influence of the ideas behind it on later generations of Frenchmen.

The eighteenth century was a transitional period in the history of crime and punishment. Patterns of crime were becoming recognizably "modern," especially in urban centers like Paris.[7] The distinction between the "laboring classes" and the "dangerous classes" was disappearing, a process probably accelerated by the Revolution.[8] The nature of punishment changed, both in form and in purpose. Prison became the basic form of punishment, continually refined as a tool for socialization in the nineteenth century, a function it did not begin to serve in the eighteenth. With the birth of the prison and the debate over the first Penal Code came the beginnings of penology, the search for a scientific theory of individual rehabilitation. And with the appreciation of forces beyond the individual that might be factors in leading men to crime, came the beginnings of criminology.

Whether the reform of the criminal justice system in the Revolution ever came close to achieving its goals is not important. The time for trial was too short. The lasting influence of the vision behind the attempt to change both law and society is important, and is the continuing heritage the eighteenth century has left for the present.

Notes

1. Edmond Seligman, *La Justice en France Pendant la Révolution 1789-1792,* pp. 459-65.

2. Funding for a new prison system to implement the mandates of a Penal Code would not be approved until the Napoleonic era. In September 1810, an imperial decree allocated 11 million francs to construct prisons for a new prison system to serve the needs of the Penal Code of 1810. The funds were again diverted to the needs of the army in Napoleon's wars. *See* Patricia O'Brien, "The Promise of Punishment: Prisons in Nineteenth-Century France," unpublished manuscript (University of California, Irvine).

3. Joanne Kaufmann, "The Critique of Criminal Justice in Eighteenth-Century France: A Study of the Changing Social Ethics of Crime and Punishment," p. 194.

4. There are no studies of crime in the Revolution based on the records of criminal courts. Richard Cobb, *Reactions to the French Revolution,* asserts that theft reached its highest point in Paris in 1797 (p. 156). While his proof is impressionistic, it would probably be supported by examination of police and court records.

5. Louis Sebastien Mercier, *Le Nouveau Paris* (Paris, 1798), pp. 200-3.

6. Jacques Godechot, *Les Institutions de la France sous la Révolution et l'Empire,* pp. 414-18, 534.

7. For the resemblance of patterns of crime described in this study with later periods, see Howard Zehr, *Crime and the Development of*

Modern Society: Patterns of Criminality in Nineteenth Century Germany and France (London: Croom Helm Ltd., 1976).

8. While I have not done enough research in the court records and in social literature of the later Revolution to trace this in detail, it seems that the pattern I observed in the early Revolution—of crime becoming a more common part of the lives of the laboring poor—would be even more distinct in the later years of Revolution. The social distinction between the honest working man and the thief would be blurred not only by the increasing numbers of workers involved in crime, but also by the change in social perception of the working classes after their political activity in the Revolution. They would be deemed "dangerous" not only as thieves of property, but also as men who stole power from its rightful holders.

APPENDIX I

A comparison between procedure to be followed in criminal trials as established by the Ordinance of 1670 and that established by the laws of the early Revolution before the establishment of criminal trial by jury

Eighteenth Century	*Revolution*
Competence	**Competence**
Jurisdiction:	*Jurisdiction:*
The tribunal nearest the scene of the crime was paramount. By this means, royal courts could assert their competence over others, especially ecclesiastical courts.	All justice was to be exercised in the name of the king. It was to be local with cantonal, municipal, district and departmental courts sufficiently numerous to be near the scene of any crime.
Appeals:	*Appeals:*
All appeals were to royal courts, especially the regional *Parlement*. By royal order, an appeal decided in one *Parlement* could be heard again in another.	Appeals from lower courts were heard by the nearest court of superior jurisdiction (e.g., cantonal courts appealed to district courts). Appeals from superior courts were heard by the Tribunal de Cassation, which determined whether proper procedure had been observed. In case of procedural error, the case was retried in the original jurisdiction.

Eighteenth Century	*Revolution*
Royal Prerogative:	*Royal Prerogative:*
The king had power to intervene in, or act outside of, the regular judicial process. He could stop judicial proceedings by a letter of grace or remission. He could pardon a convicted person. By *lettre de cachet* he could order a person imprisoned without cause.	Letters of grace, letters of remission, and all other royal powers of pardon and intervention were abolished. *Lettres de cachet* were also abolished; there was to be no imprisonment without due cause and due process of law.
Court Procedure: Arrest to Judgment	**Court Procedure: Arrest to Judgment**
Arrest:	*Arrest:*
Complaints were brought to the *commissaire* of police or to a *commissaire* of the Châtelet who made a report of the event, taking statements from witnesses and the accused. All pieces of evidence were registered with the court and retained by the secretary. The *commissaire* might be called to the scene of the crime to make the report. If there were injured parties involved, a surgeon's report had to be drawn up and signed by the attending surgeon.	The *commissaire* of the Châtelet was relieved of his functions. Police became a municipal, rather than a royal function. District committees carried out police functions until June 1790, when sections began to elect their own *commissaire* of police. In July 1791 justices of the peace were empowered equally with section *commissaires* to receive and investigate criminal complaints. Both *commissaires* and justices were to hear the complaint in the presence of *notables* or other reliable citizens.
Civil and Criminal Complaints:	*Civil and Criminal Complaints:*
Complaints could be of several types. If a private individual charged another individual with crime or injury, the case could be criminal but "with civil parties." The expenses of justice were paid by the civil parties.	Revolutionary law did not allow for civil parties in criminal cases. All expenses of justice were borne by the king. Civil actions were to be pursued in separate courts from criminal actions. The *procureur du roi* was replaced by a public

Eighteenth Century

Otherwise, the *procureur du roi* pursued the complaint and costs were borne by the king.

Denunciation and Witnesses:

If the accused was arrested because of denunciation, rather than popular clamor, the denouncer could be charged court costs if the accused were found innocent. Denunciations were made by the victim, by witnesses to the crime, and by paid police informers. The person making the denunciation did not have to participate in the trial as a witness, and his/her identity was not revealed to the accused. The *procureur du roi* issued a formal *plainte* against the accused based on testimony by witnesses and other evidence.

Investigation by the Court:

The *Information*—formal testimony of the witnesses—was drawn up in secret after the formal *plainte* was filed. One judge acted as the *juge d'instruction*, questioning the witnesses and the accused. When all evidence was assembled, it was presented in written form to the other judges who would determine the facts of the case and assign a penalty. The Ordinance of 1670 required that the *Information* be made by police or court officers other than the final judges. Witnesses were paid a *taxe*, to be determined by the

Revolution

prosecutor who decided if there were grounds for a *plainte* and by a *commissaire du roi* who served basically as an observer.

Denunciation and Witnesses:

If a complaint were based on denunciation, the identity of the denouncer was to be made known to the accused. There was no penalty for false witness. Complaints normally arose from popular clamor, not denunciation. Paid police informers disappeared. Based on statements of witnesses and other evidence, the section *commissaire* of police or justice of the peace decided if the case was to be tried as a misdemeanor by the Police Tribunal or as a crime by the regular criminal courts.

Investigation by the Court:

Revolutionary legislation required the presence of two *notables* at this stage of the trial, which was held in private—not in the public courtroom and not in the presence of the accused—and required that the *notables* sign each page of the *Information*. They were allowed to make observations at the end of the testimony, but not to interrupt the *juge d'instruction*. The presiding judge was also required to sign each page of the *Information*, on penalty of nullification of the proceedings. The *taxe* to be paid to the witnesses was set

Eighteenth Century	Revolution
juge d'instruction.	at one day's wages, to be defined by law.

Surgeon's Examination:

Either before or after the *Information* the accused was to be examined by a court-appointed surgeon to see if there were any sign of branding, either *V, GAL,* or the fleur de lys.

Surgeon's Examination:

Either before or after the *Information* the accused was to be examined by a court-appointed surgeon to see if there were any sign of branding, either *V, GAL,* or the fleur de lys.

Detention of the Accused:

If the *Information* warranted, the accused was ordered *prise de corps* or *en état d'ajournement personnel,* or *assigné pour etre ouï.* The first required arrest and imprisonment of the accused, who might already be in prison. The other two ordered the accused to be available on order of the court but did not require confinement. In most cases in which the offense merited criminal trial, the accused was arrested and held in prison.

Detention of the Accused:

At least three judges were required to sign an order of *prise de corps,* and citizens with fixed residence and stable employment were not to be ordered arrested or imprisoned without good cause. All persons arrested were to be questioned about their offense within twenty-four hours of their arrest.

Interrogation of the Accused:

The Ordinance of 1670 required the accused to swear an oath to tell the truth before being questioned about his offense. The *Interrogatoire* was conducted by the *juge d'instruction.* The accused was denied the services of a lawyer at this point or at any time during the trial.

Interrogation of the Accused:

After the decree of *prise de corps* was issued, the accused had the right to have a lawyer, appointed by the court if necessary. He was also to be given a copy of all the documents in the case by the court secretary, free of charge.

Examination of Witnesses:

After the interrogation of the accused, the case could be *reglé à l'extraordinaire.* Witnesses were recalled to verify

Examination of Witnesses:

The only change made in procedure at this point was that the identity of the witnesses was made known to the accused as soon as he

Eighteenth Century

their original testimony and to
confront the accused. If the case
was not *reglé* it was dismissed:
the accused could be declared
acquitted or simply released without acquittal. Before the confrontation, the accused was not
allowed to know the witnesses
against him.

Prosecution, Proof, Torture:

With the testimony in the case
completed, the documents were
given to the *procureur du roi*
for his recommendations, which
could include a penalty, torture,
or investigation of evidence introduced by the accused as *faits
justificatifs.* The prosecutor's
report went to the *juge rapporteur*
who reported the evidence compiled and the conclusions of the
procureur to the full court. The
accused was not present when the
evidence was reviewed. Torture
could be ordered only in cases
involving capital penalties if it
was needed to complete a proof.
The accused was interrogated
once more in court before final
sentence was passed. This could
be an interrogation under torture,
or on the *sellette* (the kneeling
stool) for serious crimes only.

Judgment:

Judgment was rendered in first
instance by a minimum of three
judges and on appeal by a minimum
of seven. If the judges disagreed on
the penalty, the most severe could

Revolution

was ordered arrested. The recall of
witnesses and their confrontation
with the accused remained the same
as it had been in the Old Regime.

Prosecution, Proof, Torture:

The assembled evidence went to the
public prosecutor and the *commissaire
du roi* for their recommendations,
submitted in writing to the judges
but not binding. The accused was
interrogated in court on the day of
the judgment, in the presence of his
lawyer, who then spoke in his defense
before judgment was passed. The use
of torture and the *sellette* were
forbidden.

Judgment:

Judgment was rendered in first
instance by a minimum of three
judges, but by ten on appeal. A
majority of three was needed to
impose the death penalty. Penalties

Eighteenth Century	*Revolution*
not be applied except with a majority of two. Penalties were to be carried out the same day they were ordered, except in the case of pregnant women, whose punishment was delayed until after the birth.	were not executed immediately. The accused was given three days to appeal. Death sentences were not carried out until a month after they were decreed, except in cases of rebellion or sedition.

Rights of Appeal

Appeals could be initiated by the accused or by the *procureur du roi.* The accused was allowed the services of a lawyer on appeal. The grounds for appeal had to be stated: the *procureur* appealed *a minima*, the legal formula designating that the penalty assigned by the court was considered insufficient. Appeals were judged by royal courts, usually the *Parlement*.

Rights of Appeal:

Appeals were initiated by the accused, within three days of the first judgment, or by the public prosecutor. The appeal was judged by one of the other departmental tribunals, or by courts designated by law for the appeal. Courts were to be at the same level of jurisdiction as the court in first instance. The choice of tribunal was left to the accused. The accused had the right to a lawyer on appeal.

Judgment Postponed:

Certain judgments were not the final resolution of the case, but were procedural extensions. The accused could be ordered *mis hors de cour*, i.e., released without being acquitted of the charges. The trial could begin over, but this was unlikely. A sentence of *plus ample information* could set the prisoner at liberty or order him detained while the court sought further proof in the case. A time limit was normally set for the investigation, but this was not required.

Judgment Postponed:

Revolutionary legislation did not specifically outlaw the procedural postponements of the Old Regime. Judges retained them at their own discretion.

Sources: Adhemar Esmein, *Histoire de la Procédure Criminelle en France* (Paris, 1882).

Collection Général des Lois 1788-An II, 23 vols. (Paris: De l'Imprimerie Royal, 1792).

APPENDIX II_____

Comparison between penalties ordered by the Châtelet in the eighteenth century with those established by the Penal Code of September 1791

Châtelet	*Penal Code*
Capital Punishment:	**Capital Punishment:**
Death by fire, by breaking on the wheel (for men only), by hanging, or by decapitation (for the nobility only)	Death by decapitation
Civil Death:	**Civil Degradation:**
Perpetual banishment	Public humiliation (men only) in a public ceremony in which the declaration of the crime was fol- lowed by the pronouncement "Your country has found you guilty of an infamous action: the law and the tribunal strips you of the quality of French citizen."
The galleys (for men)	
Prison (for women) in perpetuity	
Corporal Punishments:	**Corporal Punishments:**
Whipping	No corporal punishments
Branding *V, GAL,* or with a fleur de lys	Public exposure in the vicinity of the crime accompanied a prison term, but there were no public whip- pings or brandings
Public exposure in stocks or pillory (usually accompanied by whipping)	

Châtelet	*Penal Code*

Any or all of these, or some form of public torture, could accompany another punishment, either prison, the galleys, or banishment

Privation of Liberty:

Internment in the Salpêtrière, (a hospital/prison) for women and young offenders.

Galleys for a set term (men only)

Prison for a set term (primarily for women)

Detention in a convent (for an adulterous wife)

Banishment for a set time

Privation of Liberty:

Solitary confinement for a set time

Forced labor: in a prison, on the roads, in the ports, (as the state dictated)

Forced labor in body chains

Prison at hard labor

Detention: in prison, but not in solitary confinement and with work to do but not hard labor

Deportation

Correctional confinement for two years, minimum security, no hard labor

(All sentences involving privation of liberty to be limited, none perpetual.)

Infamous Penalties:

Amende honorable simple: ritual public apology and shame

Amende honorable "in figuris": ritual public apology while wearing a designated costume

Blâme, admonition, warning not to repeat the offense

Suspension of functions (for public officials)

Infamous Penalties:

By definition, crimes could not be punished with public infamy or shame, an act qualified as a "crime" commanded a more serious penalty

Châtelet   *Penal Code*

Libels or seditious writings burned,
publicly destroyed

Fine

Sources: Gerard Aubry, *La Jurisprudence Criminelle du Châtelet de Paris
sous le Règne de Louis XVI* (Paris: Librairie Général de Droit
et de Jurisprudence, 1971).

Collection Général des Lois 1788-An II, 23 vols. (Paris: De
l'Imprimerie Royal, 1792).

Comparison between crimes prosecuted by the Châtelet in the eighteenth century and those defined by the Penal Code of September 1791

Châtelet	*Penal Code*
Crimes Against Society:	**Crimes Against Society:**
Arson	Treason: aiding an external enemy to attack France, or revealing state secrets to an enemy
Poisoning	
Magic	Internal rebellion: mutiny by members of the armed forces
Crimes arising in prisons (riots, escapes, rebellions, etc.)	
Mendicity	Obstructing the government, interfering with a citizen's right to participate
	Falsifying government decrees
	Resisting the public authority
	Malfeasance in public office
Crimes Against Persons and Morals Offenses:	**Crimes Against Persons and Morals Offenses:**
Parricide (including murder of a parent, a spouse, or other relative)	Homicide (premeditated, accidental, and unpremeditated)
Infanticide	Assassination (attempted homicide)
Homicide (premeditated or not, or suicide)	Poisoning
	Violence

Châtelet	*Penal Code*
Violence (i.e. physical injury to another)	Causing a woman to miscarry or abort by violence
Rape and seduction (of a minor child or of a woman)	Castration
Adultery	Rape
Bigamy	Debauch
Outrage to the public morals	Bigamy

Crimes Against Property:

Larceny (simple theft)

Thefts with aggravating circumstances:
    theft with *effraction* (damage to property, breaking and entering)
    theft with violence against persons
    theft with false keys
    theft at night
    highway robbery
    theft in a church
    theft in a market or fair
    theft from an innkeeper
    theft in quantity
    theft from areas of the public faith (linens from the drying lines of a laundress, from gardens, etc.)

Swindling

Abuse of confidence by someone exercising a profession

Bankruptcy

Usury

Crimes Against Property:

Simple theft not a crime but a misdemeanor, a matter for police court

Thefts with aggravating circumstances:
    theft with violence against persons, especially on the public highway or in a house
    theft with false keys
    theft at night
    highway robbery
    theft with *effraction*
    theft with accomplices
    armed robbery
    theft from an inhabited house, an inn, boarding house, tavern, cafe, or public bath
    theft by an employee or person habitually received in a house
    theft from areas of the public faith
    theft by coachmen or messengers

Arson

Blackmail

Bombing

Destruction of dams or water vessels

Poisoning another's animals

Destroying another's legal documents

Châtelet	*Penal Code*
Crimes of Falsification:	**Crimes of Falsification:**
Forgery of written documents	Forgery of written documents
False witness	False witness
Counterfeit money	Counterfeit money
	False weights and measures

Sources: Gerard Aubry, *La Jurisprudence Criminelle du Châtelet de Paris sous le Règne de Louis XVI* (Paris: Librairie Général de Droit et de Jurisprudence, 1971).

Collection Général des Lois 1788-An II 23 vols. (Paris: De l'Imprimerie Royal, 1792.)

BIBLIOGRAPHY_____

Archival Sources

Archives Nationales, Paris
| | |
Series BB: | Minister of Justice
BB^3 | 366 Correspondence with the six provisional tribunals.
BB^5 | 356 Correspondence with the six provisional tribunals.
Series Z: | Ordinary and Special Courts, Intermediate Tribunals.
Z^3 | 2-116, Provisional Criminal Tribunals (1791-1792)
$Z^3$2-3. | Judgments: First Provisional Tribunal.
$Z^3$8-21. | Dossiers of cases judged by the First Provisional Tribunal.
$Z^3$5(17). | Laws applying to the operation of the six provisional tribunals. (The contents of these two cartons are reversed. The laws are supposed to be in carton 5, according to the Campardon index; they are actually in carton 17. Carton 5 presently contains the dossiers listed for carton 17.)
$Z^3$24-25. | Judgments: Second Provisional Tribunal.
$Z^3$28-41. | Dossiers of cases judged by the Second Provisional Tribunal.
$Z^3$42-43. | Judgments: Third Provisional Tribunal
$Z^3$46-59. | Dossiers of cases judged by the Third Provisional Tribunal.
$Z^3$60. | Judgments: Third Provisional Tribunal.
$Z^3$63-71. | Dossiers of cases judged by the Fourth Provisional Tribunal.
$Z^3$72. | Judgments: Fifth Provisional Tribunal.
$Z^3$63-71. | Dossiers of cases judged by the Fifth Provisional Tribunal.

$Z^3$100.   Judgments: Sixth Provisional Tribunal.
$Z^3$103-112. Dossiers of cases judged by the Sixth
                Provisional Tribunal.
$Z^3$115.   Miscellaneous: Pieces of judgments,
                appeals, dossiers and correspondence
                between accused persons, witnesses,
                and court personnel for which full
                dossiers could not be found.
$Z^3$116.   Inventories of cases sent to the six pro-
                visional tribunals.

Printed Sources

Douarche, Aristide. *Les Tribunaux Civils de Paris pendant la Révolution.*
2 vols. Collection de Documents Relatifs à l'Histoire de Paris pendant
la Révolution Francaise. Paris: Cerf, 1905-1907.

France. *Collection Général des Lois 1788-An II.* 23 vols. Paris: De l'Imprimerie Royal, 1792.

France. *Archives Parlementaires de 1787 à 1860.* J. Mavidal and E. Laurent
eds. (First Series: 1787-1799) 90 vols. Paris, 1867-1914.

Lacroix, Sigmond, ed. *Actes de la Commune de Paris pendant la Révolution.*
(Second Series, October 9, 1790-August 10, 1792) 8 vols. Collection de
Documents Relatifs à l'Histoire de Paris pendant la Révolution Francaise.
Paris: Cerf, 1900.

Eighteenth-Century Sources

Beccaria, Cesare Bonesana, Marquis of. *An Essay on Crimes and Punishments.*
n.t. London: Hodson, 1801.

Brissot de Warville, J.P. *Théorie des Loix Criminelles,* 2 vols. Paris: J. P.
Ailland, 1836. Republication of the original 1781 essay, with notes
and texts.

Freminville, Edme de. *Dictionnaire ou Traité de la Police.* Paris, 1775.

Gazette des Nouveau Tribunaux. 16 vols. Paris, 1791-1795. Title varies.

Gouges, Olympe de. *Projet sur la formation d'un tribunal populaire et
suprême en matière criminelle présenté le 26 Mai 1790 à l'Assemblée
Nationale.* Paris, 1790.

Jaucourt, M le Chevalier de. "Crime," *Encyclopédie ou Dictionnaire
Raisonné des Sciences, des Arts et des Métiers.* Denis Diderot, ed.
vol. 4 (1751-1765), pp. 466-467.

Manuel, Pierre. *La Police de Paris Dévoilé*. Paris, 1791.
Marat, Jean Paul. *Plan de Legislation Criminelle*. Paris: Rochette, 1790. (Originally published 1780).
Mercier, Louis Sebastien. *Tableau de Paris*. 12 vols. Amsterdam, 1783-1789.
——. *Tableau de Paris*. Amsterdam, 1782-1783.
——. *Le Nouveau Paris*. 6 vols. in 3. Paris: Fuchs. 1798.
——. *Le Nouveau Paris*. Paris, 1798.
Montesquieu, Charles Louis de Secondat, Baron de la Brede et de. *De l'Esprit des Lois*. 2 vols. Paris: Editions Garnier Frères, 1973. (Originally published 1748).
Restif de la Bretonne, Nicolas Edme. *Monsieur Nicolas*. Isidore Liseux, ed. 14 vols. Paris, 1883.
——. *Monsieur Nicolas*. Havelock Ellis, ed. R. Crowdy Mathers, trans. 6 vols. London, 1930.
——. *Les Nuits de Paris. Ou le Spectateur Nocturne*. 7 vols. London, 1788.
——. *Le Pornographe*. B. Villeneuve, ed. Paris: Bibliothèque des Curieux, 1911.
——. *La Semaine Nocturne: Sept Nuits de Paris*. Paris, 1790.
Rousseau, Jean Jacques. *Contrat Social ou Principes du Droit Politique* in *Collection Complète des Ouevres de J. J. Rousseau*. 15 vols. Geneva and Paris, 1790. Vol 6. (Originally published 1762.)
Young, Arthur. *Travels in France During the Years 1787, 1788, 1789*. Miss Bentham Edwards, ed. London: George Bell and Sons. 1900. (Originally Published 1792).

Books

Abbiateci, André et al. *Crimes et Criminalité en France 17ᵉ-18ᵉ Siècles*. Cahiers des Annales No. 33. Paris: Librairie Armand Colin. 1971.
Abensour, Leon. *La Femme et le Feminisme avant la Révolution Francaise*. Paris, 1923.
Acton, William. *Prostitution*. Peter Fryer, ed. London: MacGibbon and Kee, 1968. (Originally published 1857).
Anchel, Robert. *Crimes et Châtiments au XVIIIᵉ Siècle*. Paris, 1933.
Aubry, Gerard. *La Jurisprudence Criminelle du Châtelet de Paris sous le Règne de Louis XVI*. Paris: Librairie Général de Droit et de Jurisprudence, 1971.
Bergasse, Louis. *Un Defenseur des Principes Traditionnels sous la Révolution: Nicolas Bergasse*. Paris: Perrin, 1910.
Berriat-Saint-Prix, Ch. *Des Tribunaux et de la Procédure du Grand Criminel au XVIIIᵉ Siècle*. Paris: Auguste Aubry, 1859.

Biographie Moderne, ou Dictionnaire Biographique de Tous les Hommes Morts et Vivants. 4 vols. (second edition) Breslau: Korn, 1806.

Bouchary, Jean. *Les Faux-Monnayeurs sous la Révolution Francaise.* Paris: Marcel Rivière, 1946.

Bouvier, Jeanne. *Les Femmes pendant la Révolution. n.p.n.d.*

Brette, Armand. *Les Constituants. Liste des Députés et des Suppléants élus à l'Assemblée Constituante de 1789.* Paris: Société de l'Histoire de la Révolution Francaise, 1897.

Buisson, Henry. *La Police: Son Histoire.* (Third edition) Paris, 1950.

Bullough, Vern. *The History of Prostitution.* New Hyde Park, N.Y.: University Books, 1964.

Casenave, A.M. *État des Tribunaux à Paris, 1789-1800.* Paris, 1873. (Unfinished work, only volume I exists; it reviews the structure of the Old Regime courts at the beginning of the Revolution.)

Chevalier, Louis. *Classes Laborieuses et Classes Dangereuses.* Paris: Plon, 1958.

——. *La Formation de la Population Parisienne au XIXe Siècle.* Paris: Presses Universitaires de France, 1950.

Childs, J. Rives. *Restif de la Bretonne.* Paris: Briffaut, 1949.

Cobb, Richard. *The Police and the People: French Popular Protest, 1789-1820.* London: Oxford University Press. 1970.

——. *Reactions to the French Revolution.* London: Oxford University Press, 1972.

——. *A Second Identity.* London: Oxford University Press, 1969.

Dawes, C. R. *Restif de la Bretonne.* London: Whitefriars, 1946.

Desjardins, Albert. *Les Cahiers des États Généraux en 1789 et la Législation Criminelle.* Paris, 1883.

Deyon, Pierre. *Le Temps des Prisons: Essai sur l'Histoire de la Délinquance et les Origines du Système Pénitentiare.* Editions Universitaires: Université de Lille III, 1975.

Ellis, Madeleine B. *Rousseau's Venetian Story: An Essay upon Art and Truth in Les Confessions.* Baltimore: Johns Hopkins Press, 1966.

Esmein, Adhémar. *Histoire de la Procédure Criminelle en France.* Paris, 1882.

Fairchilds, Cissie. *Poverty and Charity in Aix-en-Provence 1640-1789.* Baltimore: Johns Hopkins University Press, 1976.

Farge, Arlette. *Le Vol d'Aliments à Paris au XVIIIe Siècle.* Paris: Plon, 1974.

Forster, Robert and Ranum, Orest, eds. *Deviants and the Abandoned in French Society.* Elborg Forster and Patricia Ranum, trans. Baltimore: Johns Hopkins University Press, 1978.

Foucault, Michel. *Discipline and Punish: The Birth of the Prison.* Alan Sheridan, trans. New York: Pantheon, 1977.

——. *Madness and Civilization.* Richard Howard, trans. New York: Pantheon Books, 1965.

Funck-Bretano, Frantz. *Restif de la Bretonne: Portraits et Documents Inédits.* Paris: A. Michel, 1928.

Furet, François, and Daumard, Adeleine. *Structures et Relations Sociales à Paris au Milieu du XVIIIe Siècle.* "Cahiers des Annales" No. 18. Paris: Librairie Armand Colin, 1961.

Garrigues, Georges. *Les Districts Parisiens pendant la Révolution Francaise.* Paris, n.p. n.d.

Godechot, Jacques. *Les Institutions de la France sous la Révolution et l'Empire.* (Second edition) Paris: Presses Universitaires de France, 1968.

Hampson, Norman. *A Social History of the French Revolution.* Toronto: University of Toronto Press, 1963.

Hay, Douglas et. al. *Albion's Fatal Tree: Crime and Society in Eighteenth Century England.* New York: Pantheon Books 1975.

Hiver, Alfred. *Histoire Critique des Institutions Judicaires de la France de 1789 à 1848.* Paris: Joubert, 1848.

Hufton, Olwen. *The Poor of Eighteenth Century France.* Oxford: The Clarendon Press, 1974.

Imbert, Jean. *Quelques Procés Criminels des XVIIe et XVIIIe Siècles.* Travaux et Recherches de la Faculté de Droit et de Sciences Économiques de Paris: Serie "Sciences Historiques" No. 2. Paris: Presses Universitaires de France, 1964.

Johnson, Douglas, ed. *French Society and the Revolution.* Cambridge: Cambridge University Press, 1976.

Kaplow, Jeffry. *The Names of Kings: The Parisian Laboring Poor in the Eighteenth Century.* New York: Basic Books, 1972.

Langbein, John H. *Prosecuting Crime in the Renaissance: England, Germany and France.* Cambridge, Mass.: Harvard University Press, 1974.

——. *Torture and the Law of Proof: Europe and England in the Ancien Regime.* Chicago: University of Chicago Press, 1976-77.

Lebegue, Ernest. *La Vie et l'Oeuvre d'un Constituant: Thouret 1746-1794.* Paris: Felix Alcan, 1910.

Lecour, Charles Jerome. *La Prostitution à Paris et à Londres 1789-1871.* (Second edition) Paris: P. Asselin, 1872.

Lepeletier, Felix. *Oeuvre de Michel Lepeletier Saint-Fargeau.* Brussels: Arnold la Cross, 1826.

Maestro, Marcello T. *Voltaire and Beccaria as Reformers of Criminal Law.* New York: Octagon Books, 1972. (Originally published by Columbia University Press, 1942).

McCloy, Shelby T. *The Humanitarian Movement in Eighteenth Century France.* Frankfort: University of Kentucky Press, 1957.

Monneraye, Jean de la. *La Crise de Logement à Paris pendant la Révolution.* Paris, 1928.

Monin, H. *L'État de Paris en 1789: Études et Documents sur l'Ancien Régime à Paris.* Collection de Documents Relatifs à l'Histoire de Paris pendant la Révolution Francaise. Paris, 1889.

Montbas, Hugues de. *La Police Parisiennne sous Louis XVI.* Paris: Hachette, 1949.

Parent-Duchatelet, J.B. *La Prostitution dans la Ville de Paris.* 2 vols. Paris, 1837.

Payne, Henry C. *The Philosophes and the People.* New Haven & London: Yale University Press, 1976.

de Polnay, Peter. *Napoleon's Police.* London: W. H. Allen, 1970.

Porter, Charles. *Restif's Novels: an Autobiography in Search of an Author.* New Haven: Yale University Press, 1967.

Poster, Mark. *The Utopian Thought of Restif de la Bretonne.* New York: New York University Press, 1971.

Radzinowicz, Leon. *Ideology and Crime.* New York: Columbia University Press, 1966.

Reinhard, Marcel. *Paris pendant la Révolution.* 2 vols. "Les Cours de Sorbonne." Paris: Centre de Documentation Universitaire, 1966.

Rothman, David. *The Discovery of the Asylum: Social Order and Disorder in the New Republic.* Boston: Little, Brown and Co. 1971.

Rudé, George. *The Crowd in the French Revolution.* Oxford: The Clarendon Press, 1959.

Sabatier, M. *Histoire de la Legislation sur les Femmes Publiques et les Lieux de Débauche.* Paris: J. P. Roret. 1828.

Scott, Samuel F. *The Response of the Royal Army to the French Revolution: The Role and Development of the Line Army 1787-93.* Oxford: Clarendon Press, 1978.

Seligman, Edmond. *La Justice en France pendant la Révolution 1789-1792.* 2 vols. Paris: Plon, 1901-1913.

Shennan, J. H. *The Parlement of Paris.* Ithaca: Cornell University Press, 1968.

Simon, Rita James. *Women and Crime,* Lexington, Mass.: D. C. Heath & Co., 1975.

Stanciu, V. V. *La Criminalité à Paris.* Paris: Centre National de la Recherche Scientifique, 1968.

Stead, Philip John. *The Police of Paris.* London: Staples Press Ltd. 1957.
Szabo, Denis, ed. *Déviance et Criminalité: Textes.* Paris: Librairie Armand Colin, 1970.
Voss, Harwin L. and Petersen, David M., eds. *Ecology, Crime, and Delinquency.* New York: Appleton-Century-Crofts, 1971.
Williams, Alan. *The Police of Paris 1718-1789.* Baton Rouge: Louisiana State University Press, 1979.
Zehr, Howard. *Crime and the Development of Modern Society: Patterns of Criminality in Nineteenth Century Germany and France.* London: Croom Helm Ltd., 1976.

Articles

Andrews, Richard M. "The Justice of the Peace of Revolutionary Paris, September 1792-November 1794," *Past and Present* 52 (November 1971): 56-105.
Beattie, J. M. "The Pattern of Crime in England 1660-1800," *Past and Present* 62 (February 1974): 47-95.
——. "Towards a Study of Crime in Eighteenth Century England: A Note on Indictments," *The Triumph of Culture: Eighteenth Century Perspectives,* ed. Paul Fritz and David Williams. Toronto: A. M. Hakkert, (1972): 299-314.
——. "The Criminality of Women in Eighteenth Century England," *Journal of Social History* 8 (Summer 1975).
Billaçois, François. "Pour une Enquête sur la Criminalité dans la France de l'Ancien Régime. *Annales E.S.C.* 22 (March-April 1967): 340-49.
Boutelet, Bernadette. "Étude par Sondage de la Criminalité du Bailliage de Pont-de-l'Arche (XVIIe-XVIIIe siècles); de la Violence au Vol; en Marche vers l'Escroquerie," *Annales de Normandie* (1962): 235-62.
Braesch, R. "Essai de Statistique de la Population Ouvrière de Paris vers 1791," *La Révolution Francaise* 62 (1912-13): 289-321.
Cameron, Ian. "The Police of Eighteenth Century France," *European Studies Review* 7, no. 1. (Jan. 1977): 47-75.
Darnton, Robert. "French History: The Case of the Wandering Eye," *New York Review of Books* 22 (April 5, 1973): 25-32.
——. "The High Enlightenment and the Low Life of Literature in Pre-Revolutionary France," *Past and Present* 51, (May 1971).
Davis, Kingsley. "The Sociology of Prostitution," *American Sociological Review* (June 1937): 744-55.
Durand, Yves. "Repartition de la Noblesse dans les Quartiers de Paris," *Contributions a l'Histoire Démographique de la Revolution Française.* Second Series, "Mémoires et Documents de la Commission d'Histoire

Économique et Sociale de la Révolution Francaise" vol. 18. Paris, 1965. 21-23.

Evans, Richard J. "Prostitution in Imperial Germany" *Past and Present* 70 (March 1975).

Gégot, Jean-Claude. "Étude par Sondage de la Criminalité dans la Bailliage de Falaise (XVIIe-XVIIIe siècle)," *Annales de Normandie* (1966): 103-164.

Goeury, Anne. "La Section Grange-Batelier pendant la Révolution," *Contributions à l'Histoire Démographique de la Révolution Francaise.* Commission d'Histoire Économique et Sociale de la Révolution Francaise" vol. 25. Paris: Bibliothèque Nationale, 1970. pp. 92-153.

Hufton, Olwen. "Begging, Vagrancy, Vagabondage and the Law: An Aspect of the Problem of Poverty in Eighteenth Century France," *European Studies Review* 2 (April 1972): 97-124.

——. "Towards an Understanding of the Poor of Eighteenth Century France," *French Government and Society 1500-1850,* ed. J. F. Bosher. London: The Athlone Press, 1973.

——. "Women in Revolution, 1789-1796," *Past and Present* 52 (November 1971): 90-108.

Ibanes, Jean. "La Population de la Place des Vosges et de ses Environs en 1791," *Contributions à l'Histoire Démographique de la Révolution Francaise.* First Series, "Mémoires et Documents de la Commission d'Histoire Économique et Sociale de la Révolution Francaise" vol. 14. Paris, 1962. 71-97.

Kaufmann, Joanne S. "In Search of Obedience: The Critique of Criminal Justice in Late Eighteenth Century France," *Proceedings of the Western Society for French History.* Santa Barbara, Calif.: 1979.

Kaplow, Jeffry. "The Culture of Poverty in Paris on the Eve of the Revolution," *International Review of Social History* 12 (1967) pt. 2: 277-91.

——. "Sur la Population Flottante de Paris à la Fin de l'Ancien Régime," *Annales Historiques de la Revolution Francaise* 187 (January-March 1967): 1-4.

Lecuir, Jean. "Criminalité et 'Moralité': Montyon, Statisticion du Parlement de Paris." *Revue d'Histoire Moderne et Contemporaine* 21 (July-Sept. 1974): 445-93.

Mackerell, John. "Criticism of Seignorial Justice in Eighteenth Century France," *French Government and Society 1500-1850,* ed. J. F. Bosher. London: The Athlone Press, 1973. 123-44.

Perrin, G. "L'Entassement de la Population dans le Paris de la Révolution: la Section des Lombards," *Contributions à l'Histoire Démographique de la Révolution Francaise.* Second Series, "Mémoires et Documents de la Commission d'Histoire Économique et Sociale de la Révolution Francaise" vol. 18. Paris, 1965. 61-77.

Pinset, Jacques. "Les Origines Instinctives de la Révolution Francaise," *Revue d'Histoire Économique et Sociale* 39 (1961): 198-228.

Rudé, George. "Prices, Wages, and Popular Movements in Paris During the French Revolution," *Economic History Review* 6: 3.

Scott, Samuel. "Problems of Law and Order during 1790, the Peaceful Year of the French Revolution," *American Historical Review*, 80:4 (Nov. 1975): 859-88.

Sevegard, Martine, "La Section de Popincourt pendant la Révolution Francaise," *Contributions à l'Histoire Démographique de la Révolution Francaise.* Third Series, "Mémoires et Documents de la Commission d'Histoire Économique et Sociale de la Révolution Francaise" vol. 25. Paris: Bibliothèque Nationale, 1970. 9-91.

Vigneron, F. Rousseau. "La Section de la Place des Fédérés pendant la Révolution, *Contributions à l'Histoire Démographique de la Révolution Francaise.* Third Series, "Mémoires et Documents de la Commission d'Histoire Économique et Sociale de la Révolution Francaise" vol. 25. Paris: Bibliothèque Nationale, 1970. 157-216.

Williams, Alan. "Patterns of Deviance in Eighteenth Century Paris," *Proceedings of the Western Society for French History,* Santa Barbara, Calif.: 1979.

Unpublished Works

Kaufman, Joanne S. "The Critique of Criminal Justice in Eighteenth Century France: A Study in the Changing Social Ethics of Crime and Punishment." Ph.D. dissertation, Harvard University, 1976.

Lafon, Jacqueline. "Recherches sur la Fin des Juridictions d'Ancien Régime pendant la Révolution: le Châtelet et le Parlement de Paris." Ph.D. dissertation, Université de Droit d'Économie et de Sciences Sociales de Paris. Université de Paris II, 1972.

O'Brien, Patricia. "The Promise of Punishment: Prisons in Nineteenth-Century France." Manuscript, University of California at Irvine, 1979.

Wills, Antoinette. "Prostitution in Old Regime France." Paper read at the Third Berkshire Conference on the History of Women, June 1976, Bryn Mawr, Pa.

——. "Moll à la Francaise: Female Criminality in Eighteenth-Century Paris." Paper presented to the Society for Eighteenth-Century Studies, May 1977, Victoria, B.C.

INDEX

About the Author

ANTOINETTE WILLS works in the Continuing Education Program at the University of Washington in Seattle. She has published articles on women's studies and political theory.